What's My
Motivation?

My thanks to everyone who has helped me, by accident or design, in the writing of this book. My special thanks to Ian Katz, Dan Glaister, Andrew Goodfellow, Tony Morris, Peter Stoddart, and lastly my family and friends, without whom, I suspect, none of this would have been possible.

Michael Simkins trained at RADA. His second job was Horrible Henry in *Dick Whittington & His Wonderful Cat* to Gary Oldman's cat. In 1985 he appeared in *A View from the Bridge* at the National Theatre and was nominated for Best Supporting Actor. He didn't win. Since then he has appeared in many West End shows including *Burn This* and *Company*. He recently played Billy Flynn in the musical *Chicago* and has been spotted encased in lycra in *Mamma Mia*. He has appeared in a trillion TV programmes, mostly as stalwart detectives or unsuspecting husbands. Movies include Disney's *Heidi* and Mike Leigh's *Topsy-Turvy*. He is regular contributor to *The Guardian*, and lives in north London with his wife but no children or pets.

What's My Motivation?

Michael Simkins

EBURY
PRESS

3 5 7 9 10 8 6 4 2

First published 2003 by Ebury Press,
An imprint of Random House,
20 Vauxhall Bridge Road, London SW1V 2SA

Random House Australia (Pty) Limited
20 Alfred Street, Milsons Point, Sydney,
New South Wales 2061, Australia

Random House New Zealand Limited
18 Poland Road, Glenfield, Auckland 10, New Zealand

Random House South Africa (Pty) Limited
Endulini, 5a Jubilee Road, Parktown 2193, South Africa

The Random House Group Limited Reg. No. 954009

www.randomhouse.co.uk

A CIP catalogue record for this book is
available from the British Library.

Photography by Mark Atkins
Cover designed by Keenan
Typeset by seagulls

Printed and bound in Great Britain by
Cox & Wyman Ltd, Reading, Berkshire

ISBN 0 091897491

contents

Need to Know 1

need to know

I really want this job.

I'm with the film director Mike Leigh in a grubby attic room somewhere off Carnaby Street. It's taken me twenty-five years to get an audition for one of his movies, and now I'm here, I'm terrified I'm going to blow it. In spite of the thousands of auditions, the hundreds of jobs, the myriad triumphs and disasters of a quarter-century clinging on to the greasy pole, these situations never seem to get any easier – particularly if it's a gig I want.

Like this one.

Hopefully the director is picking up none of this. He sits serenely in an armchair opposite me, writing the story of my life in a spiral-bound notepad, his biro twirling across the pages as he jots down fragments of my stumbling narrative. I'd been warned this might happen. Mike Leigh likes to find out about the background of actors he's interviewing for his forthcoming projects, and sometimes asks them to give a thumbnail sketch of their early years, which is as good a way to begin as any.

We've just got to me aged sixteen.

He finishes writing a sentence and looks up. 'So. What happened then?'

I've only felt genuine dread a few times in my life.

When I unintentionally hit my schoolmate Robert in the face with a cricket bat. When I had to tell Mr Farmer I was quitting my job as a sales assistant in Gamley's toy shop on the busiest weekend of the year. When I nearly drowned in a boating accident.

It is a chilly, syrupy sensation, like a seeping of battery acid.

I've been waiting for Leigh to ask this question – what

happened to me at the age of sixteen – ever since I entered the room. I had told myself we might not get this far, that he'd be so bored after hearing about the first fifteen years of my life that he'd cut straight to the improvisations, or, better still, just smile and say, 'Well, there's no need to know any more; I want you in the film.'

But he has asked. And I don't know how to answer.

Leigh holds the ballpoint over the pad and flicks to a fresh page.

'Well, to be perfectly honest …'

His fingers tighten on the pen.

'In actual fact …'

Outside in the street, someone is tipping empty wine bottles into a recycling bin. A motorbike roars past. There's no going back now. It's shit or bust.

act one

i want

Sometime in 1975 – around my sixteenth birthday – an incident occurred that blew my comfortable, middle-class upbringing violently off course. Overnight my life changed. I lost the plot and spiralled into a deep void, a dark and turbid place where no one could reach me. I recall the incident that sparked it off as if it were yesterday – indeed, I only have to close my eyes and I'm back there at once.

The school's production of Gilbert and Sullivan's operetta, *The Yeomen of the Guard*.

What's the problem? I told myself, as I settled down in the perfume-filled comfort of the stalls. There'll be some clunky old tunes, teenage boys in crêpe beards under a few hastily arranged spotlights, and an orchestra of student musicians scratching away on industrially produced violins. I'll have a laugh and be home by ten.

I should have known.

I was plunging into the world of amateur operatics, and before the end of the performance, I was hypnotized. Although we were in a school hall in suburban Brighton, I was still held captive in the Tower of London. To a grubby teenager with few academic skills and already bearing an uncanny physical resemblance to a young Claire Rayner, the world on the other side of those footlights promised all the glamour and security lacking in my real life.

The sights and sounds of the performance haunted my dreams all that night and lingered into the holidays. I started going to other shows by other companies in other halls, once a week, then twice, until I was staying out nearly every night, often going on long and treacherous journeys to exotic and far-flung destinations: Crawley, Horsham, Littlehampton … Nothing else mattered. My schoolwork, appearance and general hygiene all went to pot. They were terrible times. Even now I can't bear to think what I put my parents through.

The world into which I'd disappeared was one of draughty church halls and flickering orchestra lights; lukewarm tea and insipid orange juice served in crackly plastic beakers, and biscuits at twopence each; elderly women in wimples with unfeasibly large eyelashes and turkey-neck chins; tip-up seats and the aroma of pipe tobacco; late-night bus journeys and windswept car parks; front curtains that squealed when they were opened; rocky coves made out of hardboard and painted backdrops that rippled when you walked within five feet of them; Ruritanian princes who looked like estate agents; peeling photographs pinned to green felt display boards in musty foyers; ticket stubs; floral dresses; support tights; Grecian 2000; and adverts for the Bognor Regis Youth Mandolin Orchestra.

My Letts school diary for May 1974 records that during that month alone I attended performances of *Iolanthe* at Hurstpierpoint College, *HMS Pinafore* at the Lewes Road United Reform Church Operatic Society, *La Vie Parisienne* by the Le Roy Players at Hove Town Hall, and *Gay Times Twenty-Seven* by the Dawn Jordan School of Dancing and Movement at the Brighton Dome. I also spent a Sunday afternoon at a staging of *The Mikado* by a Czechoslovakian puppet troupe, as well as a performance of *Trial by Jury* at Tarring Infants School in which the child performers mimed from the stage while their teachers bellowed all the songs from the darkness of the wings; a night of such pointlessness that even then I remember dubbing it the Tarring Inferno.

My diary also records *An Evening of Viennese Favourites* at Eastbourne. I tried not to stoop so low as this, with its endless waltzes and blokes wrapped in cummerbunds, holding glasses of fake champagne and yelling that they 'must go back to Heidelberg, the city of romance', but if I couldn't get Gilbert and Sullivan then I made do with *Viennese Favourites* or Rodgers and Hammerstein, and if the worst came to the worst, even a scout show ('the 14th Whitehawk Troop presents *That's Showbiz*, all proceeds towards a new minibus').

I had no dignity left. Simple as that.

As my obsession deepened, I started collecting light opera memorabilia: seventy-eight records, posters from original productions and signed photographs. On one occasion I even caught a train to Reading to view the private collection held by an ex-cleric turned schoolteacher who had the largest one in the south-east – or so he assured me on the phone. Even I should have realized that visiting ex-clerics was a potentially dangerous activity for a teenager, but Peter Joslin proved the soul of discretion, holding me enthralled in his upstairs bedroom for an entire afternoon with his old programmes, sheet music covers and commemorative tea-towels, and when he finally revealed a blemished linen handkerchief supposed to have been used by Gilbert himself, it was the nearest I'd yet come to a sexual experience. Just think, it might actually have been *his* snot that caused those stains ...

I've spent time since trying to discover just why I took such a wrong turning at a time when I should have been seeking out sex, drugs and rock 'n' roll.

There were even early warning signs. I dimly remember one occasion, not long after I started to seek out this twilight world, when I found myself comparing weekends with a schoolmate. Trevor was a jokey, sporty sort of kid, who already spent most Saturday nights drinking with his mates at the Pavilion Tavern in Brighton town centre (known colloquially as the Pav Tav). This particular weekend he'd ended up at a party in Hangleton where he'd managed to get his hand inside Alison Walls's bra. Alison was the sister of a kid in my year. She was a fearsome prospect, built like a scrum-half with a line in sarcasm that could freeze you at ten paces. It was a daring raid, and he recounted the unbuttoning of her blouse and the teasing open of the bra cup with a glint of triumph in his eyes.

I didn't want to tell him how I'd spent my time, but deep down, I think I knew what I was doing. Neither Alison Walls nor anyone else with demonstrable female genitalia was ever going to allow me free access to their mammaries, rock concert or not, and something in me realized this even then. So rather than spend my weekends as a frustrated sexual spectator on the fringes of the ultimate teenage participation sport, I took my piece off the board. Alison Walls couldn't reject the lethal combination of my middle and index fingers if they were thirty miles along the coast tapping along in rhythm to the overture of Hastings Operatic Society's *Brigadoon*.

There was another reason. Going to amateur shows was warm, reassuring, constant, like dozing on the sofa on a Saturday afternoon with rain spattering the windows and the football results being read out on the radio. The productions, costumes, and moves were always the same, as comforting as James Alexander Gordon or those curling snapshots on the mantelpiece. Fifty-one weeks of the year I might have fretted over exams I couldn't pass, girls I couldn't touch, sports I couldn't play and acne I couldn't cure, but I could always flee to Titipu. There, Doris would do wardrobe, Reg would play piano for rehearsals, and Doreen would play the Third Little Maid, even if she had just celebrated her ruby wedding anniversary. It was not so much entertainment as feeling part of a complex ceremony, a semi-Masonic ritual.

But most of all, it was a haven from Alison Walls and having to get to grips with her Watney's Red Barrels.

Those two or three years now seem like a dream, a chimera, the trawlings of my darkest subconscious. The images that haunt me from that period in my life seem barely credible.

Did I really see a jolly Venetian in Crawley Operatic Society's production of *The Gondoliers* barged off the stage into the orchestra pit during the dancing of a gay cachucha, for instance?

(I did. His name was John Castleton. The St John's ambulance men said he'd had a lucky escape: eighteen inches further left and he'd have landed on the trombones.)

Was I really there at Falmer High School's *Ruddigore* when

the conductor suddenly threw his baton at the soloist, shouting, 'No, no that's bloody awful – hand it back, we're starting again.'

(I was. The conductor's name was Alan Skull. A friend of mine was once served roast badger for Sunday lunch at his house. Skull had run over the animal while driving through the back lanes near Uckfield.)

And did that female chorister really trip in the wings and accidentally set off a fire extinguisher during the rendering of 'When You Walk Through a Storm' in Burgess Hill Society's *Carousel*?

No.

No, no.

I must have imagined that.

And yet ...

My love affair died as quickly as it had begun. I'd gone to a Saturday night performance of *The Pirates of Penzance* in Horsham, and as the cast came on to take their curtain calls at the end of the show, I realized I was bored shitless. Nothing had gone wrong. Nobody had forgotten their lines. The soprano's wig hadn't fallen off. None of the chorus had tripped over the scenery. It had been a perfectly presentable evening: solid, unspectacular, thoroughly creditable. And I hated them for it. I'd come all this way on the train only to be robbed of my entertainment, and I wanted my money back.

Had it come to this?

The mistakes and mishaps and trundling ineptitude so often part and parcel of this whole, stupid, unwise, and goodwilled family of amateur musicals were now all I craved. I'd seen too many *Pirates*, too many *Pinafores*. I now needed them to be freak shows, and unless some humiliation occurred at least once a performance, I felt cheated. Their virgin enthusiasm, which had once proved so enticing, I now despised. When I was finally thrown free from my temporary oblivion, towards the end of the sixth form and on the cusp of adulthood, I found the world had changed. Harold Wilson was back in Downing Street, seatbelts had been introduced and Jimmy Savile was advertising British Rail. Worse, my mates had grown up without me. Some had passed their driving test: one or two even had their first car. They talked of studying economics at

Warwick, of heavy metal and James Taylor, of going on holiday to Yugoslavia with their girlfriends.

I had none of these things. No car, no girlfriend, no trendy clothes, no chat-up lines, and Meatloaf was still something I had with chips and peas. My schoolwork was in tatters, most of my teachers had given up on me, and the future I had always envisaged for myself, involving a decent university and a steady career as a solicitor, was a diminishing prospect. A job in a factory, I was told, was the best I could hope for.

Or was it?

But in fact, all those nights in Scout halls had left me with an ambition. I now had the belief that I could be an actor. Not just one of those amateurs, spending my life working in some stultifying job waiting for a few precious nights, but a pro who could swank about on a stage in fancy dress every night, and with a wage cheque at the end of it. I'd heard the actor Patrick Troughton on the radio describing his job as 'shouting in the evenings'.

That was what I wanted to do with my life.

But how? A visit to my local theatre provided the clue. My parents were given some free tickets to *Two and Two Make Sex* starring Patrick Cargill, and they took me along. It was the programme that pointed the way ahead. According to the biographies of the cast members, nearly all of them had trained at the Royal Academy of Dramatic Art.

If it was good enough for the Queen it would surely do for me.

I sent off for the RADA prospectus.

pieces

It's probably best that you don't know the chances of getting into drama school when you fill in your application form. They're about the same as winning the pools – worth a flutter, but don't cancel the day job. In any case, if you're taking a wise and measured view of life, you shouldn't try to be an actor in the first place.

Having sent off for the details, I decide I can afford to relax. When 'Mary' Wells, my form master, asks me which university I'm applying to, I'm able to answer, 'I'm going to drama school, sir.' Mary responds with what I take to be an encouraging smile but is probably a look of genuine pity and passes on. Surrounded by mates applying to Bristol University and Magdalen College, Oxford ('I need two As and a B and then my place is assured, if not I'll go to Southampton'), I assume much the same idea obtains for drama students. If I don't forget my words or bump into the furniture at the audition I'll be going to RADA, if not, I'll settle for Guildhall or Webber Douglas.

The RADA prospectus arrives with the royal emblem embossed on the front and the names of famous actors liberally sprinkled throughout its pages. I am informed that it was founded in 1904 by Herbert Beerbohm Tree, and that it provides a two-and-a-half-year course in all essential elements of stagecraft. It omits to mention that the Academy itself consists of nothing more than a couple of converted houses in Bloomsbury linked together by a rusting fire escape or, crucially, that it only takes in twenty-one students each year, though it regularly receives over 3,000 applications.

According to the prospectus I'm required to prepare two contrasting speeches, one Shakespeare and one modern, neither piece to be longer than three minutes. What happens to you if they exceed the stated limit isn't mentioned, but in an establishment with such long traditions I suppose a hook will appear from the wings. The only other requirements seem to be an ability to write your name and a lack of criminal convictions. And don't forget to enclose a cheque for fifteen quid, non-refundable. Your six minutes of fame is then assured. I'm expected at Gower Street in three months' time.

Two three-minute speeches with which to make an impression. Luckily my mate Alan has a dad who does a little local drama examining for East Sussex District Council.

Over a cup of tea in a café in the Lanes one Saturday morning, Alan tells me what to expect. 'For Christ's sake, stay off the beaten track. My dad has to sit through about fifty auditions a day. Start off with "To be or not to be" and they'll be pouring paraffin over themselves before you've got to the end of the first stanza.'

I decide not to ask what a stanza is.

'And you'd better decide what you're going to wear. They see so many people during the course of a day that they like to have something to write down to remember you by when they're going over everybody in the pub. My dad writes things like BT, big tits, or GS, ginger sideburns – doesn't matter what it is, just don't go there looking anonymous.'

Food for thought. I haven't got ginger sideburns, and it's now too late to grow any before the audition date. Luckily I do have big tits, courtesy of growing up in a sweet shop, but I'm not sure this piece of advice is meant for me. In any case if chest measurement was the criteria for success, our shop assistant Jean Turner should be encouraged to have a go – she'd be a good bet for a scholarship. But she's over fifty with varicose veins, an infirm mother and a passion for Sharp's Buttersnap. I'm not even sure she could afford the fifteen quid for the audition fee; not without asking my dad for a rise.

As he gets up to leave, Alan offers a final piece of advice. 'Whatever you do, don't mention at the interview that you're a fan of Gilbert and bloody Sullivan. Mention anybody you like but not them, or they'll mark you out as an AD.'

'What's AD?'

'Am Dram. Somebody who's sung "Willow Tit Willow" at the local church Christmas concert and has believed it when his mum has told him he ought to be a professional. Drama school auditions are clogged with them. Try to mention somebody a bit poncey – my dad says Chekhov is usually a good bet. You could try to slip him into the conversation ...'

My knowledge of Chekhov veered more towards the Starship Enterprise than the Russian Steppes, but I took the point.

I settle for a Shakespeare speech from *The Two Gentlemen of Verona* – a servant talking to an imaginary dog called Crab. The speech is sufficiently unknown to be a novelty item, and also includes the word 'pissing', which should mark me down as a dangerous young talent who is prepared to shock in order to achieve dramatic effect. Even if I don't get in, they might take the dog. For my modern speech, my English teacher recommends an excerpt from T.S. Eliot's *The Confidential Clerk*. I've never heard of the play or the author, but that's hardly surprising. With my exposure to classical theatre limited to Patrick Cargill using a pair of comedy chest expanders, I'm only too happy to take any advice.

I finally track down a copy of *The Confidential Clerk* at Brighton Public Library. It's a rather mournful affair, some bloke droning on about not realizing his dream of becoming a potter, but it somehow feels right; a bit melancholy, slightly sentimental, difficult to be sure what the author intended. Whatever else, it's certainly off the beaten track – the previous date stamps in the inside front cover suggests the book has been taken out twice in the last thirty years.

When I finally find the speech, somebody has circled it in pencil and written 'poof' at the top of the page. Perfect.

the phone call

Every actor recalls the moment they hear whether they've got into drama school. One actor I know received the news by post several days earlier than he was expecting. On opening the letter and finding that he'd won a scholarship, he let out a ferocious yell of triumph, leaped into the air and landed on the family cat, killing it instantly. For several seconds he stood aghast, looking down at the crushed frame of his beloved pet, a trickle of blood seeping from the nose of its otherwise inert and rapidly cooling frame. When his mother yelled down from upstairs to ask what had happened, he shouted back that he had some good news and some bad.

I'm sitting in a long dilapidated room fringed down one side by grubby full-length mirrors and on the other by ballet rails. I've just had my third recall for RADA, and I'm sitting alone, apart from my new mate Glynn Poole, who's perched on a similar iron frame chair a few feet from me. We're staring at an old black Bakelite telephone mounted on the wall at the far end, near the rusting fire escape.

Glynn Poole comes from Walsall. He's in his mid-twenties, and has a thin moustache meandering over his top lip. Glynn wants to be an actor and has been taking night classes in dance and drama, financed by working nightshifts at Cadbury's in Bournville. Consequently he smells vaguely of chocolate. Perhaps that's why I like Glynn Poole – there's something comforting about him.

The reason that Glynn and I haven't received the news of our fate by post is that we are borderlines. We've both had to come back here on a Saturday morning for a special borderliners' workshop, an hour each working with two senior tutors, and a final grilling by the Academy's principal. I've had to perform with my incontinent dog and my suspect ceramics operative for the third time in three weeks, and now I've been sent into this room to await my fate.

It's much worse now I know I'm a borderline. At the original audition it was obvious I wasn't going to get in: the odds were just too high. But then I received notification of a recall, and with it my chances of success were reduced from several thousands to one to a mere couple of hundred. Which means it might just – just – happen.

Now it's serious.

For the first recall, my mum bought me a brown two-piece suit in a new non-crease textile called Trevira. She assured me it would mark me down as a responsible student, someone who would take his studies seriously. But it made me feel like a solicitor. Whatever the merits of Trevira, it doesn't 'breathe' well (manmade fibres are notorious in this regard – I should know, I wear little else). So despite the seasonably cold weather, by the time I had walked down Gower Street from the tube station, there were dark stains spreading under my armpits.

As I descended the stairs to the audition in the Vanbrugh Theatre, a creeping paralysis started to set in. When I stepped on to the darkened stage to begin my two contrasting pieces, my right knee jiggled every time I put any weight on it and from nowhere a nervous tic began just below my left eye. I must have looked like Herbert Lom in the Pink Panther films. Somewhere out there in the darkness of the auditorium I made out three or four shadowy figures, slumped mid-stalls and lit only by a series of heavily muted desk lamps, just enough to allow them to write down 'big tits' on their audition notes. I dried stone dead in the middle of the dog speech and tripped over a chair in the wings as I left.

'You all right?' called a voice crackling with indifference from somewhere in the blackness.

'Yes, thank you,' I replied, as cheerily as I could muster.

'Good,' said the voice. 'Next please ...'

On the train home to Brighton I sat staring out of the window, trying to work through my performance. When the train stopped at East Croydon, the internationally renowned cricket commentator Richie Benaud got on and sat down next to me. The West Indies were playing Sussex at Hove and he was obviously going down to cover the match. Normally I'd have given anything to meet Richie Benaud, and I had nearly forty minutes in a railway carriage with him, plenty of time to strike up a conversation, offer him a liquorice allsort, exchange phone numbers, perhaps be invited into the commentary box. But I was not in the mood. I sensed I'd blown it and I just wanted to be left alone. I hoped he couldn't smell the pungent mix of sweat and Trevira.

The news wasn't as bad as I feared. A call from the Academy summoned me back for a special remedial session. There were six of us: four blokes and two girls. I jettisoned the Trevira two-piece in favour of something more radical, a Fred Perry T-shirt and slacks. The three sessions have gone well; in the last one the Academy's principal and final arbitrator, Hugh Cruttwell, gathered up his notes and said, 'Yes, that was better than last time, wasn't it?' It's hardly a ringing endorsement, but it's all I've got.

And at the end of it all I'm now waiting in the long room with Glynn Poole. Our one remaining task is simple: 'When the phone rings, one of you answer it and follow the instructions ...'

Glynn feels he's done well too: we're both hopeful. But we know there's only likely to be one available place to dispense among the six remedials. We haven't seen the other four for well over an hour – for all we know, they're already hanging themselves from Hungerford Bridge or ordering another bottle of champagne.

The phone rings.

Glynn and I both stare at it. He gives a nervous smile. 'Oh well,' he says in a faint West Midlands twang, 'I suppose this is it.' He walks the entire length of the room, picks up the receiver, listens without speaking, says, 'Right-oh,' and replaces it in the cradle.

'They want me to go down to the Registrar's office,' he says. 'You're to come down in three minutes. Good luck.'

With that he walks out of the room. I never see him again.

Three minutes. I knock on the Registrar's door. A tall, lean man wearing a smart blazer, Garrick Club tie and Jermyn Street suede slip-ons opens it. A smell of polished leather and old books hangs in the air around him. He extends a bony hand, his fingers immaculately manicured, shirt cuffs fastened by solid silver links extending just the right length below the cuff of his blazer. And he smiles.

'Congratulations.'

items

There is a long list of essential items to purchase if you're going to RADA. I'm studying it in secret during my tea break in the stockroom of Gamley's toy shop in Hove, where I'm currently being groomed for middle management. The stockroom is a grimy basement in the bowels of the shop, lit by a single flickering fluorescent strip light and containing a solitary tea-stained stool, a Formica table, a grubby kettle, a couple of chipped mugs and enough Scalextric track to stretch twice round the Albert Hall. I haven't yet told the manager, Mr Farmer, that I'm about to chuck it all in and send Gamley's plunging into a recruitment crisis, so every time he comes down the stairs and into the stockroom I have to shove the list back into the pocket of my Trevira two-piece and pretend I am in search of a recent delivery from Tonka.

A Trevira suit is not on the list of essential items required for the seven-term acting course, which begins in three months. But there are some equally worrying requirements – particularly if you're eighteen, still a virgin, and never in your worst nightmares imagined you'd have to encounter balletwear. In addition to a pair of dance pumps I've got to provide jazz shoes, two sets of tights and what is delicately referred to as a 'dance support belt'. The suggested stockist is a firm called Annello and Davide, whose address is Cecil Court, off St Martin's Lane in London. The checklist states I must also assemble two T-shirts, a towel, greasepaint sticks shades five and nine, a tub of cold cream and another of blending powder, and a knotted stocking top. Either I'm studying make-up or I'm going to be asked to rob a bank. The final item is a pair of braces.

Gamley's are going to take my departure badly. I've been with them for most of the autumn. They've invested a lot of time and money in my future, and rumour has it I'm being pencilled for the manager's job in their new branch in Burgess Hill. I was only taken on in the first place because I told them I was passionate about a career in dye-cast plastic miniatures and scale models, since when I've spent my days arranging displays of Airfix kits and advising children on the latest offerings from the Corgi catalogue. But, it has to be said, laughs and high drama have been few and far between here.

Customer: Do you have an XL2 Lamborghini?
Me: What, on my salary, madam?

Which, incidentally, is £17 a week before tax. Gamley's didn't get to open a branch in Burgess Hill by strewing fivers about.

I spend the next few weeks reading and re-reading the various missives from RADA in the dank, strobe-effect world of the stockroom, nipping out during my lunch break to buy the various items essential for my training, and trying to put off the day when I have to purchase the ballet accessories. I manage to stretch out the task of purchasing a hand towel to nearly a month by visiting every department store in Brighton, comparing texture of material, quality, size, nap of the cloth, even design. Eventually I plump for a small blue number made in Chile. But even as I congratulate myself on my diligence and commitment to my new vocation I know in my heart I'm a purchase nearer to having my fat arse fitted for the dance support belt.

After several weeks I catch a slow stopper up to London Victoria so that I won't bump into anyone I know and have to reveal where I'm going. A couple of stops on the Circle Line to Embankment, and I'm barely across Trafalgar Square when I see the sign swinging above the pavement a few yards ahead of me.

Annello and Davide. Male and female ballet accessories.

Before I've even stepped into the shop, a man looking like Hugh Paddick is swanning towards me with a gleam in his eye. Perhaps a career with Gamley's wouldn't be so bad after all. My own branch, a flat by the time I'm twenty-five, a regular wage, a company pension plan, plus a huge foldaway model railway layout in the attic. If he suggests measuring me for my dance support belt I'm calling the police.

But he doesn't. Nor does he burst into pitiless laughter when I tell him that I need some pumps and tights, nor that my waist-line is 36 inches. In fact his response is disarming.

'Drama school, is it?' He rummages in a couple of brown cardboard boxes on the counter.

'That's right.'

'Which one?'

'RADA.'

'Oh, the RADA?' he replies. I notice the prefix he's slipped in. Perhaps it's significant. I must remember that.

He smiles at me. 'Which colour?'

He's holding up two different shades of what the RADA obviously calls a dance support belt and Mr Farmer would call a jockstrap. One is black, the other an insistent flesh colour. I don't even have to respond. He pops the black belt into the Annello and Davide plastic bag and takes my tenner. Moments later I'm recrossing Trafalgar Square with the bag containing the tights, a pair of ballet shoes and a dance support jockstrap, and shoving the entire package into a larger Sainsbury's plastic bag fished out of a bin. The worst moment is over. I've purchased the balletwear. Now there's no turning back.

I'm going to the RADA.

bernard

A month later, and I'm sitting with Bernard inside a glass-fronted cubicle on the first floor of a building just off the sea front.

Bernard is a claimant interviewer for the Department of Health and Social Security. His job is to conduct fifteen-minute interviews throughout the day with the dispossessed from Brighton and its environs, in order to assess whether they fulfil the Government criteria for financial assistance in the form of a weekly giro cheque. I've been put with Bernard because he is the best interviewer in the building, and I'm supposed to be learning the ropes.

I don't quite know how I've got here. I was hoping to stay at Gamley's toy shop until I went to RADA, but once Mr Farmer heard that I wasn't planning to commit the next forty-seven years of my life to the firm, he asked me to leave. 'We're disappointed, quite frankly,' he'd said. 'We've invested a lot of time and trust in your future and it seems you've repaid it by going off on some hare-brained scheme just as we'd trained you up. I only hope you know what you're doing,' he'd continued. 'We had big ideas for you, Michael.'

I think he was referring to the new branch in Burgess Hill.

With no job, I panicked, and stupidly replied to an advert for trainee clerical officers at the DHSS in order to make some money in the final awkward few weeks before my new career, and now I find myself sitting here with Bernard. I haven't told him I'm going to RADA either, so I'm having to sit here and look interested. It's about 11.30 a.m., and through the reinforced glass window in front of us, we have a panoramic view of the waiting room, where sixty-odd assorted individuals are ranged on rows of plastic chairs screwed to the floor.

'So they can't be used as offensive weapons,' explains Bernard gently.

The claimants are slumped in various states of boredom, each awaiting their call over the tannoy and their chance to get hold of £18 a week.

'Mrs Haynes to booth six, please.'

Mrs Haynes gets up and walks sulkily past the line of cubicles, staring momentarily into at each one like she's visiting an aquarium. Bernard gives her a pleasant municipal smile as she leers in and points her to a booth a few yards further along.

Bernard is unflappable. His shirt is pressed, his trousers have a sharp crease in them, his shoes are brightly polished, and his hair is immaculately combed like strands of lacquered seaweed across the shiny dome of his head. Bernard never sweats. He's the only interviewer who uses a ballpoint when filling in the questionnaire. Bernard doesn't need a pencil: he never makes a mistake.

Sue, on the other hand, a large, horse-faced girl in cubicle eleven, makes lots of mistakes. Her principal blunder this morning was to allow her long, Pre-Raphaelite tresses to rest too near the tiny aperture at the bottom of the glass screen where it doesn't quite meet the desktop. Her 9.20 a.m. appointment reached through the gap, grabbed a huge fistful of hair and used it to pull her head repeatedly against the glass. She's at the county hospital right now. We're hoping she'll be back after lunch – only minor wounds and shock, the ambulance men said.

The sound of skull on glass hasn't done anything for the atmosphere out there in the waiting room. All interviews were suspended while the police were fetched and statements taken. Most of the applicants have been sitting there well over an hour now, and the air is thick with tobacco smoke and simmering frustration. But Bernard shuffles his papers, wipes his mouth with his unblemished handkerchief and takes out a new interview form.

He leans across to the tiny individual microphone on the desktop, presses the speaker button with his manicured index finger and speaks pleasantly into it. A tiny green light illuminates on the console.

'Mr O'Nions to cubicle seven, please.'

A scruffy-looking bloke gets up from somewhere at the back and begins shambling towards us. He looks as if he's slept under the pier.

'Now, Michael,' says Bernard mildly, 'we have trouble with Mr O'Nions sometimes. He can be difficult. The trick is not to lose your temper. And, of course, it helps to keep him sweet if you don't announce his name to all and sundry as Mr Onions, as I'm afraid some of my colleagues do. Always take a moment to pronounce their name properly. These little dignities can sometimes make all the difference.'

Mr O'Nions slumps into the chair on the other side of the glass. He's in a state. He's lost his latest giro and hasn't got a penny to last him through until next Wednesday. He needs a replacement.

'How did you lose it, please?' asks Bernard, beginning to write.

Mr O'Nions thinks he threw it away with some rubbish by mistake.

'It's just that you seem to have thrown your giro away by mistake three times in the last twelve weeks,' says Bernard patiently. 'I did explain last time that we couldn't continue in this fashion. I'm afraid there's nothing more I can do.'

Mr O'Nions replies that he has to have the replacement giro immediately and that if he doesn't get it he's going to walk out into the centre of Brighton and knife a child.

Bernard is impassive.

'Did you hear what I said?' repeats Mr O'Nions, jutting his jaw out and gripping the edge of the desk. 'I said I'll go into town and knife a child.'

'Nonetheless, I'm afraid I'll be unable to issue a replacement giro,' reiterates Bernard.

'Well, in that case, I'm going to do it now and *you'll be responsible*.' Mr O'Nions rises angrily, slamming the reinforced glass with his fist and kicking out hopelessly against the chair. His eyes alight on me, trembling by Bernard's side, for the first time. '*And you*,' he shouts.

I want to explain to him that there's no need to include me in all this, that I'm going off to the RADA in a few weeks to pursue a classical training in the various arts of theatrical representation, with particular emphasis on voice, movement and physical skills. But Mr O'Nions is already halfway out of the waiting room. He throws open the exit doors, before turning back to the startled throng.

'*You'll be responsible* ...' He slams the doors, descends the stairs and is lost from view.

Bernard reaches below the desk and brings out a small tartan thermos flask.

'Cup of tea?' he suggests pleasantly.

By 4 p.m. that afternoon it's even worse. Many of the claimants have been there since before lunchtime. Some are now asleep and dribbling gently, their ties loosened, heads propped against the walls. A dismantled *Daily Mirror* lies scattered in various crumpled and scuff-marked pages around the floor. Despite two ceiling fans turning gently above, the temperature is rising and tempers are unravelling.

Bernard is just finishing a small sandwich from his snackbox: sandwich spread, with the crusts cut off. He's also consumed a hard-boiled egg wrapped in foil, to which he's added salt and pepper from two small, matching plastic canisters. A couple of jam tarts lie carefully positioned on the desk. Bernard has even offered me one of them – that's the sort of man he is.

'Now then, where were we?' He takes another questionnaire from the pile on the desk and nods his head discreetly in the direction of the waiting claimants. 'If you'd care to look at what's happening out there, Michael, you'll see something quite instructive.'

I scan the small cluster of humanity simmering gently through the glass. The scene appears exactly as it has done all day. The only thing that's different is the bloody baby screaming its head off.

A large, hatchet-faced woman in a white crimplene miniskirt and stilettos is sitting a couple of rows in. She's been there about half an hour now, but in the last three or four minutes the baby she's been holding in her arms has woken and has started to cry.

With each wail the level of anxiety in the waiting room is creeping up.

'That, Michael, is Betty Camache,' says Bernard. 'An old friend of ours. Don't stare, please, just keep a discreet eye on her while I explain what's happening ...'

A mighty and ear-shattering wail from the baby brings me back to the waiting room.

'Betty Camache doesn't like waiting,' says Bernard mildly. 'She's a woman with lots to do. And hence the presence of her little boy. Look closely at her right thumb and forefinger, if you will. She's pinching the young fellow's inner thigh.'

I can. Betty's hand is almost obscured by her other arm and the baby's smock. Only a trained eye like Bernard's would spot it.

'So you see, we'll have to see Betty earlier than we really should,' continues Bernard. 'Otherwise every single interviewee from now till closing time will be so stressed as to render them impossible to interview in a frank and mature manner. And Mrs Camache knows it. As a means of sophisticated queue-jumping it really is very effective, you have to admit. And, of course, virtually undetectable. Clever, don't you think?'

He leans forward and presses the broadcast button on the microphone again. 'Mrs Camache to booth seven, please.'

The woman takes her hand away from the baby's leg, kisses him fondly on the forehead, stands with a look of triumph, and teeters towards us on her stilettos.

'Look, Bernard, there's something I have to tell you ...'

I never get any further.

Before I can blurt out my guilty secret, before Betty Camache can reach the interview chair, before Bernard can take another bite out of the jam tart with raspberry filling, the doors to the waiting room spring open with a juddering crash. The force is great enough to send the door handles flying back against the rear wall, sending chips of plaster flying into the air.

Mr O'Nions is framed in the doorway. He holds a battered suitcase.

He starts running towards the glass. He slips momentarily on a page from the discarded newspaper but it scarcely checks his progress. Barely a second or two later he's approaching the rows of cubicles at full pelt. Just as he's about to hit the glass he slides to a halt and throws the suitcase up into the air, over the top of the glass partition and into our cubicle. It lands smack on the desktop, sending Bernard's carefully prepared stack of papers and emergency ballpoints flying in all directions and flattening the tarts. Onions screams a single word – '*Bomb!*' – and runs out again.

Suddenly I'm in a Tom and Jerry cartoon; Bernard and I are through the door of the cubicle and into the office behind, leaving sheets of A4 paper fluttering gently down to the floor. Our chairs lie on their backs, rolling gently back and forth on the lino. In the office behind the cubicles it's mayhem: the occupants of all fifteen cubicles have simultaneously escaped into the room through fifteen separate doors and are now scrambling around hysterically. Sue, the one who had her head smashed earlier this morning, is cowering underneath her desk; another of the other interviewers is crouching behind some filing cabinets; I seem to have found myself behind a large yucca plant. Even Bernard has a sheen of perspiration on his forehead: he produces his handkerchief and dabs his brow with it.

Others are emerging from their hiding places.

'Who was it?' asks one.

'Bloody Onions,' says someone.

The supervisor turns to us. 'You two all right?'

'Nothing broken,' says Bernard. He smiles mildly at me, still half concealed behind the yucca. 'Well, Michael, you're seeing all human life today. You'll be a seasoned assessor before you know it.'

I'll tell them tomorrow.

ken

The DHSS has sent me on a three-day training course for clerical and executive officers. I'm one of about twenty individuals arranged at desks along three sides of a small, prefabricated office building in Hinchley Wood, just off the A3. At the front of the room, a bloke called Ken is writing figures on a shiny white board with a magic marker. The figures relate to calculations necessary for assessment of those claiming supplementary benefit with dependent children.

I'm starting at the RADA in a fortnight and I still haven't told anyone. The DHSS has spent hundreds of pounds sending me on this training course, paying my train fares, putting me up at a small commercial hotel in Tolworth in the belief that I will repay the debt with interest over the next thirty years, and entirely ignorant of the fact that I'm putting their carefully calculated *per diems* towards dance tights and hand towels.

'Michael? Did you follow that all right?'

'Sorry, Ken, didn't get the last bit.'

'Which last bit?'

'Um ...'

'Let me go through it again ...' Ken turns back to the board and begins circling the figures. He's a square-jawed, rugged-looking bloke who in a poor light could be mistaken for Bill Simpson, star of *Dr Finlay's Casebook*. Like his theatrical doppelgänger, Ken's a man's man, even though he spends his days in this prefabricated hut. You only have to look at his hairy forearms to see that.

'Now, as I just said ...'

A distant bell rings in the corridor outside. My fellow trainees are already standing up, closing notebooks, stretching, discussing whether to go to the pub for lunch, filing out into the chilly March sunshine. I smile hopefully at a huge toad-like woman who's been scowling disapprovingly at me all week: she responds by fishing in her handbag and popping an Opal Fruit into her mouth. She snaps the clasp shut and leaves without a flicker.

'Mike, can I have a word?'

Ken is wiping the board clean with a duster. When everyone else has left, he stops wiping and turns to face me.

'Mike, you don't seem too interested in what's been going on these last few days. I've got to compile a report this afternoon on each of you who've attended, and I have to say I'm going to have trouble giving you a good one. You're a nice bloke and it's fun to have you here, but I've got serious reservations about your concentration levels. Is this a fair view, or have you got something on your mind just now?'

I smile sheepishly and tell him I'm about to chuck it all in for RADA.

Seconds later I'm convinced my nose is broken.

Ken has hugged me so hard I fear he's done something to it. The left nostril is now running uncontrollably: I can see a film of snot on the shoulder of Ken's shirt.

Ken has done two things in his life since he moved from Wales in the early fifties. He's taught social security legislation in this hut, and played the leading tenor role in over thirty consecutive productions for the Hinchley Wood Amateur Operatic and Dramatic Association. He lives for his twice-yearly appearances, and he's currently rehearsing Marco in their production of Gilbert and Sullivan's *The Gondoliers*. And suddenly I see him. Not the Ken who's standing before me now, in the white short-sleeved shirt with the ballpoint pens in the breast pocket and the equations for measuring disability, but the real Ken, the one I know, in the red velvet turban, the curly black moustache, the fake tan, the eye mask, the scimitar swinging loosely from the waistband of his djellaba ...

'Were you Sid El Kar in the Dorking Operatic Society's production of *The Desert Song*?'

Ken grips me by my shoulder blades and stares into my eyes. His voice quavers out into the ether: 'If one flower grows alone in your garden ...'

Why on earth didn't I recognize him earlier? I've been staring at him all week and yet couldn't see the curly slippers for the Hush Puppies. Within seconds I'm telling him of my years spent watching amateur opera. Several fevered minutes of shared reminiscence follow, until he concludes it with another crippling bear hug.

Then he wrenches us apart and stares at me again.

'I always wanted to go to RADA,' he says, his voice thick with emotion. 'Bloody go for it, Michael. Don't do what I did. Don't end up here in thirty years ...'

He sniffs loudly, claps his hands together, and reaches for his jumper.

'Right, boyo, you and I are going for a drink to celebrate. A stiff one.' He grabs the door handle and ushers me out into the corridor.

Now I've got to tell him I only like blackcurrant and lemonade ...

That evening I don't go home as promised. The lure of London is too strong, even here in Hinchley Wood. It may only be a small dormitory town in leafy Surrey but there are red buses and adverts for West End musicals on the street hoardings, and the small commercial hotel I've been staying in has leaflets on the front desk for Madame Tussaud's and Battersea Park funfair. I'm near enough here to taste the city and to sense the bustle of Leicester Square. The blessing of Dorking's Sid El Kar feels like the final benediction of my plans, validating my attempts to untangle myself from the tentacles of the life that others had planned for me: no more Mr Farmer, no more Bernard, no Betty Camache and Mr Onions: tonight I'm going to celebrate as only a young adult single male with money in his pocket, alone in London for the first time in his life and on the threshold of manhood, can do.

I'm going to the Garrick to see Michael Crawford in *No Sex Please – We're British*.

welcome

I'm back in the room with the ballet rails and the Bakelite telephone. It's Easter 1976, the first day of the RADA course, and Glynn Poole is just a distant memory. I've been told to assemble in this room along with the twenty other successful students on which the future heritage of British theatre now rests. It seems I'm the first to arrive.

Inside, the room is exactly as it was last time I saw it, except that twenty-one of those tubular metal chairs have been arranged in a neat semi-circle. Outside, the grey winter skies have been replaced by a watery spring sunshine, which is feeling its way in through the windows. Down below me in Gower Street, a three-lane crocodile of slow-moving London traffic is juddering towards Holborn, all the emblems of London life within it: a bus, a stream of black cabs, even a vintage van with Fortnum and Mason embossed on the side.

The door flings open and a maintenance man ambles in. He's grotesque, fat, sweating. He looks like Wackford Squeers on a plumbing course. Small curranty eyes, dank blond hair glued by perspiration to his forehead, skin the colour of blotting paper, a fuzz of adolescent stubble on his cheeks and upper lip. He's dressed above the waist in a faded black singlet, and below in a pair of olive army fatigues. His feet are encased in a pair of huge, electric blue shoes. He carries what looks to be a toolbag.

He sees me and nods, walks past me to the window and looks out. 'Orright?' he says.

'Yes, thank you.'

We stand like this for a minute or two. He makes no effort to retrieve his tools from the bag, nor does he show any inclination towards looking for a problem to rectify; although God knows there are enough. One of the ballet rails has come adrift from the wall, the lino is torn and scuffed, and the automatic closing device on the door is buckled, so that every entrance into the room is followed by a high-pitched squeaking. He'll have to get a move on; the other students will be arriving in a moment. Hugh Cruttwell is due to give a welcome speech at eleven, and it's quarter to now. He won't want running repairs on an occasion such as this.

He drums on the window with one set of fingers. Most of his other arm is wedged down the back of his trousers; I can see the digits working their way into the crack. The door squeals open again and the principal of RADA strides in. He's about sixty, with prematurely white hair and a look of puzzled benevolence on his face. He's wearing a brown and white stripy shirt and carrying a vellum folder.

'Ah, Michael,' he says in a sonorous baritone. 'Welcome. Train on time, then?'

Before I can answer he sees the maintenance man.

'Hello, there,' he says amiably. Then he turns to me again. 'Have you introduced yourselves? Michael Simkins, this is Tim Spall. Congratulations, both of you, good to have you here.'

Spall grins and walks towards me. 'Wotcher,' he says, extending his right hand.

The subsequent interlude is among the most bewildering of my life. An assortment of people you'd normally cross the street to avoid walk into the room. Not one of them is wearing a tie, some aren't even wearing lace-up shoes, and nobody refers to Hugh Cruttwell as 'sir'. Two are from the United States and one from South Africa – the youngest has only just left Roedean, and the oldest is an ex-SAS Action Man type on the wrong side of thirty who seems to have got the phone numbers of at least two of the women before Cruttwell has even called for order.

With each new arrival the fragile template of my preconception is further warped: a stunning black girl with breasts the size of large honeydews, which are covered by what seems to be a lace teapot cover; a boy from Hull who behaves like Russell

Harty; a menacing lad with curly hair from Glasgow who speaks to me incomprehensibly while we're waiting; a tall, tweedy youth from Wisconsin, who's smoking a pipe ... By the time the whole complement is assembled I'm beginning to view Tim Spall as rather old-fashioned.

I had assumed that everyone was going to be like me. Or at worst, like Glynn Poole – which is me with a fragile moustache and a slight Walsall twang – but essentially white, English and middle-class. Action Man is chatting up the black girl, the Glaswegian is sharing a joke with a boy with carroty hair who looks like Tintin, and Russell Harty is lending Neville from Ashby de la Zouch some hair gel. Hugh Cruttwell is smiling benignly and sifting through his papers; he seems entirely unconcerned by this dangerous cocktail of misfits and fifth columnists he's so rashly admitted.

'We'll just wait a bit longer for our last arrival and then we'll get started,' he says.

On the basis of this lot it'll probably be Myra Hindley.

I'm never going to survive. This lot don't care about the same things as me – the operas of Gilbert and Sullivan, county cricket, the films of Laurel and Hardy, the importance of having polished shoes ...

And then the Registrar, the one with the tie and the suede slip-ons who first congratulated me on my successful remedial audition, comes into the room and passes Cruttwell a piece of paper. It's a message from our absent classmate, who's from New York. He's still at Heathrow airport where he's been held overnight at Customs for questioning. The reason for his detention is that NY has tried to bring a full set of orthopaedic leg irons into the country. Apparently, after studying his inventory, he has assumed that 'braces' means callipers, for character work, perhaps. So he's blown nearly five hundred dollars of his grant, lugged them all the way over on an aircraft, and the Customs officials at Heathrow are suspicious because he palpably doesn't require them. So they've impounded his luggage and have him in a locked room while they check the details of his passport and put the leg irons through a massive-dose X-ray machine.

It's not much, but it's a vital straw to a drowning man. I may not be the most clueless after all.

I'll stay till lunch.

class

One of the things you're warned about drama school is that you will be expertly unpicked, piece by piece, both physically and emotionally, so that you can then be reassembled in a manner receptive to the dramatic muse. In other words, Tim Spall scratching his arse is merely the hors d'oeuvre.

I'm soon discovering what they mean. By lunch on the first day I've been told I require an intensive course to correct my posture, that I'm too fat, and that my tongue string needs an operation.

The first ever lesson is at 11 a.m. with a Belgian dance teacher called Ruth-Eva Ronen. She looks like one of those plucky French women, clad only in a gabardine mac and court shoes, who harboured Resistance fighters during the Second World War.

For Ruth-Eva, vee haf to wear our dance tights.

One by one we emerge from the male and female locker rooms. A bloke from Croydon has obviously modelled himself on Leo Sayer: he arrived this morning in dungarees over a cheesecloth jerkin and Kicker boots with multi-coloured laces, and even his jazz tights are in a similarly loose-fitting stretchy material. He is going to make a mint in adverts for Coca-Cola and revivals of *Godspell*. A girl from Islington announces in breathless tones that she's already got her leotard on underneath her day clothes. My clothes are still in their cellophane wrapping – I haven't even cut the labels off in case I was fired before lunch and could get my money back. Having taken five minutes to work out how I'm supposed to wear my dance belt, I wander miserably out of the locker room and across the landing to where the others await me. They're already lined along one side of the room at the ballet rails, feet splayed at ten to two. Action Man seems to have fashioned a pair of sawn-off military dungarees. The boy from Wisconsin has put on a conventional pair of black tights and pumps, but is still holding his pipe: it's as though Sherlock Holmes had been forced to join Pan's People. At the far end of the ballet bar Tim stands in tights and his electric blue shoes, looking like a guest from the Blackpool Tower Circus.

There's no hiding place. My reflection blushes back at me from the mirrors. A layer of gelatinous fat bubbles up over the confines of the dance belt and cascades below the Fred Perry T-shirt. Ruth-Eva introduces us to our accompanist for our first dance class – a dishevelled man in a tweed jacket sitting at a battered upright next to the windows. 'Zis is Meester Blezzard,' she says.

Blezzard puts down his *Racing Post*, scans the assortment gripping the ballet rails with the resigned look of a horse who knows he's got to trot round the paddock with another group of beginners on his back, lingering just a moment on Honeydews in her figure-hugging lace tea cosy, and then lumbers into a series of arpeggios.

During the agony that is my first hour of barwork, I try to figure out where I've seen Meester Blezzard before. He's a familiar face, and in any case, I need something to take my mind off the tearing ligaments and the increasing chafing sensation where my dance support belt is digging into the soft flappy bit at the base of my scrotum. And then I recognize him – he's the pianist every morning on *Play School*. I'm shamefully impressed.

'Michael, pey attenshun, pleeze …'

Fifty minutes later it's all over. I'm walking like Hopalong Cassidy, but at least I've got through it. Hopefully it can only get better. If I keep my head down for the next 156 weeks I may make it through. As I head for the door I strike up a bogus conversation with Tintin in an attempt to meld in with the herd, but as I'm stepping into the corridor …

'Michael, ken you weyt behind a mineet, pleeze?'

Mister Blezzard pushes past me out of the door. He's ringed several horses for the day's meeting at Catterick and is off to the payphone.

'I am recommending you for Alexander Technique,' Ruth-Eva says starkly. 'You have no movement in your neck: you are too stiff. Please watch out on the noticeboards ...'

I have no idea who Alexander is, or what he might do to me. An image of me strapped down to a table while Peter Cushing stands alongside in a white coat hovers in my imagination.

Our next class is in voice production. We gather in a small, richly carpeted room lit only by an elegant desk lamp. Our tutor, Michael McCallion, sits in a plush Chesterfield armchair. His hair is immaculate, his auburn moustache and beard trimmed and waxed to perfection, his burnished Chelsea boots providing a beautiful counterpoint to the oatmeal of his cavalry twill trousers. When he speaks his voice is like the inside of a walnut whip.

'Michael,' he says, looking at me with quizzical amusement, 'let's begin with you. Why not give the class a morsel of your audition speech?'

I clear my throat and begin.

'When a man's servant shall play the cur with him, look you, it goes hard—'

'So you're from Brighton, are you?' He surveys his audience with a look of quiet satisfaction. 'Lovely town, played there as an actor once myself. Do continue.'

'Here's one that I bought as a puppy. One that I saved from drowning when three or four of his blind brothers and sisters went to it. One—'

He interrupts again with a knowing smile. 'Michael, tell me: how long have you had a constricted tongue string?'

I'm asked to repeat the opening lines of the speech. Then he gets me to say, 'Around the Rugged Rock etcetera'. As I'm speaking, he strolls noiselessly across the carpet until he's standing behind my chair. Moments later I feel his fingers smoothly gripping my lower jaw.

'Don't stop, keep going, if you would ...'

'AArfgdd Ah Arrghed Arrckkkk ...'

I can't move my lower jaw. Without it my tongue can't get up to the roof of my mouth to make the vital consonant. Suddenly I'm the love child of Terry Thomas and Roy Jenkins.

'OK, very good.' McCallion pads smoothly back to his Chesterfield. He produces an elegant fountain pen, twists off the cap with a slight flourish, and writes something on a piece of paper. His signet ring glints in the light from his desk lamp.

'You may have to have your tongue string cut.'

He flicks a speck of dust off his trousers as he speaks. It flutters past his Chelsea boots and settles on the carpet. McCallion is not so much clearing the speck as dismissing it from his presence.

'Don't be alarmed, it's not a problem.' He gives me a cool smile. 'The tendon connecting your lower palate with the underside of your tongue is a little undeveloped. A simple operation to lengthen it under a local anaesthetic and you'll be speaking like Olivier.'

Olivia who? Newton-John? I'm now recalling in my mind a horror story from grammar school: a friend of mine suffered terrible consequences when the string connecting the skin of his penis to the bell end tore off while he allegedly was drying himself over-vigorously in the shower. Apparently the place was like an abattoir. He had to go into Brighton General for an operation to reconnect it and he still couldn't play sports six months later. A severing of my tongue string sounds too close for comfort.

I stare glumly at my new classmates. Leo Sayer gives me a sympathetic smile. Roedean is already checking her tongue string. Action Man looks as if he'd like to be helping her. Tim Spall is waggling a little finger in his right ear.

During the following fifty minutes the vocal raw material on offer from the class of '76 is systematically scrutinized, dissected and evaluated. A big lumpy girl from Boston has something wrong with her s's, and an ex-luggage handler from Luton airport has sinus problems, but as we troop out across the thick shag pile and up the stairs towards the canteen, I'm only too aware that I'm the only one who has so far been prescribed major intrusive surgery. Already the field is fanning out, and we're barely out of the traps. Honeydews and Leo Sayer are already safely over the first fence, Spall, Glasgow, Action Man and Roedean a close second, with the others fast approaching. I, on the other hand, seem to have got tangled in the starting tape.

Lunch. The only category in the syllabus for which I'm uniquely qualified. But I'm already prepared for the worst. I'm here to act, to move, to dance, to express myself in physical form. My body is now my temple: family-sized bars of Galaxy and Scotch eggs are a thing of the past. It's going to need cottage cheese, pulses, high-protein tuna. And I'm ready for it. I head for the canteen at the top of the building. After a climb of sixty-three steps, I take what has to pass for a deep breath, and walk in.

The canteen is filled with ravenous students all guzzling great mountains of steaming fat. The tables are awash with treacle sponge, fish and chips, and meat pies in thick, thick gravy. A team of stoutly appointed women are lined up at the serving hatch and dishing out gigantic portions of food from enormous steel pannikins – they're all in their fifties with legs like tree trunks and voices thick from thirty years of Capstan Full Strength. Vera, Ivy and Vi – they look like extras from a Pathé News Reel about the East End during the Blitz.

I sit down with a gut-busting plate of what according to the menu blackboard is called Slumgullion. It seems to be a dish particular to this part of Gower Street – a robust combination of spaghetti, tomato sauce, low-grade mince and specks of suet.

It tastes fantastic.

Roedean sits down next to me with another student I've not yet spoken to, a sour-faced girl from Tunbridge Wells. Roedean has mini-pizza and chips, Tunbridge Wells merely a salad.

'Didn't you fancy anything?' I ask, through a mouthful of slithering pasta.

'I don't eat much,' replies Tunbridge Wells, wrinkling her nose.

'Oh well,' I chirp, my spirits rising with each forkful of nourishing slurry.

A long thin woman of about fifty with greying hair turns to speak to me from an adjoining table. She introduces herself as June Kemp, one of the other movement teachers. 'I'll make a bet with you ... what's your name?'

'Michael.'

'I'll make a bet with you, Michael: you'll be fatter in two years than you are now.' She allows herself a wry smile suggestive of battles long since fought and lost. 'They haven't got the message up here yet. I keep telling them. Eat all you want, but don't expect a job at the end of it unless they're making Fatty Arbuckle's life story. Up to you. See you for jazz dance at three – don't expect any favours.' She smiles amiably and turns back to her own meal, a plate of cottage cheese and cold baked beans.

Roedean pushes her mini-pizza away from her and returns to the serving hatch for a ham salad.

It's been a miserable morning. Corrective therapy, oral surgery, and now it sounds as if I'm likely to die of heart failure before I can get the chance to enjoy the benefits. I might as well leave now.

I'll just have some of that treacle sponge first ...

animals

I spend the summer holidays at the end of my first term at the Datsun Car Assembly Plant in Lancing, working as a pallet loader. It brings in some useful cash, and gives me a chance to see what I might be missing on out here in the real world. My foreman is a bloke called Chris, and he hates casual workers. In particular he hates university graduates. And when he hears that I'm training at RADA ...

'Oh, you're at drama school, are you?' he says. 'I suppose you'll be spending all your time pretending to be a fuckin' tree.' This last line is delivered with an overt curl of the lip, as if it is his own hard-earned cash that is funding these ludicrous activities.

Barbara Goodwin's second-term classes are a curious hybrid of acting and movement; not quite one and thankfully not quite the other. She's a placid, gently spoken woman in her forties with the face of a children's TV presenter and the manner of a stress counsellor. For much of the first term we spent our time laying on the floors of various darkened rooms and attempting to express the sensation of beads of mercury travelling up and down our various limbs.

'It's now moving up your right arm ...' says Barbara quietly as she picks her way between us. 'Now it's crossing slowly into your neck ... and now it's moving through your collarbone ...' She pads silently between our prone bodies in her stockinged feet, gently noting her impressions. 'You've got it, Stephen ... you've nearly got it, Emma ... yes, Neville, you've definitely got it ...'

I never seem to get it. It's the story of my life. I'm trying so hard to get it I'm in danger of contracting mercury poisoning. It doesn't seem to matter how hard I try: I become so desperate that I eventually take to faking a little semi-subliminal twitching of bodily extremities just to show how much mercury is forcing its way through.

'Michael, you're signalling,' says Barbara.

Then eventually, one lesson, just when I'm least expecting to, I hear her say the words I'm aching to hear:

'That's it, Michael, you've got it.'

It takes me by surprise because I've actually fallen asleep on the floor and for several minutes have been dreaming that I've been having violent sex with the girl with the pre-attached leotard from Islington in the back of a London taxi. But who's complaining? Whatever she's been doing to me it's done the trick. The mercury was obviously rising.

So now, in the second term, we progress to animals.

Barbara Goodwin's animals are one of the features of the course. Finals students have often told us that our animals are considered pivotal by members of staff to our perceived psychological restructuring. For instance, they still talk in the students' common room about Bob Goody's cow. It happened a few years back now, but rumour has it that it was sensational. I've never heard of Bob Goody, but students from other terms tell me they used to try and catch a peek at his cow through the window. It used to draw quite a crowd.

Barbara sits us all down in a semi-circle and explains the idea. She tells us we've got to choose an animal to inhabit, and that between now and the end of term we'll be spending our sessions with her mastering the inner and outer expressions of our chosen creature: its thinking, instincts, movements, the way it interacts with other animals and the environment it inhabits. She warns us to give the matter some careful consideration, to spend a few hours at London Zoo, catch the odd wildlife programme and consult a reference book or two.

She wants us to select our animal in time for our next session – Thursday, 3.30 p.m.

When we reassemble a couple of days later we've each completed our choices. Russell Harty and I have both gone for a lion. Action Man has, rather predictably in my opinion, gone for a puma, particularly as Honeydews has gone for a sheep. The girl from Boston, who seems to be piling on the pounds in accordance with the finest traditions of the Academy, has been to the Snowdon Aviary and plumped for an owl. Roedean has decided to recreate a pet she had as a child and gone for a chinchilla. Tim has sat farting in front of afternoon television in his mum's house in Battersea and gone for the first thing that came into his head.

We each pick a space in the room while Barbara pads about in bare feet, occasionally stopping to whisper confidentially in our ear. For the first thirty-five minutes we do nothing – we must just try to imagine our animal. Then we're allowed to start moving the odd limb or two. Cornelia begins to swivel her head as far round as she can get it. Roedean begins sniffing the lino. I attempt a slow, loose-limbed prowl towards the stack of chairs in the corner. Tim Spall collapses on to his side, curls up into a ball and goes to sleep.

It transpires later he's chosen a sloth.

It's all very placid, very quiet. The room is like a reference library. And then, suddenly, the air of tranquillity is shattered by Tintin. I had thought his choice of clothes odd; he came for the lesson wearing nothing but a skullcap, some dance tights and a pair of huge, steel-tipped builder's boots. And now, having not moved since the start of the lesson, he suddenly sticks his head down and charges full tilt at the storage cupboards at one side of the room. It's a sort of goose-stepping charge, as if an officer from the Third Reich had taken sudden offence at an entire wall. He hits the cupboards at about 20 mph. The crunch of skull against splintering wood is sickening. One of the doors flies open and a shelf full of battered tambourines and beanbags spills out on to the floor. Our fragile zoological representations evaporate immediately and we're twenty acting students who've witnessed a car crash. Even Tim's eyes momentarily flicker before closing again.

'Keep your intentions,' whispers Barbara.

We settle back. I try once more to imagine the lion: the slightly lobotomized look they have whenever they're at rest; the air of rumination, of laconic detachment; the sleepy way they wash themselves.

I might try that in a moment.

Barbara silently gathers up the tambourines and beanbags, and places them carefully back on the shelf. She closes the cupboard doors with hardly a click.

Suddenly Tintin goose-steps across the room and crashes his head against the door frame at high speed.

'My God, are you OK?' That was an involuntary cry from the owl.

'Keep your intentions,' whispers Barbara.

It goes on like this for the rest of the two-hour session. A period of inactivity, followed by a sudden lurch from whichever crazed animal Tintin has taken on, a sickening crash, and then silence again. By the end of the afternoon our nerves are shredded.

'And … come out of your animal slowly,' says Barbara. We wake Tim, gather up our bags of tampons, dog-eared acting biographies and Crunchie bars, and trail out. Barbara stays behind with Tintin. He's standing there, cheeks flushed, a look of intense concentration still etched on his face. As I leave I see him removing his skullcap. His forehead is bright red and a graze has appeared over his left eyebrow.

In the canteen Tintin reveals the identity of his animal, but this begs more questions than it answers. He's been inhabiting a kiwi, the curious flightless bird that looks like a rugby ball and inhabits the forests of New Zealand.

'Why did you choose that?' asks Glasgow. 'They're extinct, for fuck's sake.'

Tintin admits he has only seen an illustration – on the top of tins of Kiwi shoe polish. His dad used to use the stuff to polish his boots before going to work as a pest control officer for Barnsley Council. And as there are no examples left to tell us what it was like, he's decided to use his imagination.

Bob Goody's cow has some company at last. Tintin's kiwi from Barnsley Council is already passing into legend. And Barbara loves it. Tintin is the talk of the Academy. In Barbara's opinion he's definitely got it.

If only he lives long enough to use it.

awakening

The old folks say, 'You never forget your first kiss.'

This is true, of course.

It's also true that you never forget your first onstage kiss either. Especially as in my case they're the same event.

Especially as it could be with Tim Spall.

We've known for some time we're going to be doing a potted version of Frank Wedekind's classic piece *Spring Awakening* during our third term. It's the ideal project for students starting to find their feet, with lots of good parts and requiring minimal scenery or props. It also has the sort of dramatic structure that means you can cut it to ribbons without anybody really noticing, least of all Wedekind, who's been dead about sixty years. If I had to sum it up, I'd say it was an exploration of the conflict between repressive adulthood and adolescent sexual longings in provincial Germany, an extraordinary illumination of the teenage mind, not merely the fascination with sex but the fixation with death.

At least, that's what it says in the copy of the script I've obtained from the RADA library. Judging by the condition of the book, the piece is regularly performed. The pages are covered in thumbprints and chocolate, and some are welded together with other, more dubious substances. I can only hope they're not the result of thematic improvisations.

Not that I'm worrying about that. My problem is on page fifty-two. Scene fifteen. It took me a while to prise open the pages and now I wish I hadn't. Because it recounts a scene in which two of the adolescent boys have to attempt an exploratory mouth-to-mouth kiss. And we're talking the full monty:

Wedekind's stage directions are quite unequivocal about that. *He kisses him on the mouth.* A peck on the cheek won't do. According to the preface written by some old dodderer at Oxford, scene fifteen is a beautiful and sensitive observation of budding but as yet unformed sexual desire.

We've assembled in room thirteen to hear the casting of the parts, and I've just got some terrible feeling in the pit of my stomach that scene fifteen has got my name on it. Nothing tangible, it's just a premonition, I could be utterly wrong, but I won't relax until our director has announced how she's going to divvy up the roles.

The waiting is the worst part.

Eve Shapiro should be here by now. Eleven o'clock prompt, it said on the schedule, and she's already ten minutes late. The fact is she's probably been held up by the heatwave – London has been like a cauldron for most of the summer, and the city's crumbling infrastructure is beginning to fail. Tube trains are stalling, cars are boiling dry, Regent's Park is already the colour of old coconut matting, ice-cream vans in Trafalgar Square have doubled their prices, guardsmen have been going down like ninepins, Denis Howell has been appointed minister for drought. And if I'm going to be nominated to snog Spall, I'm going to require water, and lots of it.

Don't get me wrong, it's not that I'm not prepared to try new things; I'm aware it's all part of the unravelling and putting back together on which RADA prides itself. But this is unravelling too quickly. Remember, you're talking to a man who less than eighteen months ago walked out of a production of Seaford Musical Theatre Group's updated version of *The Gondoliers* because it was too avant-garde. I bought the ballet tights in good faith, and I wear them. That should be enough.

The others sitting here next to me in room thirteen by contrast all seem pretty cool about it. Action Man for instance, the one who's after anything in a skirt – he'd probably quite like a snog with another bloke, just to ring the changes. Leo Sayer has already declared he's anxious to prove his alternative credentials, and Neville from Ashby de la Zouch has confessed that if he hadn't got into the Academy he was going to train to be a priest, which in my book makes him halfway to nancy before he's even started. Another of our term, a Turkish Cypriot Muslim from Lewisham, may not even be eligible for scene fifteen.

I've got the list of possible parts written down here on a piece of paper, and I've done some impromptu calculations. There's a one in seven chance I'll be involved. Chances of both me and Spall being chosen I calculate at being far lower, one in forty-seven ...

Surely to God ...

I promised myself I'd stop looking at scene fifteen, but somehow it's like a scab, I can't help it. Not only does the scene involve a kiss, but the speech after it isn't much better ...

'Glowing mountains, grapes hanging down in our mouths, the evening breeze stroking the rocks like a kitten playing ...'

I'm not stroking Spall's rocks even if I have to leave the course. How Wedekind got away with that sort of dross is beyond me: but what can you expect from a dramatist who once wrote a play called *The Marquis of Keith*?

It'll be all right. Hanschen and Ernst are the parts to avoid. So long as I don't get either I'll be all right.

The odds are too high. Cruttwell casts against type: acne-ridden little rat-faces in the part of heart throbs; girls with faces like tram smashes playing the roles of glittering beauties. He casts dwarfs as Romeo, and girls with arses the size of China as Juliet. It's all in an attempt to explore the entire gamut of dramatic and imaginative possibilities while the student is still raw and malleable enough to benefit from it. He'll be looking to give that kiss to somebody who's still emotionally trussed up, behaves like a Boy Scout and looks as though his mum still buys his clothes for him.

Perhaps I'd better loosen my tie.

Glasgow is reading a novel in the corner. He's all right, I suppose. I could just about bear doing it with him, even though he's got a five o'clock shadow you could sand a floor with. Wisconsin is never without that pipe in his mouth. Tintin, Luton airport ... it's hardly a beauty pageant.

Tim is sitting on the lino, his back resting against the wall. With one hand he's investigating something between the toes of his left foot. With his other he's eating what, if my sense of smell hasn't let me down, appears to be a liver sausage sandwich. Tintin is sunning himself out on the fire escape; NY and Boston are sharing a fag; Roedean is stretching out on a ballet bar; Glasgow is staring at me with a cruel smile on his lips, as if he already knows it's going to be me. He can smell my fear.

Where the hell is Eve Shapiro? She should be here by now.

I know: I'll listen to my hamburger. That'll calm me down, make me look like the others. I fumble in my bag, feel the comforting shape lying in the bottom, bring it out, switch it on, and press it closely to my ear.

My hamburger has become a security blanket in times like this. I won it in a competition in a restaurant in Worthing last autumn. I'd been to see *South Pacific* and, to while away a few minutes before curtain up, I'd popped into a nearby Wimpy Bar. I can hardly remember filling in the competition form ('in which country is the city of Hamburg, and complete this sentence: "I like a Wimpy because" in no more than ten words'), but Head Office must have liked whatever I wrote because a few weeks later a plastic transistor radio looking exactly like a hamburger arrived in a small box, complete with volume and tone controls in the shape of tiny gherkins, and with moulded coils of mustard festooning the sides.

My ear presses on to the jagged weld of the gherkin. A few twiddles, then I hear the familiar sound of summer: the third test between England and West Indies at Edgbaston, and the voice of John Arlott.

'...So it's Boyce, with his mass of black curls, running in from the Warwick Road end, and this time Steele leaves it outside the off stump ...'

The door opens and in walks a natty little South African woman in her early fifties with a weatherbeaten face and dyed black hair. Eve Shapiro has a crisp, businesslike approach, which suggests formal cordiality just above a steely core. She apologizes for being late, sets down her handbag, plonks herself down on a chair facing us and starts sifting through a set of Xeroxed scripts.

'Michael? What are you doing?'

I would have thought it was obvious, but this is no time for flippant answers – I need to keep her onside. I switch off the hamburger and stuff it hurriedly back into the bag.

'No food in the rehearsal room, Michael, you know the rules.'

'It's all right, Eve, he's listening to it.' That's Glasgow, still smirking.

Eve scrutinizes me. 'Perhaps someone could explain?' she says with a taut smile.

'It's a radio, Eve. I won it in a contest.'

Her eyes narrow. 'Aren't you hot in that?' she asks, looking pointedly at my collar.

'No, I'm fine, thanks.'

She gives me a long investigative stare. 'Very well, can someone at least open a window?' She looks pointedly at Tim, who gets up and waddles over to the side of the room. Meanwhile she starts laying out the sheets of paper into smaller piles.

'I've got the casting sorted out, so we'll begin.'

You know how people say that when something terrible happens to them, like a mugging or the moment when the doctor tells them they've got cancer, it's as if it's happening in a dream, one in which time seems to almost stand still? 'I felt I could see it coming,' they always say. 'Even though it was only a split second before the car hit us head on, it seemed to be moving towards us in slow motion, I could remember the head of the little dog nodding on the dashboard, even the face of the driver staring back at me. I could describe every detail, I'd recognize him anywhere ...'

'Scene One ...'

I can see the car pulling out into the centre of the road from behind that articulated lorry.

'Scene Four ...' Eve's voice drones on, scene after scene, part after part, graduate after graduate ...

Apparently car travel is supposed to be an extremely safe method of transport. You've got more chance of being struck by lightning than dying in a road smash.

'Scene Twelve ...'

From somewhere very far off, a screech of brakes.

'Scene fifteen. Ernst ... Tim Spall.'

She turns a page.

'Hanschen ...'

I can smell burning rubber.

'Michael Simkins.'

Of course.

Our fenders meet. Above the slowly rearing mass of twisting metal that was once my front bonnet I can see the face of the driver. And he's eating a liver sausage sandwich.

prize fights

By the end of the fifth term, the classes and daily routines are gradually being replaced by rehearsals of plays and full-scale performances. Cruttwell's casting has been unpredictable and daring: Russell Harty has had to black up as a Negro servant in *The Little Foxes* and Honeydews has had to white up to play my mother in Molière's *Tartuffe*. I've been cast as a series of elderly men in projects ranging from Arnold Wesker to George Bernard Shaw, achieving the required effect mainly by plastering my hair with shoe whitener and sticking my stomach out. With less than a year to go we're starting to encounter the traditional set piece occasions that mark our progress through the course: the Speaking in Standard English competition; the Can You Stand Up and Entertain? event; and tonight, the most eagerly awaited of them all, the Prize Fights.

We've been learning the techniques of stage combat for five terms now in a flat-roofed annexe room wedged under the fire escape. Our tutor is an elderly man who looks like Catweazle, only five foot tall and balding, with a straggly moustache and lank hair hanging down the back of his neck. Despite his extreme age he spends all his time in a grubby T-shirt and ludicrously sagging tights, from which a set of keys to the cupboards dangle like ancient metal testicles. Catweazle's other distinguishing feature is a large divot in his domed forehead, which he claims he received after being attacked with a hammer by an unsuspecting actor in some far-flung town who returned home to find Catweazle in bed with his wife. I can well believe it; he has a louche, seaside feel about him, suggesting a bygone age of pierrot costumes on gusty sea fronts. But Catweazle knows his stage combat. During the past eighteen months he's taken us through foil, épée, rapier and dagger, broadsword and shield, and finally cutlass. And now it's time for us to put our expertise on public show.

The Prize Fights, traditionally held in the appropriately named Little Theatre, deep in the bowels of Gower Street, are one of the compulsory milestones of RADA. You have to perform a short scene with a classmate, involving both dialogue, drama and proficiency in the art of seemingly knocking the shit out of each other; how and with what it is left up to you. The evening traditionally starts with some stirring martial music over the loudspeakers, just to get the audience in the mood, after which the individual scenes are ceremoniously announced from the side of the stage by a poor conscript from the first term, who has to wear a tabard and carry a bogus medieval trumpet. Tonight it's a chubby city type called Ian who's thrown in a lucrative career in the stock market to become an actor, and who, since I gave up the habit earlier this year, is now the only student who comes to work in a tie.

It's a high-spirited evening: the audience is limited to those currently at the academy, and as the Little only holds about a hundred it's always packed to the gunnels. For the participants there are three awards on offer: the Derek Ware prize for best unarmed combat scene; the William Hobbs prize for best scene involving fighting with rapier or foil; and tonight's star prize, the Bryan Mosley award for the best overall item of stage combat.

Yes. That Bryan Mosley.

He is the actor who plays Councillor Alf Roberts in *Coronation Street*. He weighs about twenty stone, has a waistline of not less than 40 inches, is never seen without a tweed hat wedged on his bulky frame, and rarely strays from behind the safety of the counter in his corner shop. On the rare occasions he does, usually to remonstrate with Ken Barlow about the price of corned beef, he turns red and has to stop every few feet to recover his breath. And yet this is same Bryan Mosley for whose award we are all competing. The mystery of why the evening's most coveted prize is dedicated to an overweight soap star is one of the great mysteries of RADA – the notion seems ludicrous, as if James Callaghan had donated a prize for downhill skiing. But it's the truth, and I can say that with confidence because I can see Bryan Mosley in the audience, sitting between Hugh Cruttwell and Catweazle. He's even wearing a car coat much like the one popular in the environs of Wetherfield.

I've already witnessed a couple of Prize Fight evenings in previous years from the safety of the auditorium. The previous offering from the students a year above us has already gone down in folklore due to one fantastic incident, when the unofficial academy pin-up, a stunningly pretty girl called Jane from the Home Counties, accidentally exposed her breasts during a display of unarmed combat. The scene was supposed to be between two Amazonian women, who were fighting with wooden staves over some poor excuse to do with a cooking pot. Just the sight of Jane appearing in swatches of animal skin and smeared with mud would have been enough to send most of the men in the audience to bed happy, but during the frenetic stave work with her deadly Amazonian rival (a girl from Cardiff called Elin), Jane's impromptu bikini began to loosen. Many of the males in the academy had risked life and limb trying to get a peek at those breasts – one had nearly died during a foolhardy escapade on to the corrugated roof above the girls locker room the previous summer – and now suddenly they were presented to us on a plate, beautifully lit and even with a sheen of perspiration adorning them.

And now, in the autumn of 1977, nearly a year later, it's our turn; and selections have ranged from the trusty through to the absurd. Leo Sayer and the baggage handler are doing Romeo and Tybalt with rapier and dagger. Islington and Wisconsin are doing something based on what happens next in the Campari adverts when Leonard Rossiter spills drink all down Joan Collins's blouse. The thin girl from Tunbridge Wells and the plumper one from Boston are doing a scene involving mustard gas, their weapons being two huge sheets of card with which they waft the imaginary fumes in the direction of their rival. Top marks for creativity, but I somehow can't see Mosley buying it. They don't like smart-arses in The Street.

In comparison I've gone for an old warhorse: Macbeth meets

his nemesis, Macduff, in the closing moments of the Scottish play. Two huge broadswords. Two huge actors. Me and Spall.

The idea of swapping broadswords with Spall is not for the faint-hearted, and yet I've hit lucky. Spall is extraordinarily dainty on his feet. He also 'sells the blows', as we cognoscenti of the stage combat world refer to it. In other words, when Spall swipes burnished steel at a point three inches in front of your nose, it looks like he means business.

We've rehearsed the scene at every available opportunity in the past few weeks. The sequences of blows and parries have advanced from stumbling incompetence, through measured theatricality, to the point where we can do them in our sleep. Right cut to neck, step back and parry right waist, advance and head cut, parry by left breast ... so it goes on. Nearly sixty separate movements, each requiring perfect harmony and split-second precision with your partner, and all of it drizzled over with the most important ingredient, intention.

Our trump card, worked out with assistance from Catweazle, is the denouement. After three or four minutes of heart-stopping violence, Spall runs at me and launches himself into the air with an attempted drop kick at my head. It's an audacious movement, particularly for such a big bloke. For an instant Spall will actually be airborne. But it'll be OK so long as I don't flinch, assures Catweazle. So long as I stand firm with my full weight against my huge dustbin-lid-sized shield, Spall can use it as a brace from which he can make a controlled descent on to the floor. Whereupon ...

The ending is important.

'So. I've got Macbeth on his back. How do I finish him off?' I had asked Catweazle.

'Easy,' he had said. 'Take your sword and shove it up his arse.'

It's a triumph. Spall minimally lifts his back off the floor while I, and here is the trick, ever so gently, with almost courtly elegance, seemingly insert the entire blade of my broadsword carefully up inside his rectum. Spall receives the thrust in complete silence, staring up at me as I crouch over him. Not a word, not a scream. It's almost like a surgical operation. An unexpected, gloriously understated climax.

'You've cracked it,' says Catweazle.

Spall and I are the last act. The fight between Leo and the baggage handler has gone well, and the others have been received with polite applause, but the wild card in the pack, the gas fight, went down like a wet fart. We've already got one hand on the trophy.

In the minutes before our entrance, Tim and I stand in the wings, miming the endless sequences of blows in miniature with our arms. We're both dressed in shabby black leather overalls and battered armour. Spall is wearing a chain mail head-dress: he looks like Noggin the Nog. Out on the stage the stockbroker is already holding up a huge scroll and announcing us: I can see the end of his fake bugle between the drapes.

'Please welcome our final entry for tonight. Verily I request a warm welcome for the Thane of Glamis and Lord Macduff from Act V of the Scottish play ... Michael Simkins and Timothy *Spall* ...'

A huge cheer erupts from the audience.

We've chosen some Philip Glass music to underscore the fight, and as we swing on to stage, it's already kicking in, providing a murky, damaged post-apocalyptic counter-point to our apparel: saggy and moth-eared in the gloom of the wings, it now looks a million dollars, and with Tim's helmet refracting the light like some military glitter ball, he seems to have transformed from Noggin into Attila the Hun. The first set of blows cascades in a sudden flurry: the audience are already silenced by the suggestion of genuine violence by the time we go into the second manoeuvre. We're on course.

And it goes well. Really well. Tim plays Macbeth as a sort of medieval Sid Vicious, vomiting out the lines about not being killed by one of woman born with swaggering, psychotic hatred. I try to match him with an icy detachment, a Macduff who knows in his soul that his time is truly come. Before I know it we're into the final sequence, which has taken nearly three weeks to perfect. The clang of steel on steel reverberates through the tiny auditorium and up into the street. Tim lets out a banshee wail and prepares for his final attack.

I still can't explain why I flinched as he launched his drop kick. We've done it hundreds of times and it's a perfectly safe manoeuvre. God knows I've seen Mick Macmanus and Steve Logan doing it countless times on *World Of Sport*. So long as Tim can hit a solid target, he's in no danger. A rectum's worth of cold steel, and thank you very much, Mr Mosley.

But as Spall's boots are flying towards me, at the very point when I can read the words 'Property of RADA Wardrobe Dept' on their soles, I instinctively take a half-step back. Not much, perhaps two or three inches; but it's enough. Spall's feet, instead of smacking sturdily against the shield, barely make contact. Control is impossible. A split second later, the base of his skull hits the stage with a terrible crack. There's also a snapping sound. The subsequent insertion of my sword into his anus is infinitely more apologetic than even Catweazle would have recommended. Because of the way he's landed he can't arch his back to allow my blade to slide smoothly beneath him: I have to poke around in between folds of chain mail to find a route through: it takes nearly a minute, and looks as if I'm performing some medieval surgery for haemorrhoids. The Bryan Mosley prize recedes with each tentative prod.

Beneath me Tim looks dazed and disorientated. The best he can hope for is a visit to casualty up the road at University College Hospital. More likely he's going to require crutches. I wonder if NY still has those leg irons.

neville

Some actors you speak to – the ones who know a bit, who've survived – will tell you that the trick is to keep going. Just hang on in there. The business is always promising extraordinary things, not necessarily today, tomorrow perhaps, or the day after that. Just keep ticking along, the work will come in and eventually, if you're patient enough, you may get a really big break.

Then there are the other sort of actors. They say exactly the same thing, but they've believed it for too long. They are the ones who can't afford a decent car, who daren't risk having to buy a round of drinks, the ones who are getting by on ten pounds a week and talk of doing profit-share lunchtime shows above pubs in Fulham. Middle-aged blokes in balding corduroys and Dr Who scarves, drinking a bit too much and talking about the big break that is just around the corner as soon as their 'fucking agent pulls his finger out'. Meanwhile, their hopes, their marriages and their livers are gradually crushed under the weight of disappointment over the call that's never coming. But they haven't noticed: they're too busy staring at the phone.

Not that it's going to happen to me. I'll know if fate's trying to tell me something. I'll get out while there's still time. There's everything to play for – I'm not even out of the cot so why should I be worrying about pension plans? And yet, as I gaze up at this tatty announcement in the early weeks of term six, I'm strangely aware for the first time of the pressures this career is capable of exerting. The misery of being winner or loser is already claiming its first casualty, and the clues are all here before me, Blu-Tacked to the notice board in the Gower Street foyer. Neville from Ashby de la Zouch is to perform his own evening of songs from the shows in the Little Theatre, and even though we're still nearly two terms away from graduation, I know that this is the cry of a man who already senses he's never going to get off the blocks and is starting to panic.

Neville wants to be an actor more passionately than possibly any of us. Or perhaps, more accurately, he wants to be Judy Garland more than any of us. He has a strong, sinewy body, boundless energy and a mirthless laugh like the chatter of a machine gun. He never misses a class, only drinks in moderation, goes to see all the plays in the West End and talks passionately about technique and style and theatre history to anyone who'll listen. The trouble is, few people are prepared to hang around long enough to find out. They're starting to identify him as one for whom it isn't going to happen. He wants it too much. When he gets a decent role he's so anxious to be a success that he becomes unwatchable: the sinews in his neck stand out like piano wires and he acquires a look in his eye I'd only previously seen in a documentary about life in Broadmoor. All of this wouldn't matter if he had a support system, a few friends to sit him down and tell him to take his foot off the pedal, but Neville has become a pariah and consequently a loner. Just as he tries too hard on the stage, he tries too hard in the common room, and now there's a smell of desperation clinging to him.

And once you look desperate ...

The extent of his frustration and rage at his increasing marginalization is all expressed in his lurid announcement.

An evening of songs from the shows. From Gershwin to Garland. Twenty toe-tapping numbers. His personal tribute to those who put the show in showbiz.

Where's this come from? He's made no mention of it during class or in the bar, yet the look of brooding defiance that has been his trademark lately is obviously behind it. We may choose not to seek his company in the common room, or in his bed, but see if we can ignore this little lot. What's more, he's doing it entirely off his own bat. He's even paying for a trio of professional musicians to back him for the sixty-minute musical trawl. He's printed all his own flyers, arranged his own mikes and speakers, he's done everything, and all this at a time when none of us have got a minute to wipe our arse, what with rehearsals, finding agents, attending auditions, and generally preparing ourselves to leave the womb. The RADA prospectus warns that 'students should not expect to be able to have the time to take part-time jobs or casual engagements during the final terms'. We're here from 10 a.m. until midnight as it is. And yet Neville's staging a tribute to Broadway.

The same day that I see the notice I spot him sitting by himself over a tuna salad in the canteen, and wander over to ask him why he's doing it. His replies have a bogus lightness about them – it will be a laugh, why not, you're only young once, thought I'd get a few musical agents in to have a look, always wanted to be Gene Kelly, can't do any harm, ha-ha-ha – but his nostrils are instinctively flaring, the piano wires are surfacing in his neck and Broadmoor is upon him again.

'But, Neville, you're doing Nagg in Beckett's *Endgame* in a week or two. You've got to learn a huge part and then spend your entire evening in a dustbin. You don't need this.'

'Hey, fuck off, what's it to you, ha-ha-ha.' Neville tries a fluffy carefree laugh, but it sounds like the dustbin lid being thrown down a staircase.

'You'll come, won't you?' he rasps.

'Course I will—'

'Great. Let's talk about something else.' Neville knocks back a tumbler of orange juice.

'So long as I'm not rehearsing.'

'Fuck off, you won't be.' He said that too quickly: he was obviously anticipating that excuse. 'I'm doing it at five, during meal break, so you can bring in a sandwich, ha-ha-ha.' Neville smiles, showing two rows of gently grinding teeth. He's thought of everything. He's left us no easy way out.

By lunchtime on the day of the gig there's a sense of unease throughout the building. Even John, our burly receptionist on the front desk, seems tense, and he was a policeman for thirty-five years. Everyone seems to be gathering in corners discussing whether they should go to see it, and if not, what excuse they can use and how they'll meet Neville's gaze the next morning. As I run out to post a letter during the lunch break I pass a couple of men dragging in amplifying equipment through the Gower Street entrance. Neville is pointing the way down to the Little Theatre stage.

'Mike, come and meet the guys in the band.' I shake hands with Derek, Ron and Keith. The men are probably only in their mid-thirties but they look incongruous here in Gower Street with their thinning hair and Debenhams slacks and a copy of the *Daily Express* sticking out of one of their back pockets. You just don't see people like that in the RADA foyer: you only normally see them playing guitar in the back row of the Ray McVay band on *Come Dancing*.

'Good luck. Can't wait to see it,' I murmur hopefully.

'Hold on to your hat, it's going to be great,' he shouts as he disappears down the stairs and into the theatre.

Hold on to my hat?

By 4 p.m. there are reminders everywhere: tiny handbills Sellotaped to the balustrade on the staircase on every floor; piles of leaflets in the canteen; and a new glitterdust poster on the inside of the main doors. And Neville is everywhere as well, in the bar, on the stairs – 'Don't forget now ...' Student loyalty is high for a special gig, and anybody doing their own one-off thing can usually be guaranteed a full house, no problem. But the poster with the references to Judy Garland and the glitter-dust border is striking a quiet sense of unease into everyone. Even first-termers who don't know Neville from a hole in the wall are picking up the vibes. Normally they would always come to see everything – they want to see the way ahead, how they might look themselves in a year or two – and yet two of them stop me on the stairs about 4.20. They seem uncertain.

'Simmo, are you going to this cabaret thing?'

'Um ... I'm hoping to.'

'Only we're thinking of it, but we can't find anyone else who's going. Will it be any good?'

How can I answer that? Every fibre in my body wants to scream, No, don't go, that's not what you should see, in two years' time you won't be putting up posters with glitterdust round the edge with pictures of top hats drawn in magic marker, leave him be, it'll only make it worse if it becomes a spectator sport. But then I remember Neville and I fear for him. Perhaps it'll be all right after all, maybe he really will knock us dead and this will be the moment when he suddenly finds his stride, gains acceptance, taps in to that organic creative spirit that will transform him, drop his shoulders, give him the confidence and ease he so badly needs.

But if there's not even an audience …

I've got to go. If only for the sake of the other actors working with him in *Endgame* the following week. I've got to be there. And so have they, these first-termers. They'll be all right, they've six more terms in which to recover. They're young and strong …

'Yeah, it'll be a laugh … Come along. Why not?'

'OK. See you there. Thanks.' They trot off down the stairs.

It's 4.50 p.m. I finish my tea in the canteen. As I pass the students' common room on my way down, I can see the usual assortment of burst sofas and derelict chairs, the overflowing waste bins, the stained green carpet covered in cigarette burns and empty polystyrene cups. Action Man and Tintin are lolling on one of the sofas, playing cards. Glasgow is dozing in a corner.

'Coming down, chaps?'

Glasgow doesn't speak. He doesn't even look up. He doesn't have to.

When I arrive there are about twenty people already seated. Islington is sitting with Clive, a third-termer and the younger brother of the baggage handler from Luton. The *Come Dancing* trio are already on stage, tuning up and tightening snares, and a long tinselly glitter curtain hangs down from the flies. There's a printed sheet of paper in it with a running order and an illustration of a man high-kicking with a top hat and a cane. Before

I can study it, the lights start to dim, but it looks depressingly extensive.

The drummer begins a gentle drum roll and a voice talking in a fake transatlantic drawl booms out over the speakers.

'Ladies and Gentlemen, please put your hands together ... Please welcome Mr Neville *Hardwicke*!'

The voice is Neville's.

The band snap into a lively up-tempo medley from *Guys and Dolls*. Drums, guitar and electric piano. It sounds like a dinner dance at the local Rotary Club.

The curtains tremble, and Neville appears. He's wearing a spangly waistcoat, figure-hugging Lycra trousers with sequins down the side seams, and white gloves. A top hat is perched on his hair and he's carrying a cane. He grabs the microphone from its stand in the middle of the stage and launches into an ear-splitting rendering of 'Luck Be a Lady Tonight'.

An hour later he finishes with 'There's No Business Like Show Business'. Physically it's still all high kicks and winks at the audience and hands raised up to heaven for the big notes, but emotionally he finished a long time ago.

He'd thrown everything at it; a non-stop barrage of show-stopping tunes, interspersed with introductions to the band, references such as 'Here's a little tune penned by the late, great Mr Johnny Mercer', and hushed references to the memory of his beloved Judy. Each song had been performed in a harsh acid tenor with a vibrato like a dentist's drill, along with sprays of sweat and an increasingly angry expression lurking just behind the eyes. Everything he's seen on *Sunday Night at the London Palladium* is here: but Neville hasn't beaten the clock. The standing ovation hasn't materialized. In fact the show has gently deflated in front of his eyes: not instantly, just quietly, like a slow puncture. He's staked everything hoping to wham-bang-thank-you-ma'am us to our feet, cheering and shouting, calling for more, Cruttwell mounting the stage from the stalls to shake his hand and lead another volley of cheering, with us in the audience all turning to each other and nodding in approbation as we applaud, in a sort of dumb show mime of 'I've never seen anything like that in my life, have you?' Like audiences do in movies. Like they do with Judy.

But it hasn't happened. The applause throughout has been respectful, appreciative; and that's the problem. The clapping has been more like a crowd applauding a dogged half-century by a lower order batsman on the third day of a county championship match between Glamorgan and Derbyshire at Aberystwyth. And with each passing song, with each evergreen classic, with each gentle, damning-with-its-faint-praise ripple of applause, his demeanour has become more reckless. Because this is the worst of all worlds for Neville. Nothing sensational has occurred – nobody has walked out, or laughed, or anything like that. There's not even been anything to rage back at. Just thirty pairs of sympathetic eyes blinking back at him from the dark ...

By his final number his voice is starting to fail. He's looking utterly knackered. There are tiny rivulets of fake Florida tan running down from the brim of his topper; he's beginning to look like a burns victim. All passion spent. At three minutes to six he hits his final, final top note, arms stretched, sequins glittering in the pin spot, ever so slightly sharp. Blackout. Then the lights dart up again, he takes his final bow, thanks the band, and Mr Neville Hardwicke disappears for ever behind the glitter curtain. The Broadway smile is still nailed across his face, where it's been since he first appeared an hour and three minutes ago, and yet, just as he vanishes behind the tinsel strands for the last time, he allows it to drop, to be instantly replaced by a look of immense fatigue and desolation.

Only a split second later and he'd have concealed his defeat, but he eased up as he was breasting the tape. All you needed to know about Neville's evening was in that final nano-second.

First rule of acting – however bad it's been, don't drop your guard at the curtain call.

The house lights come up. Nobody moves. The only noise is the musicians starting to unplug leads, and, from somewhere far off, a distant hum of conversation from the RADA bar. It's obviously doing good business.

As I get up to leave I look across to the others, still seated.

The baggage handler's younger brother is staring at the glitter curtain.

Next to him Islington is scanning the programme. Tears are gently rolling down her face.

the tree

There comes the point in your drama school training when you can't keep pretending any longer. The fairy tale world in which we've existed – the one in which every actor gets their fair share of big parts, full employment is a matter of corporate policy, and you have no rivals for jobs, only plays you haven't read yet – is nearly over. The huge, frozen seas of the profession outside the doors to Gower Street can be heard breaking against the sides of our tiny harbour. We've got to get a job. Or at least get somebody on your side who can get you one. If nothing else, we've got to get an agent.

Hence the Tree Evening.

The Tree Evening, named in memory of our founder, Herbert Beerbohm Tree, is scheduled for the start of our seventh and final term. Every agent, every casting director, every producer who is likely to be able to take our careers forward, from the Royal Shakespeare Company through to Pyjama Tops on the pier at Weymouth ('Some nudity required') is here tonight in the Vanbrugh Theatre to see bite-sized morsels of acting performed in quick-fire succession by all twenty-one departing students. It's a bit like the auditions in reverse – we each get the chance to perform a short monologue, plus a not much longer extract with one other student. The pieces are dovetailed together at breakneck speed, with barely enough time for a lighting change or repositioning of a chair between them: approximately forty-odd extracts and scenes shoehorned into an evening two hours long. At the end of which, as the printed invitation card sent out to your future power brokers coyly suggests, 'There will be an opportunity to meet the students afterwards in the bar ...'

Were we at the Royal Academy of Music it would be something of a swish affair. The wine would be chilled, the canapés edible, the background music something cool and funky played over a set of crystal-clear loudspeakers deftly concealed in the false ceiling, between the 'hint of apricot' light bulbs and the German-made air-conditioning system.

At the RADA it's more a case of some warm Don Cortez in a plastic cup with a few bowls of Smiths' crisps to a tape of the Carpenters on a battered cassette player perched on the bar. An idea was floated of having the ladies from the canteen provide some proper food for the occasion, but the prospect of Bernard Delfont trying to force down Slumgullion and jam roly-poly at 9 p.m. was considered a non-starter.

The Tree Evening is a tough call.

It's harder to tell which part of the evening is the more terrifying – having to perform your speeches to an auditorium of stony faced potential employers, or having to meet them afterwards and pretend it's all wonderful, darling, when the truth is that most of them couldn't fancy you fried. Of the two, the bar room get-together is probably the more excruciating by a short head: at least that's my opinion, as I sit in a fetid dressing room below stage. Already the tannoy system is broadcasting a low hum of conversation, as the various invitees amble in. Rumour has it that Gillian Diamond, Head of Casting for the National Theatre, is going to be here, that Jeremy Conway and Denis Sallinger, two of the country's most powerful theatrical agents, have returned their invites with a promise to attend, or at least to send a representative from their agency. A nod from just one of these, in fact from nearly anyone in the auditorium, and I could be away, out of the traps, heading towards my first job.

But first I have to impress them with my speech.

I've chosen an extract from Shakespeare's *Two Gentlemen of Verona*, in which a servant talks to an imaginary dog.

Yes, I know.

I've been at this Academy, arguably the world's finest, for seven terms, studying voice, movement, dancing, Restoration comedy, improvisation, stage fighting and singing, gaining proficiency certificates in standard English pronunciation, in unarmed combat and tumbling, and playing roles in productions as diverse as Molière, George Bernard Shaw and Wedekind, and yet I'm still doing the same audition speech I used to get in here.

Do you think the pitiful irony has escaped me? The tutor programming the evening, Geoff, has tried to forestall my creeping sense of self-loathing. 'No, no, Mike, it doesn't matter if it's the same speech, it's a good one and you do it well. Why not?' But his honeyed words can't deflect a terrible sense that when push comes to shove, I haven't moved on at all. I'm exiting a revolving door I entered nearly 800 days before.

I've got to go on. It's nearly my turn – I can hear Roedean launching into something from Caryl Churchill's *Top Girls*, and I'm only two items after her. I've got a date with destiny and an unfunny Shakespearean comedy speech.

First rule of acting, don't drop your guard at the curtain call. Second rule of acting, don't expect Shakespearian comedy to be anything other than tedious.

That's what hurts: three years ago I had an excuse for choosing Shakespeare comedy because I knew no better, whereas now … I've seen countless productions of the Bard during the last seven terms and in virtually every one some poor sod has to come on in a pair of tights carrying a pig's bladder on a stick, and try to wrench some laughs out of Shakespeare's best one-liners.

'Sowter will cry out on't, though it be as rank as a fox …'

'Yes yes, he teaches boys the horn-brook. What is a, b, spelt backwards with a horn on his head?'

And my favourite:

'I said the deer was not a *huad credo*; 'twas a pricket.'

You can hardly see Les Dawson losing much sleep.

Luckily my dog speech hasn't got anything quite like that, but it has got, 'Didst ever see me make water against a gentlewoman's farthingale?'

I can already hear the sound of the tipping up of seats before I've even got to it.

~

A few minutes after curtain down we trail into the dingy bar. I try to stick close to Tintin and Russell Harty. None of us thought we did very well, so with any luck we'll all be ignored, though my duologue went a little better than the dog. I'd plumped for a scene from Noel Coward's old warhorse, *Tonight At 8.30*, a dusty and over-whimsical piece about a couple of old ham variety actors, husband and wife, bickering in a dressing room somewhere in the thirties, and in truth, Islington and I got a couple of laughs with it. Well, Islington got the laughs, but as I stand forlornly among the throng I tell myself that it was my feed lines that gave them to her. There must be someone in the audience who spotted my contribution and who's looking for a feed. Surely?

But there isn't. The only feed they're looking for are the nibbles. Slowly, inexorably, the employers find the ones they want 'the opportunity to meet'. By 10 p.m. the trend is clearly established: Tim Spall is surrounded by a gaggle of important-looking executives; Honeydews is talking to a film producer; Gillian Diamond from the National is engaged in a long conversation about government funding for the arts with Tintin and Wisconsin; even Action Man has found a fellow sports enthusiast to talk to about the recent World Cup in Argentina; and Glasgow has been pursued by somebody from BBC Scotland about a new lunchtime series set in a small Highland village. Russell Harty, who wants to go into musicals, has been whisked away to a corner by somebody who's trying to put on a version of *The Boyfriend* to tour schools in the Lowestoft area. Which leaves me.

Time to cut my losses. I'm going back home to Brighton; if I don't walk too fast to the tube station I could justify having to leave now to get the 11.05 from Victoria. I pick up my bags and make for the exit doors. Just as I'm leaving, somebody touches my arm. I turn round to find a well-dressed man in his forties, still holding a notebook and pen, and smiling at me.

'Excuse me, are you Michael Simkins?' he asks, checking his programme.

'I am.'

'Well, I must say it's nice to have an opportunity to meet you.'

'Yes?'

'Yes, I've been meaning to pop over to have a word all night,' he says.

My sphincter tightens.

'Do your parents own a sweet shop in Brighton?'

'They do.'

'I thought I recognized the name. No "p" in Simkins did it. Most unusual. I live in Kemp Town – I used to come in there every day on my way to the station.' He shakes my hand vigorously. 'Really enjoyed it tonight.'

'Thanks. You are ...?'

'Oh, my firm is supplying the wine for the event this evening.'

With that he smiles and wanders away. I never find out who he is. Or whether I should have asked him for a job in his off licence. Thirty minutes later I'm staring at the indicator board on the station concourse. My train comes up. Semi-fast to Clapham Junction, East Croydon, and straight back to where I started from.

the card

The final weeks of the course are when you put away childish things, and begin to concentrate on even more childish things: getting an agent, some publicity photos, a snappy begging letter, a decent haircut and a job.

There is a further minor obstacle that the profession throws at you, just to make it more interesting. In 1978 you also have to get an Equity card.

Equity is the actors' trade union. You have to be a member in order to work, and in order to be a member you have to obtain a card. Equity controls how many new cards are issued each year, and as part of this policy of closed shop they allow each regional theatre company to have two – *two* – new cards each year, to be divvied up between the hundreds of graduates pouring out from every dramatic orifice.

The only other way of getting one is to do topless dancing in Majorca. Strip clubs in Mediterranean resorts always seem to have an endless supply, nobody knows why. Either that or you can apply to the Donovan Maule Theatre in Nairobi, a far-flung outpost of the empire still staging Agatha Christies to ex-pats. But I get heatstroke on Brighton beach, so I'm going to have to ask a regional rep for one.

Even if I'm successful I'm still not allowed to work within a fifty-mile radius of London until I've clocked up forty-two weeks of paid employment. Those are the rules. No matter if you've got wonderful reviews in your first acting job at Pitlochry and a London producer wants to bring you into the West End. Sorry, darling, you've only got eleven weeks on your card. Never mind, there's always *The Ghost Train* at Bangor-on-Tees. After that we'll see.

During my final term there's only one thing on my mind: how to persuade a regional theatre to give me one of their cards. Actually there are two things on my mind, the other being a first-term student from Rochdale with whom I've fallen hopelessly, sickeningly in love. In between writing hundreds of applications for auditions to all corners of the country I spend every waking hour trying to bump casually into her on any possible pretext: on the stairs between classes; in the canteen; in one of any fifteen pubs within a ten-minute radius of the Academy. I can't sleep or eat for thinking about her, so much so that she's achieving what seven terms of dance classes couldn't – I'm losing my big tits. Good for my personal ego, but it rules out those dancing clubs in Majorca.

Every day the building is alight with fresh rumours of the whereabouts of these bloody cards. Leo Sayer has heard on the grapevine that Lancaster Rep have got one to offer.

'A mate of mine was in this morning, they're auditioning drama school leavers this afternoon down at the YMCA on Tottenham Court Road. They're casting three plays, *Epsom Downs*, *Abigail's Party* and *The Gingerbread Man*.' Suddenly every student who hasn't managed to get representation from the Tree Evening is queuing at the one available payphone, or worse, legging it down the road to try to gate-crash the Lancaster auditions. By 4 p.m. the rumour has run into the sands; the Turkish Cypriot waited there all through lunch break and beyond, only to be told by the associate director that Lancaster's two available cards have gone to somebody from Webber-Douglas and the administrator's eldest daughter, who's studying agriculture at Wye College but who fancies a go at acting.

Later, in the Montague Arms in Torrington Place, at the end of another nerve-shredding day, it all ignites again. A group of us are enjoying an end-of-day pint, when Wisconsin wanders in. I'm on my normal blackcurrant and lemonade but if it needs a half of sweet cider to press my masculine credentials with Rochdale I'm prepared to do it.

'I don't know if you guys are interested, but my flatmate has just rung to say he's heard that Exeter Rep are holding auditions tomorrow at a church hall off Horseferry Road for *Privates on Parade* and *The Late Edwina Black*.'

'Is there a card?' someone shouts hoarsely.

'Jeez yes, why do you think I'm tellin' you?'

It doesn't matter to Wisconsin – being from Wisconsin he isn't allowed to join British Equity anyway and is soon to return to the States to try his luck in their rep equivalent, 'summer stock'. Within seconds the bar is empty; my classmates stream back to their digs to write personal letters. Only Rochdale and I are left, marooned among the upturned stools and dead crisp packets. Oh, and Wisconsin.

'Like another drink?' I try to disguise the pleading note in my voice beneath a insouciant, seen-it-all-before final-term-graduate world weariness.

'No, ta,' she says, 'I'll be getting back.'

'I'll walk with you to the tube.'

'I've got my bike, thanks.' Rochdale is already gathering up her impossibly lovely straw basket in those tired, sinuous, exquisite northern working girl's hands.

'I'll have another,' drawls Wisconsin. He sits down beside me, blocking my escape. 'Have you seen that Somerset Maugham revival at the National yet?'

And she's gone.

Then, around mid-term, my luck starts to change. It may be because I've lost about three stone, or perhaps all this training is subliminally, imperceptibly, beginning to pay off, but firstly I get cast as the lead role for the very final production of the course – Shakespeare's *Much Ado About Nothing* in the main theatre. It's going to be a biggie, our last hurrah. When the curtain falls on the last of our scheduled ten performances, we will immediately all become out-of-work actors. That'll be it.

Secondly I get my first audition. After 200 handwritten letters I get a reply out of the blue from the Marlowe Theatre Company in Canterbury. It's the offer of what is called a general audition at the London Welsh Centre in Gray's Inn Road. This

Thursday, 10.40 a.m. Please bring two contrasting pieces.
Thirdly, I ask Rochdale out for a spaghetti.
And she just says yes.

audition

Fourthly: I have two new contrasting audition pieces.

Thank Christ. At last I can jettison the dog. Actually, these days it's more of an albatross. In its place, a snatch of Benedick, and a piece by Harold Pinter from *No Man's Land*.

Pinter is a good author to have up your sleeve for auditions. For a start, none of it makes much sense, and so long as you invest your particular excerpt with a little latent menace you'll look as if you know what you're doing. Secondly, all Pinter's speeches are pregnant with sudden pauses and unexpected silences, which gives you time to remember your lines when you dry stone dead, which you're almost certain to do with a waiting room full of rivals baying for your blood. So I learn the speech about Briggs getting lost in the regions of Bolsover Street, and decide to use it for Canterbury. A fresh start.

Rochdale agrees it's a good idea. We're sitting at the Spaghetti House on the corner of Goodge Street and Tottenham Court Road. We're alone at last – not even Wisconsin has been able to find us – it's nearly twenty to one and all the other diners have gone home. A bloke looking like an extra from La Dolce Vita is mopping the floor in between my feet.

'We'd better be going,' she says.

'Yup.'

'Where are you staying?'

'I'm going back to Brighton.'

I'm always going back to Brighton. My mum will have laid out some ham sandwiches and a bowl of oxtail soup for me on the dining table for when I get in.

'What time's your train?'

'Quarter to one.'

'That's in six minutes.'

We amble down Gower Street, her pushing her bicycle, me droning on about Pinter and Canterbury, and just how tough it is to be a final-term student, and trying to ignore the reality of my wristwatch. My next train home now will be the 3.05 slow stopper; I'll be getting into Brighton just in time to come back again for tomorrow morning.

At the corner of Holborn and Monmouth Street she kisses my cheek. 'I'm looking after my sister's flat in Victoria,' she says. 'She's away on holiday for a month. I can put you up for the night. You'll have to get a taxi. Eccleston Place, behind the bus station.'

My audition for Canterbury is the following morning. Rochdale gets up early, goes to a local deli, and comes back to bed with coffee and croissants. I feel utterly fantastic. It's odd – the events of the last eight hours have done more than voice, dancing, Alexander technique or stage fighting, to make me feel like a proper actor at last. Rochdale throws on an old sweater and sees me to the door of her flat. 'Get the job,' she whispers.

The Welsh Centre is a large building near King's Cross with echoing corridors of scuffed parquet. Adverts for male voice choirs and language courses are pinned everywhere, and a faint odour of socks clings to the furniture. Soon after eleven I'm shown into a large airy room with Velux windows. There are two men, the director of the company, a thin nervy man named Carson with receding hair and a goatee beard, and a younger man called Hayes who looks like he should be teaching metalwork at a technical college.

'What have you got for us, Michael?' asks Carson, already busily writing down something about me on a form. I tell them and the two men settle back and try to look interested. In a nearby room someone is practising 'Summertime' on the violin.

The speeches go well. Benedick loosens them up, then the slam dunk: Briggs, heavy with suggested violence, a speech consisting almost entirely of road directions in the Warren Street area. At the end of it Carson looks at me and smiles.

'Very good,' he says. 'I enjoyed that very much. Can you give us a moment?'

He turns to Hayes and begins muttering while I try to look unconcerned. I stare out of the window at the parapet of an adjoining wall. The decomposing body of a pigeon lays trapped on a coil of razor wire: its unblinking eye socket stares back disapprovingly. I find myself recalling Glynn Poole, the bloke from Walsall who auditioned with me three years before. I wonder if he's still at Cadbury's.

'Michael? This is what we think,' says Carson. 'You've probably seen the schedule for the autumn season at the Marlowe – it's pretty robust stuff, we're doing a comedy, then a musical, followed by a Shakespeare, and finishing off with the Christmas pantomime.' He glances briefly at his assistant before continuing. 'We like what you did very much ... but we're wondering if you have anything a bit more ... up front.'

Up front? I've done nothing I can think of. Chekhov, Wedekind, Ibsen, Wesker ... none of it up front. And I'm not letting out the dog again. Not after last night. No going back.

'I can't think of anything, I'm afraid.'

'For instance, do you know any Victorian monologues?'

'I'm afraid not.'

'Any music hall songs?'

'Sorry.'

'Any good bits of dramatic poetry you could reel off for us?'

I can feel the Equity card squeezing out under the door and off down the Gray's Inn Road.

'What about some Gilbert and Sullivan?' suggests Hayes, leaning forward. 'We'd only need to hear a snatch. Could you sing us a bit of that?'

'Which opera do you want?'

prizes

It's the last night of the course.

One of the idiosyncrasies of RADA is that there are various awards for good acting. There are nearly thirty, ranging from the Gold Award for best student of the course down to the Warrington Minge award for best performance of a Rattigan play by an Irishman. The recipients get a small trophy or a cheque for a few pounds, and their names are subsequently inscribed in red ink on huge roll of honour boards, which festoon every bit of available wall space in the foyer of the building. You too can find your name rubbing shoulders with Patricia Hayes, Peter Barkworth, Albert Finney, Alan Bates, and my favourite, the 1967 winner for Restoration comedy, Noble Shropshire. With a name like that he should be guaranteed a job with the RSC for life.

With more awards than students you can pick up a small supermarket trolley-full if you're canny. Even I've managed to collect one. Some of them are worth a lot of money: the Bancroft, for instance, is worth several hundred pounds and your name on a board alongside Charles Laughton (1926). Others, such as mine, the William Poel award for best verse speaking delivered in a standard English accent, is a cheque for two guineas and a book on acting by the donator, William Poel, which has been out of print for nearly twenty years.

The biggest award is reserved for tonight. After curtain down on the final performance of *Much Ado About Nothing*, the entire final term, the staff, the tutors, doormen, Vi, Vera and Ivy from the canteen, even the man who comes to fix the heating system, cram into the bar for a final drink and the presentation of the coveted Ronson.

The Ronson is a relatively new addition, sponsored by the makers of the electric safety razor. Along with the certificate the male and female winners are also guaranteed front-page coverage in tomorrow's national press. A useful start.

There's never been any doubt who's going to win it for the men. Tim Spall is the outstanding actor of the term. He's already picked up the Gold and about six other gongs for a series of audacious performances, including a week blacked up as Othello. The female award is more open. Any one of three or four could be in with a chance – Roedean for her performance in a couple of comedies, Boston as Beatrice, Tunbridge Wells as Lulu. In fact it goes to Honeydews for a dark, sensual Antigone with her dark, sensual voice and her dark, sensual attitude to the whole course. The photographers crowd in, she and Tim strike pleased but relaxed-about-it poses for the morning papers, the managing director of Ronson Enterprises UK hands over the cheques, more smiles, more photos and the press go away happy. You can see tomorrow's headlines: 'Reaching For The Stars', 'A Warm Hand On Their Opening'.

The staff members make their excuses and leave as soon as the flash bulbs have stopped, just lingering long enough to wish us luck and encourage us to keep in touch: McCallion is going to his house in France for the summer, Catweazle is writing a book on stage combat, and Ruth-Eva Ronen has some railway lines to blow up near Bruges. But for the twenty-one of us who, as from about 10.15 tonight, are suddenly unemployed, these final few minutes of studentdom have got to be wrung dry. Somebody has rigged up a sound system in the bar, somebody else has located the leftover bottles of Don Cortez, and the night disintegrates slowly from celebration, through partying, into maudlin sentiment and finally incoherence. All the while Harry the night porter sits stoically at the front desk reading the *Daily Mirror* – he knows this is going to be an all-nighter. Addresses are swapped, undying friendships are declared, promises to resurrect college productions in the upstairs of dingy pubs off the King's Road if nothing else comes up are instantly made. I hang around on the periphery of the desperate revelling, unwilling to leave the building for the last time and break the spell, but aware that Rochdale is staying in a friend's flat in Fulham for a couple of nights and is expecting me to drop by.

The flat in Fulham wins. Bye-bye, Tim. Safe flight home, NY. See you, Tintin. At 2 a.m. I stamp out into Gower Street. It's the first night of August and the air is still warm. A night bus takes me down to Sloane Square, and from there it's only three steps to heaven.

The next morning – Sunday – doesn't feel much different. If I concentrate hard enough I can still believe nothing has changed; I could still be a student. Rochdale has got to go back to her home town for the summer: she's going to tell her boyfriend about us and get some work in an industrial laundry to build up her funds before returning to London for her second term. But for me it's different. What am I supposed to do now? Sign on? Answer the ads in the back pages of *The Stage* ('Lively, outgoing performers required for cruise ships: basic tap essential')? Stay in London and hang around Leicester Square? Return permanently to Brighton and get a job in one of the sea-front hotels till the phone rings? Gamley's toy shop? I've no idea. All I know is that I haven't heard anything from the Marlowe Theatre, Canterbury, and that the woman I can't live without is returning to the back of buggery.

I leave around lunchtime. We're going to meet up in a couple of weekends, perhaps rent a hotel room for a night, take stock. I can look for digs here in town, somewhere to base myself near to her for when she returns to the course in September. But as my train trundles through the suburbs of south London I suddenly recall a promise dimly made in the depths of the frenzied partying last night. Boston has to hang around town till Monday evening to wait for her flight back to the States and I said she could come down to Brighton for the Sunday, stay at my parents' place for the night, kill some time, look around, sample some English seaside, maybe visit the Royal Pavilion. I think she said if I didn't hear otherwise she'd be down around tea-time.

I'm right. Boston turns up during the opening credits of *Songs of Praise* with an overnight bag and some flowers for my mum. We stroll along the pier, ending up in a pub in the Lanes where we spend the evening retracing our memories and predicting the various fates in store for our classmates before returning around 11 p.m. She has the spare room in the attic, the one next to mine.

I'm woken at 4 a.m. Boston is sitting on the end of my bed, clad only in bra and pants.

'What's wrong?' I ask her blearily.

'Oh, nothing. I couldn't sleep. Thought you might like some company.'

This is a moment I've often dreamt about, ever since I was in the stockroom at Gamley's. Waking up to find a girl wearing only bra and pants asking if I'd like some company. Be careful what you wish for.

I like Boston. She's sweet, she's kind, she's a good actress, and if you like a Rubenesque figure (and who am I to start pronouncing?) and don't mind an unsightly pimple she's always had on the tip of her nose, she's a looker.

A few weeks ago ...

'Thanks anyway,' I smile. I squeeze her hand. She gives me a watery little version back and leaves the room. A few moments later I hear the bedsprings creak across the landing.

The next morning I walk her back to the station. She gives me a stiff hug at the ticket barrier and wishes me all the best for the future. I promise to keep in touch: neither of us mention last night's incident. She climbs into a carriage and the train creaks away from the barrier. I hang around on the platform, expecting her to lean out of the window and wave, but the window stays shut. A minute longer and it's round the curve and out of sight.

When I get back home there's a letter for me. It's postmarked London, Sunday night. The writing on the envelope is Rochdale's hand.

'Dear Michael ...'

She couldn't tell me face to face, didn't want to ruin my last night, and sends me whispered wishes of sunny smiles. I want to run back to the station and retrieve Boston; to ask her for another go tonight. This time I won't be so bloody honourable. I'll take my chance.

The next few days pass in a black miasma. I've no drama school, no job, no idea what to do with my days, and now no lover. I read the letter a trillion times, scanning it for any sign of hope. It remains stubbornly mono-interpretable. I sincerely have no idea how I'm going to be able to live without her.

On the following Friday morning I'm lying in bed, still asleep at 10 a.m. Apart from going up to the DHSS – to sign on, not to get my job back – I've rarely been outside my room all week. Mum knocks on the door and comes in with a letter for me postmarked Canterbury. It's the offer of a nineteen-week contract, to play as cast in four productions, starting first week in September, £45 per week. Provisional Equity Card included.

Starting Monday, 7 September. Details of first call to follow.

It's the trip of a lifetime. From Rochdale to Canterbury in a single moment. Probably just as well. It would never have worked.

act two

pro

Ninety per cent of all actors are out of work at any one time. That's what they all tell you. The business is colossally over-subscribed, and you can expect to have an average net annual income of about £1500.

Still interested?

And what they don't tell you is that the same ten per cent of actors tend to work all of the time, the rest spending their entire lives working in bookshops, driving delivery vans or waiting tables. Talent has nothing to do with it – apparently strategy and luck are what you need. So it's actually very simple. I've just got to make sure I'm in the ten per cent.

The Equity contract arrives sometime in mid-August, and frankly it's something of anticlimax. For a start it's printed on impossibly thin paper, the sort usually associated with begging letters from charities working in Malawi, and when I sign my name at the bottom the ballpoint tears a hole in the page before I've even completed my signature. It's mostly small print, with lots of crossings out in thick black biro and sub-clauses asking you to initial where indicated, and there are several references to an organization with the unfortunate acronym of SWET: the Society of West End Theatres. There are three copies, one original and two carbon underneath – original to be returned to the theatre, blue copy to be forwarded to Equity, yellow copy to be retained 'for my own files'.

I'd better buy a file.

The crucial clause is number seven. I'm to 'play as cast', which is to acting what allocation on arrival is to the package holiday industry. In other words you have no idea what you're going to get until you turn up. Technically you are legally guaranteed at least an appearance on stage in each of the four shows, but if they choose to cast you in all four as a tree that's their prerogative. The Marlowe Theatre, Canterbury is under no obligation to give me a single spoken line throughout the entire nineteen-week season. But hey – what's nineteen weeks? Only another twenty-one more and I'll have the forty I need to enable me to work within fifty miles of Marble Arch.

There are four plays – the season is starting with *The Bed Before Yesterday* by Ben Travers, followed by *Joseph and His Amazing Technicolor Dreamcoat, Twelfth Night*, and finally *Dick Whittington and His Wonderful Cat*. I seem to be on something referred to as a special Equity 'Low', meaning I'm on a figure below the minimum agreed wage. When I shake the envelope a digs list flutters out, plus a stencilled diagram of a human body to which I'm supposed to add my relevant measurements and send back at once to the wardrobe department. I'm to present myself in the circle bar of the theatre at 2 p.m. on 7 September, for a get-together and read-through of the first play.

My train arrives in Canterbury at about noon. The journey from Brighton is impossibly romantic, involving changes at Hastings and Ashford, and wending its way along by the coast before meandering through the comforting contours of the South Downs and into Kent. Even the names of the stations seem to have been lifted from an Ealing comedy: Guestling Halt, Three Oaks, Appledore, and, perhaps more relevantly, Ham Street. As we lurch into Canterbury I half expect to find Will Hay waiting with a luggage trolley.

I'm so busy trying to pull my suitcases off the train and on to the platform that I'm utterly unprepared for the sight that greets me when I eventually turn round. It's heart-stopping. I can almost feel the pupils of my eyes dilating as I take it in.

I'm staring at a poster advertising *The Bed Before Yesterday*.

It's a cheap, badly drawn art deco drawing of a man and a woman locked in an embrace, all straight lines and sharp angles. Underneath are phrases like 'forthcoming attraction' and 'uproarious comedy'. The poster is already peeling, and the pinks and reds that form the backdrop to the illustration have already faded under the assault of several weeks' weather. It doesn't matter. If I weren't so exhilarated I'd probably be cringing with embarrassment at the cheesiness of it all. Gotta sing, gotta dance and all that crap. How clichéd can you get? Mickey Rooney would struggle to match the inane grin smeared across my features just now. One day I'll look back and wince that I could have experienced such a tinsel town parody of showbiz excitement at the sight of my first theatre poster. But not now. Not yet. Knowing that I'm being paid to appear in something being advertised on the outside wall of the gents' lavatory on platform two of Canterbury East southern region is bliss.

Bliss on a stick.

digs

That evening I find myself on the doorstep of a Georgian style house 'a few doors along from the theatre' according to the digs list, which I'm still clutching in my right hand. I press the door-bell and an Avon-calling chime sounds somewhere in the house. After several moments a small, heavily powdered woman in her sixties opens the door. She looks like Sandy Powell.

'Mrs Willey?'

'Yes. Are you Michael? Come in.'

A haze of talcum powder hangs above her, and an over-powering smell of Yardley's soap hits me as I step into the hall.

Finding accommodation in a strange town is a perennial prob-lem for an actor. Company digs lists are supposed give you some help, but they're impenetrable documents, frequently inaccurate, out of date, and the cause of more trouble than they're worth. Rows of names and addresses, some with 'use of kitchen' or even 'run of house'; others with 'own bathroom', 'must like dogs', 'leading men only', or in Mrs Willey's case, 'a few doors along from the theatre'. It's impossible to tell by reading them what to expect. On a special 'Equity Low' my priorities are simple: I've gone for the cheapest. I'm at Mrs Willey for £7 per week.

'And all the flies you can kill,' roars the leading actor, Alan, a weatherbeaten man in his early fifties who chain-smokes Capstans, when I mention it at the read through. He lets out a huge throaty guffaw, which makes all the glasses behind the bar tinkle in unison.

In truth, nobody seems to have heard of Mrs Willey, which is worrying because Alan has done twenty-seven productions here and another cast member, a large, amiable man called Philip in his late forties with a fondness for yellow turtlenecks, is close behind with twenty-one. The theatre secretary informs me during coffee me that Mrs Willey is a recent addition to the inventory and was a response to an appeal inserted by the theatre in the local paper.

I don't know whether I want my liaison with Mrs Willey to succeed or not. Because bad digs – stinking, terrible, flea-infested digs I have known – are the social currency of professional actors, the ice-breaker, the theatrical equivalent of dogs sniffing each other's rears. Not for them route directions or complaints about the weather. During the read-through of *The Bed Before Yesterday*, apart from when we were actually reading the play, conversation consisted entirely of story after story about digs.

'Have you stayed at that one in Darlington next to the cemetery? Well, I was there last year in *Bell, Book and Candle* and ...'

I want to join in, to be a part of that bonding, to match their anecdotes of blocked sinks, rampant divorcees and inedible food. All the cast of *The Bed Before Yesterday* seem to have their own memories of the one next to the cemetery in Darlington, or if not, one that's even worse, or worse still, or you won't believe this, but I was doing *Spring and Port Wine* in Redcar and ...

By the end of the read-through they seem to have known each other for years, even though none of them have ever worked together before. Every actor has their favourite story. Philip, the one with the turtleneck, tells of a house on the outskirts of Hull where he was greeted on arrival by a sixty-year-old hunchback man and a woman in her thirties with dyed blonde hair. While she went to make them all a nice cup of tea the hunchback invited him into their lounge, where the hardest of hard-core porn videos was playing on the television set.

'Then the wife brings in the tea things wearing full tennis gear ...'

The stories tumble out. Lisa, who's in her mid-twenties and playing Ella, the juve lead, tells a long and involved story about a flat in Basingstoke.

'So, my second night there I wake up around three and, fuck me, there's a bloke standing in a monk's habit at the foot of my bed – and *I can see through him*!' She strikes a mock terrified pose, her hands held up by her face like Faye Wray seeing King Kong, fingers splayed in music hall terror.

Alan laughs throatily and reaches for another Capstan, Philip fiddles happily with his turtleneck, and John from Worcester, whom I already suspect might be gay, gurgles in enjoyment and gives me a little twinkly smile. On and on it goes, the cast bonding with each new horror story, until it seems as if their entire lives had been leading inexorably up to this moment of meeting one another in the circle bar of the Marlowe Theatre.

'... And whenever our landlady shouted up the stairs that breakfast was ready we'd shout back, "You can't frighten us ..."'

I want my own story. Hence my ambiguity about Mrs Willey's. It all looks too ordinary here, too calm, too quiet. I want to be part of the conversation tomorrow morning, and to be part of the conversation *I* have to have something to say. I want to see Lisa scream, John gurgle, Philip fiddle with his turtleneck: I want Alan to make those glasses behind the bar rattle together with his phlegmy laughter because of something I said. And if I have to be sexually assaulted by Mrs Willey at 3 a.m. to do so I'll consider it a price well worth paying.

And yet, as I'm shown round Mrs Willey's manicured home, with its ticking clocks, volumes of Patience Strong and bowls of pot-pourri on window sills, I know it's not going to happen. The atmosphere is already worryingly formal – her offer of a cup of tea has been followed by the arrival of a set of bone china cups, silver sugar basins and dainty tongs, all of which look terrifyingly expensive – in fact, there's barely a surface in the entire house that doesn't house some priceless knick-knack. I'd hoped to find something more like home: pairs of pants warming on radiators; leaking biros in the fruit basket; earthenware mugs with interiors like toilet bowls. I'd feel happier then because I'm almost certain to drop one of these priceless ceramics in the course of the next nineteen weeks, and I don't want to break Mrs Willey's heart.

After tea I follow two portly legs clad in elasticated stockings up several flights of stairs. The attic room which is to be my home for the next five months may be sparse, but it's neat and clean, with a polished wooden floor, chintz curtains and impressive views of the cathedral through its sloping windows. There's a single truckle bed with a white bedspread, a tiny sink with an antique jug and ewer on a washstand next to it and a Binatone radio alarm clock on the top of the chest of drawers. What's more, it's even set to the correct time. Mrs Willey is obviously a woman with standards.

And yet ... What was it that Alan said this afternoon?

'I hope you'll be happy here, Michael,' says Mrs Willey.

'I'm sure I will be.'

What was it? A single piece of advice he gave me about landladies ...

'Please let me know if there's anything you want,' says Mrs Willey.

'Thank you. I will.'

For Christ's sake. What did he tell me to look out for?

'Just treat the house as your own,' says Mrs Willey.

She turns to leave. I've no idea when I'm supposed to pay her the first week's rent, but I suppose I can leave it until after I've unpacked. It may all be a bit *People's Friend* here, but at £7 a week I suppose I should be glad.

Then I remember what Alan told me. Look for the photos.

He gave me the nugget of advice as I walked here. Alan was on his way to find some fish and chips, and as he ambled alongside me down St Margaret's Street he told me to look out for signed photos of previous tenants on the walls.

'Most of the good landladies have them,' he'd said. 'The old dears like having actors around; in fact most of them are a bit star struck. If your Mrs Willey has got lots of signed photos of actors nobody's ever heard of hanging above the fireplace, chances are they'll be of actors who've come back several times. Which means they like staying there. Which means she's sympathetic to our needs. Which means she's not going to insist on telling you her life story every evening after rehearsals. If you get a chance, try and see what they've written along with their signature. "Lovely as always, see you next time" and she's probably all right. "I'll never forget my time here as long as I live" and you should fake an epileptic fit and get the hell out as quick as you can. Good luck. Let me know how it goes.'

As I lumbered off down the road with my suitcase, Alan had shouted one final word of advice. 'Look out for a photo of a bloke called Freddie Lees. Freddie's stayed everywhere in Britain. Nobody knows more about digs. If he's left his mark on the wall you can take that as the actors' equivalent of an AA five star.'

I've seen plenty of china dogs in the last twenty minutes. But no actors. And unless he bears an uncanny resemblance to Sir Winston Churchill, no photographs of Freddie Lees. RADA made no mention of this in their training. What to do?

Mrs Willey checks her step at the attic door, turns sheepishly to face me and studies me a moment through a pair of thick bi-focals.

'One thing, Michael,' she says.

It's obviously rent time.

'I would be grateful if you would make sure you weren't in the house between eleven and five on weekdays. Only I usually have some friends round to play cards and ...'

She licks her lips nervously.

'I don't want them to know I'm taking in theatricals. So if you could keep away till tea-time I'd very much appreciate it. I'm sorry to have to ask. Hope it won't be inconvenient.'

By lunchtime next day Alan has arranged for me to move in to a room above the local Reject Pottery Shop. The room is owned by a couple he knows who work for Canterbury Social Services. It's a top-floor bedsit with bits of broken furniture, a grubby galley kitchen in the corner, a double bed, which, when you lie in the middle, sags so much that you can't see over the sides, and a litter tray of three-week-old cat shit in the corner. A line of filthy earthenware mugs hang from rusting kitchen hooks over the draining board.

When I try to slide my suitcase under the bed I discover a fried egg on the carpet.

Lisa's going to love that one. If I can't make her scream now I might as well go home.

I'll take it.

preparation

It's now October, and I'm sitting in the dressing room on a sunny Thursday afternoon during the interval of a schools matinée performance of *Twelfth Night*. Around me the other actors in the dressing room are getting into character for the second half of the play, each in their own idiosyncratic manner. Feste the jester is reading *Titbits*. Andrew Aguecheek is trying to see if he can lob pages of rolled-up script into the brim of an upturned hat lying on a shelf on the other side of the room. Antonio is twirling a pocket watch round and round by a chain hooked over his right index finger. And finally Orsino, Duke of Illyria, is searching through Yellow Pages to find a garage that will do an MOT on his car between the matinée and the evening. I'm staring out of the window and sweating: though that may be because I'm wearing a padded stomach and leggings, a Harris tweed shooting jacket, woollen gloves, a tweed hat, plus fours, knee-length knickerbocker socks and calf-length leather boots.

I'm far too young for the part of Sir Toby Belch, but the original choice ducked out with only a week till rehearsals when out of the blue he got a week's filming on *Howard's Way*. He'll earn as much in three days as he would have done in the entire run of *Twelfth Night* and will be put up in a fancy hotel in Southampton for the duration as well. That's how the business works: we only ever get offered jobs because somebody else before us in the queue hasn't fancied doing them. I've no doubt that if Paul Newman had expressed his desire to have a crack at the Marlowe autumn season I wouldn't have got a sniff. But he didn't. The *Canterbury Evening Messenger* didn't seem to like my performance, but who cares? With the play on this year's GCSE syllabus we're playing to full houses, and by sharing a communal dressing room with hardened old pros I'm learning fast.

For example: if you want to quieten an audience of disruptive teenagers, speak your lines softer rather than louder. They'll instinctively shut up so as to find out what you're saying.

Or what about this: if you have an overwhelming desire to sneeze in the middle of an important speech you can override it by biting your top lip. This sends a nervous response to the brain, which temporarily distracts it from the instinct to shower your fellow actors.

Never leave your descent to the stage from the dressing room till the last minute – you never know when the actors before you may suddenly cut a page of dialogue.

Keep in with the stage doorman; he wields more power than anyone else in the building, so an occasional fiver dropped into his hand as you leave on a Saturday night will ensure phone messages get copied down, letters get left in your pigeon hole, and the old woman you naively got chatting to in the coffee bar who, too late, you discovered is the local crackpot and is now calling every afternoon with scrawled messages quoting the New Testament, gets politely discouraged.

Empty your bladder before getting into a padded stomach piece and woollen suit.

Always wear underpants.

Martin doesn't wear underpants. Ever. Until this afternoon's performance, his disregard for underpants was one of his favourite topics of conversation – he was almost evangelical about it. He is from somewhere near Sheffield, where the non-observance of underpants seems to be a badge of honour. He says he likes to feel the sensation of his 'ragman's trumpet' rubbing against the trouser material while he's performing – it makes him feel alive. I'll take his word for it.

Martin is playing Sebastian, Viola's twin brother, cruelly separated during the Act One shipwreck scene (ingeniously suggested in this production by a sound effects tape of crashing waves combined with flashing lights). With a shock of closely curling black hair, dark hazel eyes and a pair of tight moleskin breeches, he's proving a hit with the hoards of local teenage schoolgirls bussed in by Kent County Education Authority, many of whom are flocking to the stage door after the perform-ance to get his autograph and leave him scrawled love notes. Following this afternoon's performance, Martin should have a particularly large crowd of Lolitas, because in the middle of his scene with Antonio, he slipped over on the stage and split his moleskins from arsehole to breakfast time, exposing a particu-larly fine example of horn and rhythm section to the close scrutiny of five hundred ecstatic teenagers.

I knew something disastrous had occurred when I heard a burst of delighted screams emanating from the auditorium, followed closely by a cacophony of giggling that lasted until the interval and obliterated at least ten minutes of the Bard's greatest prose. Actors quickly become adept at knowing when and where to expect audience reaction, and if the anticipated sound pattern is broken, their heads instinctively bob up from the *Guardian* crossword towards the show relay system. Seconds later and with the auditorium still in uproar, Martin passed me in the wings, still vainly trying to stuff his genitals inside the loose flaps of material where once his crutch would have been. I had to go on myself a few seconds later and didn't make much of a fist of it.

Martin's in the wardrobe department now, having the seams of the moleskins restitched and reinforced for the second half by Jill, the wardrobe mistress. Meanwhile Becky, the most junior of the assistant stage managers, has been despatched to our local Marks and Spencer for a pair of Y-fronts. Normally the show relay would now be broadcasting nothing more frenetic than the scraping of wooden spoons on ice-cream tubs: today it's pande-monium out there.

Comedy and tragedy are first cousins. Whoever said that knew a fair bit.

The tannoy summons us all to the stage for the second half. One by one the other actors meander out of the room and down towards the stage. I'm just adjusting my plus-fours and prepar-ing to follow them when the phone rings. It's Syd, the stage doorman; can he have a word?

'Syd, if it's about me laughing onstage—'

It's not. Syd doesn't know what the hell I'm talking about. He's got a call on the line from someone called Lisa from my term at RADA – have I got time to take it?

I haven't spoken to Islington since our promise to keep in touch with each other in the mawkish embers of the last night party. In fact, I haven't spoken to any one of them. Despite my protestations of undying friendship, somehow the offer of the Equity card obliterated the necessity to hang on to them a minute longer. But we've still a few minutes till curtain up and it would be nice to hear from her. Perhaps she's joining for the panto?

'Hello, how are you?'

'Sorry to disturb you, Mike. I was going to leave a message, I thought you'd be on stage. Have you got a moment?'

A glance out of the open window reveals Becky still puffing back along the road with a Marks and Spencer's bag. They're unlikely to unleash Martin again without safely securing it all in, so it's likely to be a few minutes yet.

'Sure. What is it?'

'I've got some bad news ... '

It takes a minute or two to compute. Our classmate, the girl from Tunbridge Wells, has died. She can't have been more than six months older than me. I never really got to know her well because we were rarely cast together and in any case I found her rather surly. But dead? The explanation is starkly simple: she suffered from a rare and serious blood disorder, a fact she had kept entirely hidden from the rest of us for nearly two and a half years – hence her bilious disposition and her even more bilious skin colour. Despite a lifetime of illness and excessive pain, she'd managed to finish the course and had just got her first job offer, a lunchtime production at the King's Head pub in Islington. But she never made it to the read-through. She died in a train carriage somewhere between Clapham Junction and Victoria after a sudden and fatal complication sometime last month. Islington's only just heard and is now phoning round.

There's no time for further explanation. Beginners for Act Two are already being summoned over the relay. I promise to call her back at the end of the performance and replace the receiver. As I get up I catch sight of myself in the mirror: huge false moustache, absurdly reddened cheeks, unconvincing eye bags, wobbly crow's feet, a twenty-something trying to look about forty years older. The *Canterbury Evening Messenger* had said that 'the performance was heavily scarred by the youthfulness of the actor'. I'm sitting here trying to look looking like James Robertson Justice and my classmate from RADA hasn't even made it to her twenty-third birthday.

There's a knock on the door.

David, the theatre administrator, a mild-mannered chap in his forties, peers round the door. He notices at once my look of surprise – David rarely comes backstage unless the toilets are blocked.

'Michael, sorry to bother you, have you got a moment?'

'Look, David, if it's about my laughing—'

'I just wanted to tell you, we had a burglary last night and you won't have a chicken leg this afternoon ... or probably for the rest of the run.'

David's job as administrator is basically to keep the theatre from the edge of bankruptcy. It's an invidious task. In addition to the miserable Arts Council grant that enforces him to pay his actors their special 'Equity Low', he spends most of his time trying to persuade local firms and businesses what a great advertising method as well as a public relations triumph it would be for them to sponsor one of the productions. Sometimes he hits lucky and a major employer in south-east Kent bungs him a couple of grand in return for their corporate name being linked with a particular show – in fact, he was saying only the other day that he's on the brink of clinching a multi-pound deal that will harness our forthcoming production of *Dick Whittington and His Wonderful Cat* with Brewer's World of Wallpapers, for all your wallpapering needs, branches in Folkestone and Margate.

But more often than not he has to be content with the loan of some footling prop or piece of specialist equipment in return for a mention in the programme or some freebies. For instance, the recent production of *Joseph and His Amazing Technicolor Dreamcoat* was indebted to Luff's of Whitstable for supplying all the timber, Barrett's of Herne Bay for the toy pistols, and Kennard's of Northgate for the loan of the accordion. *Twelfth Night* couldn't get any sponsors at all – apparently 'Shakespeare isn't sexy' – but a friend of his had a contact with Buxted Poultry and Meat Products of Sussex, and he managed to persuade them to donate fifty-five frozen chickens for the scene in which I'm supposed to eat one – it barely saved us thirty quid on the budget but you can't afford to picky when you're running a third division repertory theatre. Thirty quid is nearly a week's wages for some poor sod.

(Me.)

So we've had fifty-five chickens, which are securely kept in a huge industrial fridge located by the stage management office. The lid is padlocked after each one is removed, and just for good measure a load of spare stage weights, huge great iron pucks used for ballasting pieces of scenery, are stacked on top each night; just in case anyone fancies swiping a couple for supper on their way home.

'The whole lot's gone,' David mutters. 'We discovered it at lunchtime. Whoever nicked them would have had to not only break the padlock but remove nearly a ton of cast iron. They even put the bastards back on top afterwards so no one would notice. It was obviously an inside job, so if you hear anything ...'

An inside job. That's a terrible accusation. We're like a family here at the Marlowe Theatre. And yet his accusation makes sense – the notion of Kent's criminal fraternity bothering to plan a daring heist just to remove fifty-five frozen chickens from a weighted fridge doesn't add up.

'Anyway, there'll be no more chicken, I'm afraid. You'll have to make do with peanut butter sandwiches ...' David is already disappearing behind the door.

Another summons crackles over the relay. I can't eat peanut butter. I was given some as a child and it brings me out in a violent rash. The notion of that happening with me marooned on stage in a tweed suit doesn't bear thinking about. It would make the incident with Martin's trumpet look like *Jackanory*.

There's a knock on the door.

It's the associate director, Chris Hayes. He's currently running the theatre while his boss, Carson, is on a sabbatical, apparently studying street theatre in Senegal.

'Chris, if it's about—'

'No, I've just popped in to tell you the casting's up on the board for the panto, so when you get a minute ...'

Dick Whittington begins rehearsing on Monday. There are hundreds of parts for a young drama school graduate – street sellers, jolly sailors, guards at the Sultan of Morocco's Palace, King Rat's henchman, numerous small parts and chorus for the voyage to the Orient and the desert island and the revelations on Highgate Hill. I'm probably playing most of them.

'Can you tell me now?'

'Sure. You're playing Dame. Sarah the Cook. You're happy in drag, I take it?'

Without waiting for a reply, he closes the door softly behind him.

There must be some mistake. Twenty-one-year-olds don't get Dame. Terry Scott gets Dame. Arthur Askey gets Dame. I've never even seen a proper panto.

As I clatter down the stairs to the wings I find myself a few steps behind Martin, newly pinned from the wardrobe. Normally at this time, with his big fight ahead of him and the prospect of a pubescent grab bag at the end of it, he would be in full spate. This afternoon he descends the stairs in flinty silence. The seams of his moleskins are criss-crossed with what appears to be nautical twine: they look as if they could now survive a small controlled explosion. He looks round and mistakes my intense study of his reinforced gusset for notice of an imminent wisecrack. He stabs a finger at me.

'Don't say a fucking word.'

Martin's exposed himself to a load of schoolgirls, Emma's

died on a train, someone's swiped fifty-five frozen chickens and I'm Sarah the cook. Just another day in rep. Perhaps the last fact is a hoax. I scan the assortment of grubby announcements, rehearsal calls, health and safety regs, offers of reduced membership at gyms and special offers in local tanning shops. And there it is – the cast for *Dick Whittington and His Wonderful Cat*.

Sarah the Cook: Michael Simkins.

Syd the doorman leans out from his cubbyhole. 'Heard the news?' he says.

Emma's death? Sarah the Cook? The poultry heist? The debacle of Martin's genitals?

Syd lifts up the local evening paper. 'Pope's dropped dead.'

panto

Pantomime is not so much a show, more a number of set pieces. The mums and dads, boys and girls who make up the bulk of the panto audience come every year – in fact, for many of them, it's the only time they'd be seen dead inside a theatre – and they want it all to be the same as they remember from last time. Or rather, the same but different. It is a bit like the Last Night at the Proms, with the Dame as the centrepiece. She's 'Land of Hope and Glory'.

There's the wallpapering scene: 'Now I'll give you this big mallet to knock the nail in with, and when I nod my head I want you to hit it ...'

There's the community song sheet: 'Now it's the turn of all those up there in the ashtrays to have a go ...'

And there's the parade at the end with Sarah the Cook teetering down from the back in an outrageous frock in the shape of a giant jelly: 'Merry Christmas, everyone, Merry Christmas ...'

These are the defining moments by which my Sarah the Cook will be judged out in the car park, in the chip shop, on the bus home.

The kids love Sarah, and the mums and dads love watching their kids loving Sarah, and when I enter in my moulded blancmange at the end of the first performance there's a genuine cheer of affection. I only make one mistake in the entire evening. And it's not with the wallpapering, nor the walk down, nor the community song sheet. It's not even in the show.

The mistake I make with Sarah the Cook is in deciding to get rat-arsed for the first time in my life at the after-show party in the full knowledge that I've got a shoppers' matinée performance the following morning, Christmas Eve, at 10 a.m.

Until the moment when Jill from wardrobe leans over with that bottle of warm German wine with the picture of the dancing bear on the label, I've never touched the stuff. Don't like the taste, seen what it does to people, you shouldn't need to drink to have a good time, all the usual hand-me-down notions from my parents. But there are some times when you've just got to let go and live a little. And what better time than having just survived your first pantomime Dame. Particularly as the party's being held in the room below mine in the Reject Pottery Shop.

Clive, who's playing one of the broker's men, has invited everyone back for a celebratory bash. We're all there now: the street sellers, sultan's guards, stage management, Jill from wardrobe, and the girls who sell the ice cream in the interval. Even Syd on the stage door is having a drink, and he's got diabetes and has to take special pills otherwise he gets upset and confused. The room is already thick with tobacco smoke and the mantelpiece is festooned with plastic cups and bowls of crisps. A couple of the girls in the ensemble have fetched in a bulk purchase of French bread and cheese, which they're sawing into chunks on the lino by the bed. Time to relax, to let my hair down. I'm nearly at the end of my season with Canterbury and I've done my first Dame. What can go wrong?

I was shitting myself in the wings as I waited to enter on my kiddies' scooter. What happens if none of my gags work? I had thought. What would happen if all the mums and dads, boys and girls just sat there thinking, Who's this adolescent twat? For an extra tenner we could have driven up to Bromley and seen Roy Hudd ... After all, what did I have to offer? A pair of falsies, a bright red frock held together with Velcro, and a shopping basket full of things for Alderman Fitzwarren's supper.

Mother-in-law pie. That's cold shoulder and tongue.

Windmill pudding. If it goes round we'll all get a bit.

Roast octopus. It's not as good as chicken but everyone gets a leg.

Three gags, and I got three laughs. I was off and running. Before I was halfway through the first verse of my song some of the mums and dads, boys and girls were beginning to clap along, and the aisles were already ankle deep in discarded sweet wrappers. Three hundred faces all guzzling boxes of Quality Street were smiling back up at me. Thank Christ. Canterbury was looking for a good time, and so long as I didn't get in their way they would make sure they got it.

Jill from the wardrobe is an attractive little freckly thing with long auburn hair, and before I can say I don't drink, she's fetched me a plastic cup from the sideboard, emptied the ash out of it, and filled it with a liberal measure of Liebfraumilch. Clive has put on a record of Steeleye Span singing 'All Round My Hat' and most of the rest of the staff of the theatre are twirling each other round. Even Syd's spinning around and he wears a raised right shoe. Before I can protest that I don't like the taste of it, that I'll be fine with this blackcurrant and lemonade, Jill arranges my fingers round the cup, lifts it to my lips and makes me take a swig. I try to remonstrate again and the wine goes down the wrong hole which makes me cough, a rivulet of the tepid wine streaming down my jumper and on to my jeans. We're both laughing. Jill thinks I'm a scream. It's all rather sexy.

The wallpapering scene, sponsored by Brewer's of Folkestone, for all your wallpapering needs, was a more complicated matter. The trick here was to cause sufficient mayhem to delight all the mums and dads, boys and girls, but not to leave the stage in so dangerous a state as to render it a death trap for anybody subsequently trying to walk across it. Our Dick Whittington, a Scottish actress with a dyed blonde Louise Brooks haircut, a singing voice like Lee Marvin and legs like hams, had already complained that her pivotal moment, the scene following the wallpaper paste in which she hears Bow Bells telling her to turn again on Highgate Hill, was impossible to act because the stage was like a skid pan. She'd even threatened to call her agent. She is a household name north of the borders due to the fact she's currently featured in a telly advert for porridge oats, which is why she's taken to throwing her not-inconsiderable weight about. She'd been using words like intention, truth and subtext a lot just recently. I even heard her ask the director to explain what her motivation was for taking the sausages out of the trunk.

I suspect she's hasn't got the idea of panto.

All these images come fizzing into my head as I sit there in the warm fug of Clive's bedsit in the Reject Pottery Shop. I'm on my third glass now and the wine is beginning to taste less like anti-freeze and more like Tizer. In fact it's not bad. Nor is Jill. Funny, I never noticed it until now. She's sitting opposite me on the sofa. Having just finished knotting my shoelaces together, she's now throwing crisps at Clive, who's sitting on the carpet with John from Worcester, the one with the gurgly laugh, discussing the winter of discontent (Labour's, not Shakespeare's) and whether the piles of rubbish currently mounting up in the cathedral car park are reason enough to bring in the troops. Madeline from the chorus and Syd are doing a duet of 'Summer Lovin'' along to a cassette tape. She's doing the John Travolta and Syd is filling in the Olivia Newton-John.

'Summer dreams, ripped at the seams … But oh, those sum-eh-er … nyy-hyyyyttttsssss …'

The only balls-up I made this evening was in the community song sheet. Put it down to inexperience. It won't happen again – I'll get it right for the next performance. Which, as I focus uncertainly on Clive's alarm clock on the battered cupboard beside his bed, appears to be now only eight hours away.

One of the traditions of panto is that before the community song sheet, the Dame is supposed to spend a couple of minutes by herself on stage with a hand-held mike, reading out any birthday greetings and Christmas wishes requested by members of the audience. Usually they're just scrawlings on tiny scraps of paper and handed to the front-of-house manager or delivered to Syd during the interval by sheepish parents. Not too many: three or four a show is more than enough. It only takes a minute or two, and they enjoy it. References to local folk from neighbouring boroughs and towns makes them feel special. Just don't let it get out of hand, I was warned by King Rat. 'And whatever you do, don't make it sound like you're inviting the recipient to join you on the stage. Don't let them get out of their seats. It's not *Opportunity Knocks*. Get on with it, or you'll be there all bloody night.'

I should have listened. A few more minutes, a quick chorus or two of 'Does Santa Claus Sleep with His Whiskers?', the walk down, final bows, Merry Christmas everyone, and it would all be over, at least until the shoppers' matinée the following morning. I read out a few messages, congratulations to kiddies on passing their grade four life-saving medal or being a brave little scout during his latest stay in hospital, love from Auntie Rose, and I was just about to ask for the song sheet to be lowered from the flies when I saw this old boiler advancing down the left-hand aisle and pushing a terrified child in front of her. With the lyrics unfurling behind me in letters three feet high, the pair mounted the wooden steps bridging the orchestra pit and up on to the stage. 'Go on, go on,' the boiler was yelling at the tot; and suddenly he was standing beside me. I had no gags up my sleeve, no idle chit-chat, just a terrible blankness where Sarah the Cook's naturally winning ways with little children should be.

After a couple of desultory questions – 'What's your favourite colour?' ('Don't know,') 'Which football team do you support?' (Kent only has one, Gillingham, and he'd never heard if it.) – and suicidally, 'Are you enjoying yourself?' ('No.'), the house manager appeared from nowhere, took his hand and helped him back down and into the proudly heaving bosom of his mother. I'd spent nearly an hour and a half gaining the sympathies of the people of Canterbury; another couple of minutes of that child and I would have lost them for ever.

It's not until my fifth glass of German wine that I realize how drink loosens you up, makes you feel uninhibited, gives you a sense of all being right with the world. We're on to something called hock now. Despite my breaking my sexual duck with Rochdale behind Victoria bus station in the summer I haven't so far managed to follow it up since I started at Canterbury, and it all seems a long time ago, but Jill from the wardrobe is looking prettier with each gulp. Then again, so is Madeleine; and I never realized how striking Syd is. These are my mates, my pals: this is where I want to be, for the rest of my days, sitting here in this dusty smoke-filled room smelling of one-bar electric fires and flannelette sheets, with 'You Ain't Seen Nothing Yet' by

Bachmann Turner Overdrive pounding out on the music centre and the room spinning delightfully in front of me. It's nearly 3 a.m., I should go: even if I get through the shoppers' matinée I've got another performance in the afternoon.

But just then Jill leans over and pours me a cup of Rioja.

I'll just try this and then I'll be off.

I don't recall much of the next few hours. I vaguely remember the other surviving party-goers were playing a game of guessing old television theme tunes: I remember shouting the word Bonanza repeatedly as I was hauled up the stairs.

I think I spent quite a few minutes trying to convince Madeline that there was a fried egg somewhere in the room and that if she could find it I'd let her make love to me. I then have a dim memory of urinating out of my attic window into the street below sometime around 7 a.m., and that's all I recall until I wake up around eight to find myself throwing up on the bedspread.

dr footlights

Christmas Eve, and I'm sitting with King Rat in the snack bar attached to the casualty department of Kent and Canterbury Royal Infirmary. I'm wearing jeans, a thick sweater, one shoe, false eyelashes, scarlet lipstick and a large beauty spot on one cheek. Becky the stage manager was originally going to bring me here in her old mini traveller, but King Rat has rather taken a shine to me and in any case he drives a Volvo, one of those big ones built for Swedish winters: large enough at any rate for me to be able to stretch my leg out straight, so long as I sit in the back seat. We've been sitting here now for the best part of three hours, but I'm assured as soon as they've developed the X-rays I can go home. King Rat is currently finishing off the remains of somebody's half-eaten tub of Ski yoghurt from an adjoining table, and, in between mouthfuls, expounding his theories about Dr Footlights.

Dr Footlights is the name given to the curious mystical process that overtakes an actor when he is struck down with sudden illness or infirmity, but still has a performance to get through. The show must go on, and there are hundreds of stories of how poor old Jorkins struggled through a performance of *Dear Brutus* at Wolverhampton, even though he'd just fallen skull-first on to a circular saw on his way to the theatre, how he gallantly made it to the final curtain even though he was having to hold his head in both hands to stop his brains slopping out on to the stage, yet once the curtain was down, he never spoke again, spending the rest of his days in a nursing home in Penge.

It's not surprising really. Theatres are dangerous places, full of dark corners, swinging scenery and unwashed stagehands making pots of tea in the green room with teaspoons not cleaned since they were used to scrape the mouse droppings off the floor after the last vermin infestation. No matter if your arse is dropping out due to a dodgy prawn sandwich before the show, Dr Footlights always gets you through. King Rat believes in this received wisdom. He says it's to do with the actor's instinct – the unique dread a performer feels at the prospect of letting down his loyal and doting public. I suspect it's more to do with the unique dread at the prospect of somebody else climbing into our costume and making a better fist of the part, but King Rat is having none of it. He maintains that when the endorphins take over, numbing out all pain and stress until the body can better cope, the most superhuman achievements are possible. He says it's the theatre equivalent of all those GIs in Vietnam who only discovered they'd lost most of their bottom half when they were finally out of the paddy fields and safely back in the Chinook.

Dr Footlights is like that. It gets you through when every conventional scintilla of medical wisdom tells you that you should be writhing in agony.

King Rat is eating a packet of peanuts found on a window ledge and recalling a time when he appeared in the original production of *Hair* in the sixties.

'So I'm underneath this table, naked as the day I was born, and my cue comes to leap out and start singing my solo verse, and just as I'm clambering out from between the table legs somebody's left foot kicks me full tilt in the mouth.'

He proceeds to give a demonstration with a mouthful of peanuts of how he managed to complete the verse successfully despite spitting most of his front teeth out between breaths. King Rat's own teeth are the colour of peanuts anyway, courtesy of thirty years of smoking roll-ups, so the dramatization is particularly graphic. Having successfully completed it, he retrieves the peanuts from the hospital floor.

That man is an actor to his boots.

King Rat likes the notion of Dr Footlights. I believe in it now, because I've just done one and a half performances of *Dick Whittington and His Wonderful Cat* on a left ankle three times its normal size. It happened during the shoppers' matinée: I slipped on some paste during the wallpapering scene. I wasn't looking where I was going. In fact, I wasn't looking at all. Keeping my eyes closed whenever possible seemed to be the only way of getting through with the hangover from the previous night. But then Clive came on with his bucket of paste and chucked the whole lot straight at me, and either he misjudged the quantity or I was just feeling more sensitive than usual, because when it hit me, it was like being felled by a left cross from Joe Bugner. Before I knew it I was staggering about the stage with my false eyelashes glued together and about three tons of something resembling elephant cum all over me. In the meantime the stage had turned into what the porridge oats girl would call a skidpan, and I slipped and went over on my ankle.

Since when I've struggled through a performance and a half despite feeling nauseous any time I put the slightest weight on it. So far as King Rat is concerned, his notion is proved again by the fact that I fainted dead away in the wings seconds after curtain down second house, still in full drag. I recall nothing for several seconds until a vague image of a huge rodent slapping my face brought me to my senses.

King Rat is reminiscing over half a can of Coke somebody has left abandoned at a nearby table. 'So anyway, this girl had a miscarriage in the toilet during the interval of *Godspell*, but bless her, she cleaned herself up and got back out there for the second half. Had to, you see Mike – no understudy. Brave girl ... even did the splits ...' King Rat takes a swig and lobs another KP Jungle Fresh into the air and catches it languorously in his mouth.

The nurse pokes her head round the café doors. 'Sorry, Mr Simkins, it's going to be a couple more hours yet. We're getting the usual flood of Christmas Eve drinking stunts. We'll get to you as soon as we can. Anything I can get you in the meantime?'

The voice next to me assures her we'll be fine – in fact, this reminds him of a previous Christmas Eve when he was playing Scrooge in Torquay ...

I wonder if she could rustle up the number for Rentokil?

last night

One of the oldest theatrical sayings is 'Leave 'Em Laughing'. Don't outstay your welcome. You've done well, the audience love you, so don't give them the chance to see the joins. It's good advice.

One of the problems of pantomime is that it doesn't know when to take the hint, a bit like the neighbour you invite round for mince pies and sherry on Christmas Eve and who's still there when you're putting on your pyjamas and filling your hot water bottle. Regional theatres rely on pantomime as the one time in the year when they can guarantee full houses and shore up their failing coffers, and frankly, they tend to abuse the spirit of goodwill.

That's why I'm still doing Sarah the Cook in late January.

The show is now like a bottle of Babycham that's been opened and then left out overnight. It may still have its festive wrapping and the little Bambi figure on the label with a Santa hat draped over its horns, but the whole thing lost its fizz long ago. The final week of the show we're playing to half-full houses of people now mired deep in the financial aftershocks of Christmas blow-outs and January sales, and wondering how they're going to escape bankruptcy. They don't want to know whether Santa Claus sleeps with his whiskers inside or outside the sheets: they're thinking about whether they're going to have to appear in Maidstone County Court for non-payment of hire purchase instalments on that leather sofa and matching pouffe. The weather's terrible, the bank balance is farcical, the news is awful: there's a lorry drivers' strike, a work to rule on the railways, the Prime Minister is saying, 'Crisis, what crisis?' and yet we're still standing up there shouting, 'Happy New Year, everyone, Happy New Year ...'

On 19 January the show is put out of its misery. I swap phone numbers and addresses with everyone within a hundred-yard radius of the theatre, including Syd and the security guard in the car park to whom I've not yet spoken. Actors have an infinite ability to become sentimental about people they've been calling 'that fucking cunt' for the last three months, and the circle bar on the final night is full of the scratching of ballpoints in address books and the sound of flesh on car coat as they embrace people they'd normally cross the street to avoid.

The only two who aren't speaking are Porridge Oats, who played Dick, and King Rat. Tonight during the final performance – at the conclusion of the boxing match that brings the evening to a successful end for the forces of good, and with Dick Whittington standing triumphant astride the prostrate figure of her arch-enemy – King Rat decided to do what he's been threatening to do for the past sixty-one performances: namely, take his thick, flesh-coloured, four-foot, phallus-like rat's tail and slowly raise it between her legs while she was singing her reprise of 'Gold, Silver, Diamonds, Emeralds'. Porridge Oats went for him in the wings during the curtain call and is threatening to report him to Equity for sexual harassment.

As we descend the stairs from the circle bar for the last time, we glimpse Olde London Towne through the rear doors of the auditorium. It's already matchwood – a team of stage-hands and local hired casuals have torn down the designer's precious creation within twenty minutes of curtain down. No sentiment here: just get it in the skip and let's get home before two. One by one we scatter to the four winds. Philip with the turtleneck is going back to Worcester to do *Erpingham Camp*. Helen is joining a national tour of *The Rocky Horror Show*. John is going to Morocco with his boyfriend for a break. King Rat is doing a new thriller at Guildford by a bloke he swears is called Hugh Janus. The others will be signing on the dole on Monday morning.

And me?

Well, I don't have to worry now. I can spend my time sprawling in bed, staring out of the window while eating toasted marshmallows and just waiting for the phone to ring. Because I've got myself an agent.

I'd written to him some months ago at the start of the season, and unbeknown to me he'd come down on the train to have a shuftie from the anonymity of the stalls. He obviously liked what he saw because this week I received a letter from him stating that if I were still looking for representation he'd like to take me on. In fact, to quote the letter verbatim, he'd been 'struck by my unexpectedly mature stage presence ...'

I'm only sorry he hadn't been able to stay for the second half. The scene in which I did the balloon dance for the Sultan of Morocco was probably my best moment.

cameos

Why don't actors look out of the window in the morning?

Because they'd have nothing to do in the afternoon.

I hit my first serious bout of unemployment in the early months of 1980. My agent assures me it's a good sign. He says that the business will be getting the message that this actor has plans, that I'm not content to take the first thing that comes along. He assures me it will pay tremendous dividends in the long run.

I've no complaint with that. I just wish he'd explain it to my bank manager. Another Friday night is looming, the time of the week when actors are at their most vulnerable. The rest of the world is settling down for the weekend. Outside in the street I can see the general public streaming home with their wage cheques in their pockets and shopping for all the family, and it's going to be a long time here in this bedsit till Monday morning at ten when the world opens for business and the faint glimmer of hope stirs afresh. But just as I'm uncorking the cooking sherry the phone rings ...

'Michael, it's Simon.'

'Simon who?'

'Simon, director of *The Winter's Tale*. I hope you don't mind me calling you at home but you may recall you wrote your number on your audition form and I just thought I'd ring to have a debrief about your decision. Not that I want to put any pressure on you, I've got far too much respect for you to do that ...'

Never let the director of a job you've turned down have your home phone number. Because once they have that, you're dead in the water. That's what your agent is for – he's supposed to form a protective membrane between you and the potential employer, to translate your reaction to the opposing party into

honeyed words and weaselly phrases, which can enable negotiation and position-shifting to take place without the threat of
writs. Agents act as arbitrators between employer and employee
so that in the period between the job interview and the first
rehearsal you need never have to speak to each other. Then you
can all pretend to be best buddies on the first day because the
agent has dealt with all the nasty stuff for you.

For which he takes 10 per cent of everything you earn.

For instance, I've just said to my agent: 'Tell the director of
his second-rate theatre on the outskirts of Surrey if he thinks I'm
happy to be stuck doing three virtual walk-on parts in the same
play, thereby condemning myself to standing around upstage all
evening in a succession of terrible hats, he's an even bigger mug
than I thought when I met him ...'

This is transmitted to the theatre director as: 'Michael is
thrilled to be offered the chance of working with you but feels
that he would like the opportunity to contribute more exten-
sively to the overall production. He's wondering if the part of
Autolycus, a part in which he believes he could express himself
more profoundly, has been cast yet?'

It works both ways, of course. The director of the second-
rate theatre on the outskirts of Surrey replies: 'Who the hell does
your client think he is? Does he realize I've got nearly five thousand other actors all ripping my arm off to do these walk-ons?
Does he seriously believe for one moment that we haven't cast
Autolycus weeks ago with an actor much better known and, if
you want the truth, more talent in his little finger?'

This is passed back to me as: 'They thought your suggestion
about Autolycus a very interesting one, Michael, and I think
they're genuinely regretful that it didn't occur to them before.
Sadly, they've already signed somebody else up now and don't
think they can withdraw the offer, but they want to stress how
keen they are to have your personal skills aboard this project...'

And eventually it's resolved. Or not. Perhaps we meet in the
middle with an extra fiver, or a slightly better part, or we don't.
Often some other sweetener will be employed – one actor I heard
of signed up to a year's contract at the RSC on the understanding

he could bring his Jack Russell into the dressing room during performances. Perhaps you'll get your own mini-fridge, or a measly mention at the bottom of the poster in letters so small they look like a supermarket bar code. There are hundreds of ways round apparently insuperable problems ... or there aren't. It's your agent's job to protect you from all the greasy fumbling and get the best deal he can.

But once the director has got your home phone number and the enemy can invade your citadel ...

Simon has rung me in my bedsit in Brighton, where I've been living for the past three months since moving out of my parents' house soon after returning from Canterbury. The flat is far enough away for me to feel I've finally broken the shackles of studentship and to assert my independence as an adult male making his own way in the world in his chosen profession and at last standing alone, yet near enough for me to take round my dirty washing and still be back before the end of the advert break. Since going with this international theatrical agent I've been trying to up my profile a bit, and had already turned down the offer of these three separate small parts: so why does Simon want to ring me now, and on a Friday evening?

'I'm only really calling to say how sorry I am it hasn't worked out. I know the parts we're offering are only ...'

Offering. Note the use of present tense. That means it's not too late. I could change my mind. But hang on – only three hours ago I told my agent to inform him he could shove them up his arse ...

'... I know they're only cameos, but they're really pivotal parts and I just wanted to make sure you knew how integral I feel they are to the production ...'

Aahhh ... Cameo. My defences are already breached, and the hoards are pouring across the drawbridge. I must be strong. Remember my first instincts and prepare to repel boarders ...

In all the lexicography of actor-speak, there's no single word that is used so often or possesses such nuance of meaning as 'cameo'. If Jack Nicholson only had one scene in a movie you can bet that he'd grip the wrists of friends at dinner parties and whisper, 'But it's a cameo.' The word is a godsend. For those of you who've never asked an actor about the size of his part, cameo is a word that means small but suggests big. It means that although the character may only be on stage for thirty seconds, he plays an essential part in the action of the play. Which brings us to the next crucial term. Pivotal.

Pivotal is the word often associated with cameos; cameos must be pivotal, otherwise they're merely rotten parts. An actor I was talking to in a pub on the seafront the other week was telling me how he was persuaded to do the role of a hansom cab driver in a play because it was described to him as a pivotal cameo. He found out too late he only had one line, which was, 'Thank'ee, Guv.'

But Simon's still talking. And I think I just heard the word 'integral'.

Integral suggests integrity. All actors need to be thought of as having integrity. Any job decision can be justified if you can keep a shred of integrity. The actor playing Bungle the bear in *Rainbow* knows how much delight he's giving to the nation's children by signing up to a seventy-third consecutive series, so he can still claim integrity. The three Porsches standing in his driveway are merely incidental to the valuable public service he's performing. And now Simon has just used the three words in the same sentence.

And I'm already thinking, perhaps I've made a terrible mistake.

OK, so the cameos on offer are only a sea captain, a royal lord and a doctor. Granted, if you take the total number of lines each character speaks and put them all into a single speech it would last about fourteen seconds. But, as Simon is explaining now, and I must say he's making a spirited case, 'The play can't happen without them ...'

'... The point is, Mike, that the sea captain has to row the prince to the deserted island and leave him on the shore to be eaten by the wild animals, the noble lord is the one who sums up the shock and surprise of the entire Sicilian court when he exclaims: "My Royal Liege..." And as for the doctor, I need hardly spell it out ...'

'No?'

'Well, since you ask, I mean, it's obvious, isn't it? The doctor has to break the news to the King that his wife is dead. It's the single most important and profound speech of the piece. It rocks the entire universe of the play, throwing the geoid off centre and hurtling the characters on to the path of destruction and of course, ultimate redemption ... '

Geoid? They're throat sweets, aren't they?

In any case, I'm having trouble with his description of the doctor's contribution as a 'speech'. All he says is: 'She's dead, my lord.' Four words. Added to which, if it's a Shakespearean doctor, the chances are I'll have to come on in one of those felt bonnets with side flaps that make people look like Piglet. Unless he's updating it, in which case it'll be flak jackets or surgical gowns. Either way it's not much to get hold of.

'Anyway, I respect your decision but just wanted to check that you knew how I felt about them as director. Only ...'

There's a long pause. Only what? He seems to have tailed off. Business psychologists say that this is the critical moment of any discussion. In matters of delicate negotiation, with both sides vying for supremacy, for the vital compromise from the opposing side, the winner is always the one who doesn't break the critical silence ...

I last three seconds.

'Only what?'

'... Well, only that, we all felt here in the office that you'd just be so *good* in it ...'

Five minutes later he rings off, wishing me a good weekend. I've agreed to think it over.

bear

Six weeks later I'm sitting in a terrible hat in the stalls of a second-rate theatre on the outskirts of Surrey.

Someone told me recently that there are two types of directors. Blockers and wankers. Blockers are the ones who meticulously plot out each move of every actor in the first week, brooking no argument or query until the process is complete, after which, if you're lucky, you can negotiate. Working with a blocker can feel a bit like being in the army: their theory is that even if the original scaffolding of moves and positions proves to be entirely unhelpful, at least it gives everyone a basis from which to argue. Wankers, or the beanbag brigade as they're sometimes called, prefer the opposite methodology, by which nothing is decided upon until the dress rehearsal. Tell-tale signs of wankers are a predilection to improvisational hot-seating, complex role-play games, and terms like 'Fluidity, Choice and Intention'. Of the two sorts, most actors prefer blockers – at least they're certain to cobble something together for the first night, even if it's terrible. An incompetent wanker will leave you vulnerable and clueless, and then when the press tear into your chaotic, unformed, one-note shambles of a performance, will heap the blame squarely on your head for your intransigence and reluctance to embark on this complex emotional journey.

Simon is an unusual hybrid, in that he's both a blocker and a wanker. That takes some doing. He's spent two weeks sitting round a table pontificating on the various allegorical allusions and classical references, and then has lost his nerve in the final few days since when he's been pushing us round the stage hysterically as if he's General Jumbo with his model army in the *Beano*.

The play is, in any case, a notoriously difficult one, involving complex court scenes, and an unwieldy transformation to a pastoral-comedy motif for most of the second half. In addition, it has the single most difficult theatrical moment to stage successfully in the entire history of the stage:

'Exit Pursued By A Bear.'

Shakespeare must have been struggling for ideas when he came up with this way of disposing of the character of Antigonus, and it presents tough choices for the modern-day director. Do you go for something abstract, a roaring and a flashing of lights, perhaps with him cowering in terror and gibbering furiously at some imaginary spectre that none of the audience can see? As a method of getting rid of people in episodes of *Dr Who* it works well, but occurring out of the blue like this in the middle of an otherwise classic tragedy you risk the audience thinking the actor's having an epileptic fit.

So what about the more traditionalist stance of having some poor assistant stage manager being required to lurch on in a bear costume and chasing the actor into the wings, to be followed seconds later by a blood-curdling scream?

That's OK too, so long as you know that his appearance will be greeted with a guffaw of derision.

Simon has decided to go for the reality option, and he's talked big about making it a genuinely frightening moment. One of the assistant stage managers, a burly teenager called Glen, has been dragooned into playing the part of the bear: yet at the run-through in the rehearsal room last week, admittedly without the crucial assistance of an animal skin, his effort was frankly pitiful. In Barbara Goodwin's terms, he hadn't got it. So Simon's hopes rest largely on the belief that the designer could produce for him a realistic outfit: I've even heard him describe this as essential to his plans.

But at this afternoon's technical rehearsal he's suffered a massive setback. Unknown to him, the designer has tried to save some money by recycling the badger costume left over from their Christmas production of *The Wind in the Willows*. Instead of starting from scratch he's disguised that particular badgery head shape that badgers have with some extra pieces of fur, and has managed to obliterate the telltale white flecks at the side of the muzzle with some spray paint; but if he had any fears that it still looked like a badger, the snorts of barely suppressed laughter coming from theatre staff and cast members during the technical rehearsal merely confirmed his worst fears. It looked as if Kenneth Grahame had adapted the *Texas Chainsaw Massacre*.

Consequently, Simon's in a foul mood. There's nothing more calculated to put a director in a vile temper than raucous laughter during the tech, and he's looking for trouble. You should never try to communicate with a director in this frame of mind; they're on the lookout for a whipping boy, some innocent low-status nonentity at whom they can direct their wrath. So I'm just sitting here in the stalls at the end of the rehearsal waiting to hear what's going to happen next and trying to keep my head down.

Which isn't easy when you're wearing a two-foot felt doctor's hat that makes you look like Piglet.

Anyway, I've got my own problems to sort out.

I should have trusted my instincts, switched on the answerphone and continued with the cooking sherry, because it's proving even more difficult to do anything with my three cameos than I'd feared.

Take my sea captain. All he says is the entire play is: ''Tis a wild night.' Four words. I've tried stressing ''tis', 'a', 'wild', and 'night', in alternate weeks. Nothing.

Or my doctor: 'She's dead, my lord.' Four different words to play with, yet it still remains page-bound. I'd even toyed with rearranging them in a different order, that's how frustrated I was.

My noble lord fares even less well. Compared with his predecessors' four words apiece, he can only muster a feeble three: 'My Royal Liege!', barked reflexively in response to the announcement that his sovereign is disinheriting his son and heir. This afternoon I wasn't even accurate with the text: I'd become so preoccupied about a piece of elastic somewhere in my leggings that was wrapped too tightly round my thigh that I got distracted and came out with 'My Real Lorge!'

Seven terms at the RADA, thousands of pounds of taxpayers' money, all those certificates and prizes, and this is the best I can come up with. But Simon's already spotted me lurking here by the fire exit: he's picking his way along a row of upturned seats and is rapidly approaching in my direction. No way out.

'Michael, I wanted a word with you ...'

He slumps down next to me. I try to remain cool and unconcerned. This hat isn't helping.

'Look, Michael. I didn't want to say this in front of the others so it's best I take this opportunity now. The point is, I've given you three parts and you're playing them all exactly the same.' His mouth curves in a humourless smile. 'I wonder if you could possibly do something about it before tomorrow night. I'd be grateful ...'

Before I can respond, the designer crashes in through the fire exit doors. He's clutching a paintbrush and his face is a mask of anxiety and fear. He's already speaking as he enters. 'Simon, I've got good news about the bear ...'

He wants Simon to say something friendly and encouraging but the director merely swivels his humourless smile around 180 degrees on its turret and fixes him with it.

'Yes, we've found a firm in London who've got the equipment. They can have it down here by first thing in the morning. I've persuaded them to make a special journey. You'll have dry ice by tomorrow's performance ...'

Oh dear. Dry ice. The last refuge of the embattled director. I didn't realize the situation was so grave. From the look on Simon's face he was hoping for something better, like a new bear costume perhaps, but with this designer's track record he'd probably end up with the Honey Monster. As it is, both he and the designer know that with enough dry ice they can rescue virtually any naff moment. It's the oldest trick in the book. Pump enough of the stuff on to the stage just before Glen's attack and the swirling white cloud will safely transform a six-foot badger into nothing more discernible than a vague animal-like shape illuminated through opaque mist ... Most of the stalls will be coughing so much they won't be looking anyway, and those that are will be wondering what that terrible hissing sound is. It's desperate, but it might just work.

'Is that all right?' asks the designer, pitiably.

'It'll have to be, won't it?' Simon rises and walks out of the auditorium. 'Tell everyone there'll be notes in the circle bar in ten minutes. That includes the fucking badger ...'

I spend a sleepless night. *Three parts exactly the same* ... The words keep running around my head. And I've only got eleven words at my disposal. And then an old adage comes back to me from my training. I think it was advice intended for parts of more than four words a throw, but nonetheless a nugget of pure gold surely just as applicable to cameos as to leads: 'When you are struggling to unlock a part, at all times return to the text. Ask yourself – what is the character trying to say?'

I lie in bed long into the night with the Penguin edition of *A Winter's Tale* propped up in front of me. Think!

What was the purpose of ''Tis a wild night'?

What emotions stir the doctor to announce, 'She's dead, my lord'?

And as for 'My Royal Liege'?

At all times return to the text ... Eventually the book drops gently on to the bedspread and I fall into a fitful sleep.

The next evening I play the doctor with a stoop, the sea captain as a Cockney and leave the nobleman as he is. It works a treat.

car

Actors are very popular people.

Everybody likes talking to actors. I can almost sense the relief whenever I walk into a party. 'Meet Mike, he's an actor,' says the host, and suddenly I'm surrounded by quantity surveyors, estate agents, and schoolteachers all wanting to know what they might have seen me in (most likely the DHSS), have I ever met anyone famous (Yes, Coco the Clown at the opening of the Brighton Tesco when I was six), and how I learn all those lines. (What lines?) And in all honesty I like it, we all do, because it's nice to be wanted, to be asked your opinion on the crisis in the Middle East, to have your views coveted and your jokes laughed at. It makes a change from all those blank faces and unreturned phone calls we get in our work. We may say we don't like talking about ourselves but we're pretending.

Yes, everybody loves an actor. Unless, of course, you're asking them for car insurance.

When it comes to providing us with mortgages, bank loans or motor cover I'm beginning to realize we're somewhere between stuntmen and serial killers in the list of desirable clients. The popular perception is that we are reckless hell-raisers who think nothing of getting behind the wheel after an all-night bender of booze and drugs, usually with some international celebrity in the passenger seat whose insurance claim should they go through the windscreen would bankrupt the entire company.

Three years out of RADA, I've passed my driving test and have purchased my first status symbol, an ageing white Renault Six I've spotted on a garage forecourt in Hove. It may have a thatched radiator, Henry Ford's sandwiches on the front seat and a sign on the dashboard that reads 'Fasten Thy Seatbelt', but it's mine. And even if I won't be able to afford to put any petrol in it, I can at least polish it on a Sunday morning.

All I've got to do now is get it insured.

I'm standing outside the AA office in the precinct in Churchill Square. 'Let Us Insure You' reads a sign in the window. Right then, mateys. Western Road is stretching away into the distance, and somewhere at the far end, just as the road curves and is lost from view, will be Gamley's toy shop and the model department that nearly trapped me for ever in the basement. And I'm suddenly thinking, I want more than anything to drive this Renault Six past Gamley's with the window down and something loud and funky blasting out on the car stereo, Abba or Brotherhood of Man perhaps; I want Mr Farmer to look up and see me. I want him to know I've made it, that I've won the William Poel memorial prize for best verse speaking delivered in a standard English accent at RADA and scored a bullseye with my sea captain. With the help of the AA, I'll soon be able to. The Renault is parked at a friend's house a bare ten-minute walk from here. A few forms to fill, a hastily written cheque, and I can be outside Gamley's in less than half an hour. I push the door and walk in.

A young man in horn-rimmed glasses and wearing one of those quasi-military jerseys so favoured by the organization is sitting behind a spacious counter. According to a small lapel badge on his right breast he's called Howard. When I announce the reason for my visit he gives me a broad smile and asks me to take a seat. He even offers me a Fox's glacier mint from a small bowl on the table-top. We're obviously going to be best mates. While I suck away happily, Howard rummages in his desk for the appropriate forms. 'Just a few questions,' he says. 'Shouldn't take too long.'

And indeed it doesn't. Type of car, size of engine, will it be garaged on-street or off-road, third party or fully comp? I've been here barely a minute and already we're on to question seven. The box marked 'Occupation'.

'Actor,' I reply, with a cheeky smile. Bless him, he can't get many interesting people to talk to, stuck here in his terrible sweater every day. I'm looking forward to brightening his morning:

I've even got my answers ready. A few choice morsels of theatrical tittle-tattle, a little advice on voice production and coping with nerves, now where do I sign?

But Howard isn't smiling. In fact, he's looking anxiously at his notes. 'I'm afraid I'll have to refer this to Head Office. Just a moment.' He picks up a nearby phone and waits for his supervisor to respond. Eventually the phone is answered.

Howard turns away from me and cups his hand over the mouthpiece. 'Sorry to bother you, sir,' he mutters, 'but I've got a third-party fire and theft Renault Six and an actor.'

I consider asking to have a word about the billing. But Howard is already feverishly jotting down a complicated set of instructions on how to proceed. At length he turns back to me.

'Are you in the theatre or on television?' he asks.

'Theatre,' I reply, omitting the fact that this is through necessity rather than choice. We don't need to dwell on my TV career. When it starts I'll be the first to bring it up in conversation. Hopefully that's it. Howard relays my response and waits for further instructions while I daydream about the look on Mr Farmer's face. But there's more.

'What was your last role?'

'The part of Hickory Wood in *One for the Pot* at the Brewhouse Theatre, Taunton.'

What the hell has this to do with my driving ability? Howard is writing my answer down and relaying it to the supervisor at the same time. The relaying of this latest information seems to wrong-foot the supervisor. Again Howard turns back to me.

'How do you spell "Hickory"?'

A further minute passes while whoever is on the end of the phone receives the correct spelling and writes it down. More instructions. Howard's brow crumples slightly.

'Would you describe it as a lead role or a support role?'

'Is this really necessary?'

'I'm afraid it is,' says Howard. Apparently actors don't fit into their usual framework of risk assessment criteria. He's very sorry.

'What was the question again?'

'Lead or support. How would you describe it?'

I reply that as I had fifty-one separate entrances in the play, it could be safely counted as a lead part. After a few seconds whispered conversation into the phone, he looks up at me again.

'Er ... could you give some idea of what you had to do in it?'

'Look, I had to lift up a Scotsman's kilt and squirt the contents of a soda siphon up it,' I rasp. 'Are you going to give me some car insurance?'

'I'm sorry, sir, I'm just following company rules,' bleats Howard. He turns away again to communicate to his supervisor the single funniest moment of the play. I can only hope that Head Office isn't in Glasgow. Both Howard and the supervisor then have to write down the entire incident of the kilt and the soda siphon. There isn't enough room on the form for even a concise description of John Chapman's uproarious romp, and more minutes pass while he searches for another piece of paper on which to continue the answer. But at last it's completed. Surely now that will be it.

Howard turns to me again. His brow is covered with a thin film of sweat.

'Would you describe it as a drama or a comedy?'

'It's a bloody farce,' I roar. 'And so is this.'

I march out of the office.

Three days later I return. This time I'm wearing a shirt and tie, beige trousers and shoes that look like Cornish pasties. And this time a different employee is on duty – someone called Spencer.

I've had a hunch and it's time to back it.

'I'd like to arrange some car insurance, please,' I beam.

Ten questions later we get to occupation.

'Drama teacher,' I reply, giving Spencer a good look at my corduroy jacket with the suede elbow pads. Five minutes after that I'm driving along Western Road. Gamley's is approaching fast. And I'm in luck. Mr Farmer is in the window, arranging a display for the new polar adventurer Action Man.

The window mechanism isn't winding down properly at the moment but that won't stop me. I turn up the stereo and put my foot to the floor.

The car accelerates to a heady 27 mph. I press out a steady rhythmic tattoo on the horn.

The horn seems to be temporarily out of order as well. But at the last moment he turns to look out the window.

'Kisses for me, save all your kisses for me ...'

amy

Not long after the incident with Howard I get the chance to meet the man I've most wanted to work with since I bought my first dance belt. As well as his status as the most prolific and consistently funny playwright in the English-speaking theatre, Alan Ayckbourn also runs and directs his own company of actors up at a theatre in the tiny seaside town of Scarborough in North Yorkshire. I long to be there, part of a committed group of actors working together under the direction of a man touched by genius. I trot out my Pinter and Shakespeare for him at the audition, trying to resist the temptation to ask for his autograph, and return home to stare balefully at the phone. I'm offered a six-month contract the following week.

My train clatters into Scarborough railway station soon after five on an April evening. The seafront is bathed in that chill sunshine which makes you yearn for spring; what's more, the taxi driver, upon discovering that I'm joining the theatre company, insists on a short detour so I can have a glimpse at the outside of the famed Stephen Joseph Theatre on my way to my digs. I'm therefore rather nonplussed when he pulls up outside the ground floor of a dilapidated ex-primary school situated right next to Scarborough bus station. The top floor seems to be used as a technical college and the entire edifice faces a muddy slope at the top of which stands the local branch of Tesco.

Perhaps the driver is confused. After all, there are a lot of theatres to choose from. This summer the world's most successful living playwright is going to be vying for custom with Max Jaffa and his Concert Orchestra at the Spa Pavilion, Cannon and Ball at the Futurist, Keith Harris and Orville the Duck at the

Opera House, and a surviving rump of the once-legendary Black and White Minstrels at the Floral Hall. There are even daily displays of famous sea battles involving tiny remote-controlled galleons on the boating lake at Peasholme Park: that alone could eat into our matinée audiences. We'll have to be on top form.

A brightly painted sign above the doorway to what was obviously once the entrance to the infants' cloakroom confirms my driver's local knowledge. This is indeed the Stephen Joseph Theatre.

A few minutes later the taxi dumps me in the middle of what seems to be a brand-new housing estate on the Seamer Road. 'Dick and Amy Shortle, clean room, use of kitchen, non-smokers preferred, friendly, relaxed atmosphere'. Nearby, people are washing their cars and clipping hedges. Mrs Shortle, a tall stocky woman in her early forties, answers the door and welcomes me in: her husband will be back later. Everything here looks as if it's only just come out of its wrappings: the hallway is decorated with tasteful prints, and a box of crisp white tissues stands on a polished telephone table; even the local directory has a vinyl cover on it. There's a smell of washing powder. Mrs Shortle – 'Please call me Amy' – shakes my hand and welcomes me into the lounge.

'You're our first actor,' she says. 'We only put our names down on the digs list this season. It seemed a pity to have the spare room going to waste, so we thought ...'

I return her reassuring smile. I feel I'm on a stand at the Ideal Home Exhibition. God knows how she and her husband are going to take to me trying to make cheese on toast at 2 a.m., and with the walls looking like they're made out of plasterboard I'll have to go easy on the late-night curries. Still, it's clean and tidy, and Amy Shortle is much more welcoming than the mummified Mrs Willey ever was. She's even brought me a few provisions, just to get me started: tea bags, long life milk, some jammy dodgers.

'I'll show you to your room, shall I?' she says.

I follow her up a balsa wood staircase to a small landing. Three identical doors lead off, all newly glossed in white to complement the pristine, mulberry-coloured carpet.

'That's our room,' says Mrs Shortle, indicating the far door. 'This one here is the bathroom. You'll find clean towels in the airing cupboard. And this is yours.' She opens the last door and I walk in.

A single bed, immaculately made, dominates the room. On the walls are posters of Bjorn Borg and Adam Ant. The one shelf is neatly stacked with old *Jackie* annuals and books about pony jumping. At the top of the bed I can just make out a quilted velour headboard. It's only just visible behind a mountain of cuddly toys: there must be about thirty of them, arranged with infinite care on top of one another: teddies, gonks, curious little squashy penguins, woollen dolls, each one carefully placed so that they're all sitting upright and staring out at something in the middle distance which only they can see.

'We've kept it exactly as it was,' says Mrs Shortle, gazing round the room with a fond smile. A schoolbag lies in the corner next to the dressing table next to a tennis racquet. A small framed print of a teenage girl with flushed cheeks blowing out the candles on a birthday cake stands next to an alarm clock on the bedside cabinet. Various sets of board games lie stacked on top of the wardrobe: Cluedo, Mousetrap, Connect 4.

'Of course we don't blame the lorry driver,' she adds. 'He's got to live with it for the rest of his life ...'

superstition

Actors are very superstitious.

There are any number of things you mustn't do in a theatre. You must never utter the word Macbeth; the play is associated with misfortune and there's a long incidence of disaster and tragedy befalling people and projects where the word has been casually mentioned. Mention the dreaded M word in a dressing room and you'll be asked to go outside, turn round three times, spit, and knock on the door to request permission to re-enter. You should, of course, always refer to it simply as the Scottish play.

Another tradition: you must never wish another actor 'Good Luck'. Instead, you should employ the post-ironic epithet 'Break a Leg', thus forestalling bad fortune by the use of self-regarding irony.

Worst of all, you must never whistle backstage. Only last December I was threatened with physical violence by Frank the theatre carpenter for violating this simple golden rule, although he admitted afterwards it had less to do with superstition and more with the fact that I'd been whistling 'Stop the Cavalry' by Jona Lewie outside his workshop for the past forty-five minutes.

Those are just a selection. For a full inventory of acts likely to bring doom and destruction raining down on an actor's head, just ask Irene, the Scarborough stage manager; she's the repository for all theatre folklore, customs and general witchcraft, coming as she does from a long family tradition of theatre technicians from the Scottish Highlands. She never steps on the cracks between paving stones, avoids walking under ladders even during scenery fit-ups, and carries a rabbit's foot around in her stage dungarees during performances. She's also as broad as she is tall and weighs nearly twenty stone, but she assures us it's glandular. Bad luck.

In any case, I don't believe all that stuff. It's luvvie hokum, something for the memoirs.

It's May 1981, my second summer working in Scarborough. The town itself is a breezy knockabout sort of place, filled from spring till autumn with hordes of holidaymakers from Leeds to Glasgow all wandering round the town in huge impromptu crocodiles under Tupperware skies, wrapped in pac-a-macs and eating chips out of polystyrene trays. The Stephen Joseph Theatre, a theatre in-the-round, on the other hand, is an entirely unfamiliar concept in populist entertainment. There are no curtains, no wings, no doors or walls, no cumbersome scenery, no proscenium arch, no upstage, no downstage, no cheating left or right: just a central acting space encircled by rows of seats set on a steep rake in every direction, with access for both audience and actors through one of three vomitoriums ('voms') from which the performers burst on to the stage as if from the midst of the spectators. The front row are close enough to touch you without leaving their seats: I was kicked in the shins by a man crossing his legs the other week, or at least that's what he claimed in the bar afterwards.

At first it was disconcerting, being able to read the labels on the ties of old gents and smell the particular perfume worn by office girls. When somebody sneezed you could feel the film of mucus hitting your cheeks, and with the audience able to scrutinize you in the smallest detail you're always likely to get accosted in the bar afterwards by some anorak whose zip has broken, particularly in my first play when I had to appear in RAF uniform ('I noticed that you only had one set of lapel buttons on your tunic, young man, whereas in fact, I happen to know that at the time the RAF had a double set and a cream lanyard'). Nonetheless, I'm a complete theatre-in-the-round convert. What on earth are we all doing, facing front like that?

'Shouting in the evenings,' Troughton called it. Ludicrous. We're presenting two plays in repertoire this summer: the latest Ayckbourn offering, a dark comedy called *Season's Greetings*, and, starting tonight, another piece by a local author. *Tapster* is set in the saloon bar of an old-fashioned English pub and tells the story of a small family business struggling to maintain their independence in the modern cut-throat commercial world of Thatcher's Britain following the death of the patriarch, old Sam.

It's *Tapster* that has caused all the problems with Irene ...

Act One: The lights rise to reveal the saloon bar of the Lost Shepherd; stools, pumps, tables and chairs, all the trappings of a traditional pub, except that a full-size coffin is placed neatly along the length of the bar top.

When Irene read that she went the colour of parchment and her voice trembled with foreboding. Short of announcing we were doing a production of the Scottish play set in a ladder factory and starring Ronnie Ronalde and Roger Whittaker, it couldn't have been worse news.

'D'ya no ken?' she muttered darkly at the read-through. 'You surely canna' hav' a coffin in a theatre. You'll bring calamity doon on yer heids.'

From day one Irene wouldn't have anything to do with the project, refusing even to go near the coffin during rehearsals even though it was only a mock-up created by Frank in the carpenter's workshops: and when it came to the fit-up onstage she threatened to hand in her resignation when asked to help position it on the stage. Eventually an uneasy compromise was reached with Irene directing the placement of the bleached ash wood casket from the edge of the vom, stroking her rabbit's foot furiously as she did so. Nonetheless, she remained adamant: misfortune would strike one of us before the end of the run.

'It's merely a matter o' time,' she says to anyone who'll listen.

Silly cow.

World premieres don't come along very often. When they do they're a unique set of circumstances. There's no template of experience, no history of past productions to draw on, no predecessors in the part to ring up and ask how they did it: in short, no sense of what to expect. Will it work? Will the audience treat it as a comedy or a tragedy? Will the author's *coup de théâtre* at the end of the play prove to be a seminal moment in theatre history or a damp squib: or worse still, just quietly baffling. All the usual first night tensions of getting a play on are increased tenfold with new writing.

My own anxiety is further heightened by the fact that my character opens the play. I'm first onstage in the role of Thomas, the owner's dour and reliable twenty-something son. Wandering on to the bar-room set, dressed in overalls and wiping my hands on an oily rag, I deliver the first line of the evening (shouted to someone offstage): 'Can we get this place cleared up? It's like a pigsty in here.'

One of the problems of theatre-in-the-round, at least at Scarborough, is that the audience can only get to their seats by walking across the acting space: expensive or bulky props can't be placed on the set until the last person is seated, in case they're nicked or disturbed. The coffin isn't a problem, as it's already resting on the bar top at the start so can be safely positioned before the doors are opened. But there's another item, a huge brass scuttle filled to the brim with great chunks of loose coal, which has to be positioned centre stage before the play can commence. Once the house lights have faded, Irene, dressed discreetly in black jeans, black T-shirt and black plimsolls must hurry up one of the voms with the container of coal, place it quietly on the correct spot and hurry off again (taking care not to inadvertently brush against the coffin in case she gets turned into a monster person): after which the stage lights fade up and the play can begin.

On the first night I'm waiting to begin the play in the comforting darkness backstage while a few yards away, the last of the audience are fussing their way to their seats: Irene stands in the darkness next to me, her glasses glinting feebly in the half-light. From a few yards up the vom I can hear (and if I peek round the corner I can see) them arriving. It may not include the national press and West End producers as it would if it were an Ayckbourn premiere, but, nonetheless, all the other usual suspects are here. There's the Mayor and Mayoress of Scarborough picking their way past the coffin. There's the chairman of the theatre board crossing past the bar pumps. There's the Managing Director of Plaxton's motor coaches, followed by the *Scarborough Evening Mercury* theatre critic, weaving their way between the bar stools.

Tonight, just as planned, Irene lumbers up the vom in the dark with the scuttle. The audience are already quietening, the buzz of pre-show chit-chat already stilled by the blackout and replaced by the silent expectation of the drama to come. But tonight the drama occurs sooner than any of us can anticipate.

Irene trips on the carpet while running full pelt with the scuttle and goes down like an elephant being shot mid-charge on the African veldt, showering the audience with huge lumps of anthracite while they're sitting there in complete darkness and unable to defend themselves.

I sense something is wrong when I hear the sound of Irene's plimsoll catching on a floorboard, followed a split second later by a noise like a horsehair sofa being dropped from a great height. A few seconds later she limps back past me in the dark. The stage lights rise. We're off.

I wander up the vom to begin the action. My feet are now making an unfamiliar scrunching sound that wasn't there before. And then I see why. The sight that greets my entrance is chilling. It looks like the aftermath of a boiler explosion: coal lies strewn everywhere, on the floor, on top of the coffin, in the aisles, on people's laps. Everywhere I look men and women are rubbing limbs or holding their cheeks; a woman in a pale two-piece is whimpering softly; a couple are inspecting their tickets to see if they'd inadvertently stumbled into the Grumbleweeds at the Opera House by mistake. The Lady Mayoress is attempting to dislodge a huge lump of the stuff from her chain of office. In the back row the associate director, Robin, is holding his head in his hands. And there, in the middle of the stage, lying among the smokeless briquettes like some ritualistic offering, is Irene's lucky rabbit's foot.

'Can we get this place cleared up? It's like a pigsty in here.'

The evening never really recovers. Every time the lights dim the audience flinch, and there's a steady rush for the exit during the bows. In the bar afterwards Irene sits with her knee up on a chair and an ice pack round one of her wrists, and is adamant: the presence of the coffin caused it. When Graeme, the actor playing old Sam, offers to give me a lift home to the digs we share, Irene looks up briefly from the family-sized bag of ready-salted crisps she's hoovering up and tells us to watch out on the road. 'The day's nay over yet ...' she says, fumbling for her recovered rabbit's foot through her dungarees.

'Stupid bitch,' says Graeme, as we climb into his car.

But we drive home along Falsgrave at an unusually sober 18 mph.

He even stops to indicate before pulling out of the car park.

any which way

Actors who've done a lot of farce – 'farceurs' – say the trick of the thing is that the central character must try to keep his dignity even though his world is falling apart around him. However many air hostesses are hidden in his wardrobe, however unlikely the arrival of his wife at the worst possible moment, however ludicrous his explanations to all and sundry, it only remains funny if the hero is still striving to maintain some self-respect. If there's nothing at stake, there's nothing to laugh at.

My time at Scarborough is over before I know it. Fifteen months, seven full-length plays plus three lunchtime musicals and a couple of late-night entertainments in the bar. It's been the best time, but I'm anxious now to get back to London and pick up the strands of my life again, particularly as the town is closing down for the winter. It's now September, and all day the beach has been deserted: a fierce wind has been strafing the seafront, with most of the remaining tourists hunkered down in local cafés glugging back the Horlicks or ambling aimlessly round Marks and Spencer in the High Street. A forlorn troupe of donkeys crowding together for protection on the sand has been the only evidence that the town is supposed to be a holiday resort. Scarborough even in late summer is more like the Gulag Archipelago once the sun's gone in.

We've finished our last-but-one performance of *Season's Greetings* and are on our way back to our digs. Graeme swings the Renault Fuego into Springbank Terrace at 35 mph without signalling and my heart leaps: the dustbin has been moved, the lights are already on in the hallway, and Lucy's black Chelsea boots are lined up on the carpet underneath the coat rack. She's here.

I met Lucy at an audition last year and we've been an item

ever since: which is the other reason for wanting to get back to London. She's the daughter of a well-known impresario and has been trying her hand at acting since graduating from university. I haven't seen much of her recently as she's down there while I'm stuck up here, but no matter – she's fierce, competitive, sexy, enthusiastic, ambitious, quick-witted, and above all has a wonderfully keen sense of humour, all of which I'm hoping to reacquaint myself with tonight as she's has come up on the National Express coach to spend the weekend with me.

Number 19, Springbank Terrace is the best digs in the town: though it had little to beat as my only previous accommodation apart from my one night at Amy Shortle's was a dusty attic room in a house owned by a man whom I suspected was the Yorkshire Ripper. It is owned by the son of the local vicar, an affable young man called Anthony Tubbs, and he's the dream landlord – as well as a young man of Christian principles and a keen supporter of the theatre, he lives well away from the premises, keeps the property well maintained, requests a very modest rent, and never visits without letting us know he's coming so we've got time to clear up the wine bottles and empty the ashtrays beforehand. He also doesn't mind girlfriends stopping the weekend, which is a liberal approach not universally found in landlords. Come to think of it, he's an archetype of the incompetent but well-meaning middle-class sort of bloke that Ayckbourn seems to be able to write about better than anyone.

Graeme opens the lounge door with his knee and we lumber in with our shopping to where Lucy is squatting on the sofa wrapped in my dressing gown watching the TV. She's warm and pink from having just had a bath, her shoulder-length auburn hair is clean and shiny and her freckles are even more noticeable than usual. She looks truly beautiful. And what's more she's overjoyed to see me and gives me a ferocious hug while Graeme diplomatically moves through into the kitchen to prepare supper. He begins sawing the French sticks and arranging a variety of cheeses on the breadboard. The film he wanted to watch has already started on ITV, a comedy starring Clint Eastwood, Sondra Locke and a large orang-utan.

'What's it like?' he calls.

'I haven't really been following,' Lucy yells back.

I give her a playful kiss on her ear. 'How was your bath?'

'Fine.' Her voice lowers to a whisper. 'But I've got something to tell you.'

Graeme wanders in with a couple of cans of Skol and plonks them down next to us. 'Enjoy,' he says expansively before returning to the kitchen.

'What's wrong?'

'Nothing. Only ... something's happened.'

'What is it?'

'Well, I had a bath.'

She stares at the screen. An orang-utan is walking into a bar. 'Yes?'

'And afterwards I was lying on the floor in your dressing gown watching the telly.'

The orang-utan climbs on to a tall stool and opens a can of beer.

'And there was this film on starring Al Pacino ...'

'And?'

'And I started feeling a bit ...'

'A bit what?'

'Well, a bit ... fruity.'

'You what?'

Graeme ambles in with a jar of silverskin onions. He watches the screen for a moment while the orang-utan picks up a bowl of pretzels and tips them over his head.

'Good stuff,' he remarks. He returns to the kitchen.

I turn back to Lucy. 'So what happened?'

'So I undid the dressing gown and started ...'

'Yes?'

'Well ... I knew you'd be at least an hour or two so ... so I started ...'

'What?'

'Having a wank.'

The orang-utan has just put some coins on the bar top.

'*You what*?'

'Sshh! No need to shout.'

I glance into the kitchen. Graeme is rummaging in the fridge. 'Is that it?'

'No ... um ... the fact is ... I was just in the middle of it when your landlord walked in.'

'Here we are,' says Graeme, walking in with a cheeseboard. He sits heavily in a single chair next to us, reaches for the bottle opener, and stares at the departing ape. 'Anyone tell me what's going on?' he says.

I've got to think. No need to panic, it could happen to anyone. Perhaps I should get Lucy out of the lounge and into the kitchen, the bedroom, anywhere, just so that I can find out the extent of the damage first-hand. Maybe it won't be as bad as I'm imagining and he didn't notice anything. Maybe she was able to recover before he looked round the door frame, perhaps he's got glaucoma ...

Who am I kidding? Anthony Tubbs, landlord, vicar's son and man of principle, has walked into his house to find a strange woman masturbating on his shag pile in a borrowed dressing gown. It must have looked like a scene from *Caligula*. Whatever else I do, I've got to ring him and apologize, make some attempt to salvage the situation, and I've got to do it now, before tomorrow morning. It's already 11.15 p.m., and with every second that ticks away the situation can only get worse: he may be knocking on Alan Ayckbourn's door in town and demanding to know why the world's most celebrated playwright is employing perverts and deviants in light comedy-of-manners, he may ...

Come to think of it, he'd better not refer to them as light comedy-of manners, at least not to Alan's face. Not if he wants a sympathetic hearing.

The only phone in the house is in here, in the lounge, next to where Graeme is slumped. And Clint Eastwood is now fumbling for Sondra Locke's bra strap; blokes never leave a television set if there's a chance of some gratuitous nudity, particularly not blokes of Graeme's age. And then I remember. There's an extension phone in Graeme's bedroom, the front one above the lounge. I never normally use it, but tonight ...

'Just going to the loo.'

Thirty seconds later I'm in Graeme's bedroom; my mouth feels as if I've been sucking pennies. The bed is cluttered with a snooker cue and various garish sweaters that are Graeme's trademark. I clear a space, perch on the edge of the bed, and pick up the receiver. I've absolutely no idea what I'm going to say.

The phone rings endlessly on and on. Nobody there. I'll have to hang up ...

'Hello?'

It's Anthony. His voice sounds grainy and dulled. In the background I can dimly make out a television blaring.

'Anthony, it's Mike.'

'Mike who?'

'Mike Simkins. Your tenant at Springbank.'

Silence. I plunge on.

'Look, Anthony, there's something I'd like to say to you.'

'Yes?'

I take a deep breath. 'Yes, I just want you to know that I am profoundly sorry for what occurred here this evening. I've just been informed as to what happened and I can only register my shock and embarrassment at the disgraceful position you found yourself placed in. I'm fully aware that you may want to terminate our arrangement immediately and you would be perfectly warranted in doing so, but if you could possibly see your way to finding some forgiveness I can vouchsafe you on my honour that tonight's events were a complete and isolated incident, that you need never fear that anything like that will happen again, and that your magnanimity would be rewarded in every particular.'

Thank God I've run out of breath: I'm starting to sound like Leonard Sachs on *The Good Old Days*.

Silence.

'Anthony?'

'Yes, Mike, I'm still here. Sorry, I was asleep. But it's just as well you've rung.'

A pause.

Then he continues. 'I can't believe this has happened again.'

Again? Jesus, how many times has Lucy done this for him?

'Michael?'

'Yes, Anthony, I'm still here. Sorry, I was ... You mean this has happened before?'

'Yes, several times. I'm getting fed up with it to tell you the truth.'

'Yes. Yes I'd imagine ...'

'This time my hand's gone completely numb.'

I sit there in the semi-darkness of Graeme's bedroom. I suddenly seem to be spinning into a performance of *Two and Two Make Sex*. All I need is Patrick Cargill and some chest expanders.

'What happens is I drop off in front of the telly and fall asleep on my arm. It's completely dead.'

Silence.

'Michael?'

'Yes, Anthony, I'm still here, sorry.'

'Don't apologize, I've only myself to blame. I can feel the blood coming back now. It'll be hell for a minute or two but I reckon you might have saved my hand. Thank God you called.'

'Oh. Well. That's great.'

'What was it you wanted?'

'Nothing.'

'Is there a problem at the house? I didn't catch what you said a minute or two back, I was still a bit groggy, but I can come round now if—'

'No. No. It's all fine. Very nice.'

'Good.'

'Right. Well, I'll be off then.'

'Yes, of course. Night.'

'Goodnight, Anthony.'

I replace the receiver. I don't pretend to understand any of that, but the fact is I've still got a roof over my head. I trot down to the lounge and collapse back on to the sofa. Lucy barely glances at me.

Hey, this monkey's good.

~

Two hours later I feel Lucy's head turning to face mine on the pillow.

'I'm sorry about tonight. It was silly. I don't know why I did it.'

I kiss her eyelids. 'Don't worry. It was just how you felt. It's quite a compliment actually. Anyway, I sorted it all out.'

'What do you mean?'

'When I left you in the lounge I went upstairs and called Tubbs on the extension. Don't know how I did it but it turned out all right. I explained how it was and he was fine about it. Almost unconcerned in fact. Barely seemed to recall it.'

Silence.

'Lucy?'

'No, when I said I don't know why I did it – what I meant was—'

'Forget it. It's sorted. Just take a bit more care next time—'

'No, when I said I don't know why I did it—'

I find her lips in the dark with my right index finger and touch them lightly. 'I said don't worry. I've sorted it.'

'I meant that I made it up.'

We spend the rest of the night practising our own version of shouting in the evenings.

Lucy stays for a couple more days. After the verbal maelstrom of 3 a.m. (only ended by Graeme throwing one of his golf clubs against the dividing bedroom wall), and a following morning of virtual silence, we manage, fragment by grudging fragment, to make it up. By lunch the next day we're on speaking terms and by the evening restoring full sexual relations; on the Sunday we even take a trip to see a late-night performance of a comic hypnotist at the Floral Hall. But something has changed. Such a cataclysmic difference of opinion as to what constitutes having a laugh leaves little confidence in a future together, and when Lucy gets a call from her agent to return early to London for an audition there's a silent but tangible sigh of relief from both of us. The relationship can be put out of its misery.

The London coach is nearly full but she finds a seat over the wheel arch towards the back. She's apologized for the twentieth time for her practical joke, pleading that she just said it on the spur of the moment because she knew the house was owned by a vicar's son and she thought it would appeal to my sense of humour. She'd never imagined in her wildest dreams ...

We wave stiffly at each other as Service 561 via Leeds and Peterborough crawls away from the bus station in a fog of diesel fumes. As her window glides past me she presses her face unhappily to the window, and then it's gone, revealing a huge hoarding for the *Grumbleweeds' Summer Spectacular Laughter Show* on the wall of the bus station. 'Scarborough's zaniest comedy evening' shrieks the banner title.

Underneath is a full-size picture of five men dressed in lederhosen and leather skullcaps. With their hands cupped to their mouths, they yell silently across at me.

offer

There have been some marvellous job offers since I've been with my agent: only last year it was an international spy movie shooting on location in the Caribbean, then a luscious period drama over the entire summer in the Cotswolds, and only last month a major new play by Christopher Hampton beginning at the Royal Court with a guaranteed transfer to New York. The only trouble is, none of them have been for me. These lucrative propositions have been for other actors on my agent's list, who've chosen to call his other line to discuss them with him at the exact moment of his annual call to me. So, can I just hold a minute, please, Martin.

Sorry. Michael.

I'm standing at the payphone next to the scenery dock at Scarborough. A column of ten-pence pieces is piled on the top of the unit in front of me, courtesy of the cashier in the box office. I've already used five of them since calling. 'He's just on another line,' his assistant has explained. 'I'll put you on hold, is that all right?'

I ram another coin into the unit. 'Would he rather call me back when he's got more time?'

'No no, he very much wants to speak to you. He's on a call to the States but he looks like he's wrapping it up. He's just finishing, I'll put you through ...'

A call to the States? Perhaps it's all about to take off for me at last. Perhaps the review in the *Scarborough Evening News* describing my performance in *Tapster* as 'funny and moving' has been read by Scorsese.

My agent's voice breaks in, a deep chocolate tone, full of claret and the Garrick Club and afternoons in the pavilion at

Lord's. 'Mike, thanks for holding on. How's Scarborough? Looking forward to coming home?'

'Well—'

'I'm only sorry I never made it up to see you – we've just been so busy down here. But no need really, I already know you're a class act, it would only have confirmed the obvious ...' He gives a nervous laugh, hoping this morsel of flattery will explain his non-appearance over a five-month season.

'I got a message saying you wanted to speak to me.'

'It's good news. You've had a straight offer. Starts in a few weeks. They don't even need to see you. Isn't that great?'

'What is it? The new Coppola movie?'

'No, not Coppola – hang on while I get my notes.' Agents rarely acknowledge irony. A rustling of papers. 'Here we are. It's a nativity musical written by Tony Hatch for the Connaught Theatre, Worthing.'

That's the thing about this business. It keeps you in your place.

'When for? Christmas?'

'More than that. Christmas plural. There are two of them.'

He goes on to explain. So far as I can make out between the pips, the Connaught, Worthing, has done a particularly crafty piece of marketing, scheduling what seems to be a Christmas show in December, only to then schedule another different one over the Christmas break itself, thereby hopefully duping parents into having to fork out twice. *Rock Nativity* is a rock 'n' roll musical retelling of the story: if you don't read the small print in the brochure you'd think this would be the one to take the family to see for their annual treat. But no sooner have you got home and settled down to *The Two Ronnies* when your youngest waves a leaflet in your face and says what's all this about *The Wizard Of Oz*? It's opening on 22 December, so you'd better get your coat on again, rush down there on the bus and cough up for another family-sized booking.

By the time my agent has explained all this I've got through a further ninety pence.

'So you'd be starting with King Herod in *Rock Nativity*. Nice part apparently, melodramatic baddie, one nice song, rehearsals start on tenth of October. You won't be rehearsing in the theatre, but they've arranged a space in an anteroom in the Worthing Chamber of Commerce. They've asked me to say this because the council operates a no-smoking policy. But you don't smoke, do you?'

I ram in another ten-pence piece.

'No.'

'Well, this looks like it's working out then.' My agent sounds dismayingly keen that my status as a non-smoker seems to be the clincher. 'Two and a half weeks rehearsal, and then the first night is on—'

Someone is speaking to him.

'Michael, sorry, can you hold a moment, there's an urgent call come in. Don't go away, I'll get rid of them.'

He holds the receiver to his chest. Through the steady thump of his heartbeat and the rustlings of the plastic moulding scraping on rayon I pick up tantalizing snatches echoing down the phone.

'... picked up at JFK ...Waldorf Hotel ... Three and a half per cent of gross ... McQueen thinks he can work with that ... your private car ...'

He comes back on. 'Sorry, Mike, where were we?'

'In an anteroom of Worthing Chamber of Commerce I think.'

'Ah yes.' He tries a light laugh. 'King Herod, two and a half weeks playing, extra matinées, I'm afraid, Wednesday, Friday and Saturdays. No more money for those so you'll be paid the standard fee.'

'Which is?'

More pips. I pump in more coins and signal frantically to a nearby cleaner mopping the corridor that I need some more. She puts down her bucket and starts to fumble in her purse.

'Sorry, what was that?'

'£130 a week. They've asked me to point out they don't anticipate any overtime.'

'But presumably there's subsistence?'

Subsistence is the special payment that theatres are required to pay actors for the first twelve weeks of a job to help them with settling-in expenses, applicable for any actor having to work at a venue more than twenty miles from his home address. Subsistence is important – sometimes the extra dosh can make the difference between sinking and swimming. Particularly on £130 a week and no overtime.

'I'm afraid not. They're counting your home address as Brighton. You don't have your own place in London yet, do you?'

'No, not yet.'

'Well, I'm afraid they'd expect you to live at home. Brighton to Worthing is apparently only seventeen miles so you wouldn't qualify. In fact they stress it's a pre-requisite of offering you the job. Still,' he continues hopefully, 'you'll be able to see your mum and dad. Think of all that home cooking!'

I was.

'And it gets better. They also want you to play Cowardly Lion in *The Wizard of Oz*. It opens three nights after *Rock Nativity* closes so you'd be rehearsing one while you'll playing the other – ah, hang on, Mike, someone on the other line, won't be a sec ...'

My money's running out. The cleaner is broke. Luckily Irene is passing: I signal frenetically and she fishes a fresh stock of ten-pence pieces out of her purse for me. Meanwhile my agent is in full spate on another line:

'Two thousand a week for the filming period ... you'll get your entire fee again if it's sold to the States, which it will be ...' His heart is beating faster; probably the thought of all that 10 per cent flooding in to his Swiss bank account from my Cowardly Lion.

'Sorry, Mike, where were we?'

'Cowardly Lion and my mum's oxtail soup.'

'Yup, Cowardly Lion. Great part. Put 'em up and all that; you'll steal the show. They'd want you to double with the Kansas farmhand in the first scene of course, but you'd expect that, wouldn't you?'

You would at Worthing. I'll probably be tearing tickets in the auditorium if they have their way.

'And that goes until fifteenth of January. Extra for Boxing Day, about another fifteen quid.'

Someone has filled the wipe-easy message board next to the phone with illustrations of hundreds of tiny steaming cups of tea, all delicately drawn in pencil. Someone else has written 'Irving

Wardle fucks' across the board in big black magic marker. Irving Wardle is the theatre critic for *The Times* and, on occasions, probably does, but this phrase has obviously been scrawled by someone still smarting from an unflattering review.

'So, what do you think?' says my agent. 'What shall I tell them? Do you want to do it?'

I can hear a phone ringing in the background again. I stare at the wipe-easy board. Irving Wardle fucks.

'I'd like to think about it for a day or two. There's a lot to consider.'

'Only they need a decision by the end of today or they'll have to move on.'

'I'll do it.'

'Great. I'll get back to them. I think it's a good career move, they run a pretty tight outfit down there. Anyway, how are you up there? All going well is it? How's Lucy?'

'Not so good I'm afraid. We've—'

'Mike, I'm so sorry, I'll have to go. Someone on the other line.'

The pipping sound again. I can just make out my agent's voice saying, 'Alec, how lovely to hear you, I've just heard that Broadway's back on ...'

My money runs out. The call has cost me two hours' wages. King Herod, Cowardly Lion, no subsistence, rehearsing in Worthing Chamber of Commerce, my mum's oxtail soup again every night, plus a Kansas farmhand.

I replace the receiver and turn round. Irene is standing at the far end of the corridor stroking her rabbit's foot.

hatch

A scientist conducts an experiment to see if dogs mirror the qualities of their owners.

An architect's dog is brought into the room where a pile of bones is laying on the floor, and it immediately assembles them into a tiny pyramid.

A mathematician's dog is then led in, and rearranges them so that they spell out a complex algebraic formula.

Finally an actor's dog is hauled in. It eats the bones, shags the other two dogs and asks if it can go home early.

Actors are essentially creatures of habit. We always behave according to certain genetic principles, which, try as we might, we can't seem to change. But we're also loving, kind, sympathetic, enthusiastic, and remarkably open-minded, so long as we're talking about ourselves: 'But enough of me, what did *you* think of my performance?'

More than anything else, we love a good bitch. In fact, the sooner we can get to the pub and bite the hands that feed us the happier we are, which is why I'm sitting in the public bar of the Wheatsheaf in Worthing High Street with my new friends on the evening of our first day of rehearsals. There's a big bonding session going on with an abusive commentary on the management and staff of the Connaught Theatre the common currency. The air is blue with invective against our new employers, and with each new complaint and shared grievance the closer we're becoming. As you join us, the topic of conversation is whether we should all up and leave, just collectively walk into the manager's office first thing tomorrow and tell him unequivocally – we want out.

Actors really do say 'I want out' when they threaten to leave a job. In times of great drama or crisis (which, in an average actor's day, occurs about once every twenty minutes), actors always slip into the language of B-movie Hollywood: 'I want out'; or 'Now, just hang on one minute here'. (I've even heard this prefixed by 'Whoa', but to be fair, the actress concerned had just been told she was too fat to fit into her costume, so she can be excused.)

Today's ructions have not been caused by the no-smoking policy in the rehearsal space, nor the fact that there's no reduction for cast members in the tiny café at the front of the foyer that serves macaroni cheese and lukewarm coffee at lunchtime – although both of these could have easily sparked the protests now flaring round this beer-sodden table. No, it's the fact that we're not being given the dots for the show.

The dots are, of course, the vocal score of the words and music. If you're rehearsing a musical the least you expect is to be given the dots. But for some reason, as yet unexplained by the management but almost certainly connected with financial prudence, we aren't being provided with them. This despite *Rock Nativity* running at around two and a half hours in duration, including solos, duets, choruses, several trickily updated carols and a complex quasi-Handelian aria for when the baby Jesus is born, not to mention a tricky little close harmony number in the style of 'Don't Sleep in the Subway'. We're talking twenty numbers; nearly thirty if you include the reprises.

Yet no dots. We're supposed to learn it all by dogged repetition in rehearsals.

It's disgraceful.

Not that any of us can read a note of music. Even if we were given the dots we wouldn't know what to do with them, but that's not the point. No, the whole point of actors being given the dots is so we can sit in the pub after rehearsals, stare blankly at them and then bitch all night about the fact we can't read music and what do they expect, we're actors not singers, and how impossible it's going to be to get it all under our belts.

This is why we have dots. They're a badge of honour. But someone in the higher echelons of the Connaught Theatre,

Worthing, someone who has fatally underestimated the important function that having something to whinge about fulfils in the psyche of the average actor, has decided that as none of us can read a note of music in the first place they might as well save a whole heap of money by not bothering to issue them: '£8.50 a copy, that's £127.50 plus postage and packing. We could build the set of the entire show for that money and still have some left over for the yellow brick road. Tell 'em to bring in a cassette recorder.'

If any of us round the public bar in the Wheatsheaf on Worthing High Street had any balls we'd be saying, 'I want out.'

And we'd say it big time.

But of course we haven't any balls. Actors never have. Actors are always threatening to go up to the management and tell them where they can stick it. 'We'll see how tough they are when they realize I might actually walk,' we proclaim loudly to our peers in the pub, but the moment any of the management hove into view we transform instantly into fawning sops. The only actor I've ever known who had the courage to put his indispensability to the test received the reply, 'Well, if you must you must.' Needless to say, he mustn't.

We're a curious rag-bag of actors sitting here in the Wheatsheaf. Looking round I get the sense that none of my new colleagues has ever done any well-paid work. They're clinging on to the edges of the business. Nearly everyone has frayed cuffs or scuffed shoes, and several obviously have a credit account at Millets. Most tellingly, nearly all of us seem to live just within a 25-mile radius of the theatre. The Angel Gabriel lives in Durrington-on-Sea, a particularly bleak dormitory town further along the coast; one of the Wise Men has a maisonette in Portslade; the Bethlehem innkeeper still lives with his parents in Sompting; and the Virgin Mary has a small flat in central Brighton, just up by the old hospital at Fiveways Circus above a second-hand dress shop called Finesse. You know the one.

In case I am giving you the impression that the management have cynically tried to save money by recruiting anybody with two hands and a head from within the subsistence boundary, I should point out there are one or two creatures from more exotic locations as well – one of the shepherds comes all the way from Peterborough, and there's an old bloke with a bald head, a long auburn beard and a voice like Zippy out of *Rainbow* who has waived his right to subsistence to get the job, even though he lives in Surrey and is technically well outside the catchment area. Buster Merryfield has a particularly odd history, which he recounted to us over the lunch break in a nearby greasy spoon. He's been a bank manager all his life, but has always been passionate about amateur dramatics, and now he's retired on a company pension, and has decided to give acting a go at the age of sixty. He's doubling as a Wise Man and the Wizard of Oz, and it's only his second job. He's like a kid at a funfair.

Poor sap. Doesn't he know how difficult it is? Actors with profiles like Robert Redford and eyes like Paul Newman who've spent three years at the RADA can't even get work at the moment, so what chance has a little, fat, bald bank manager from Godalming? He's destined to have his heart broken. The odds against him making it are stupendous. I might have a word with him at the end of the contract, just to ask him quietly if he's sure it's the right career move. Because unless that old geezer who plays Grandad in that new sitcom *Only Fools and Horses* suddenly keels over I can't see there's a hope in hell for dear old Buster.

The story of *Rock Nativity* is, of course, known to everyone. Joseph, a bodybuilder from Weybridge with a neck thicker than his head and a voice modelled on David Cassidy, and his wife Mary, the one who lives above Finesse, have to go to Bethlehem to be taxed. There's no room at the inn so they're forced to shelter in a stable, where the Angel Gabriel appears above them on a tiny balcony in a pair of white woolly tights with a worrying interlacing shoestring affair around the crotch, a silk shirt open to the waist, magnolia-coloured paper-mâché wings and what appear to be a pair of wrestling boots and he says to Joseph:

> *Don't be afraid,*
> *Don't be afraid,*

You're a good man,
You've led a Gooh-ooh-ood Life.

Then Mary goes off stage to give birth to the baby Jesus and soon afterwards is visited by three shepherds, one from Peterborough, the second from Portslade and the third a retired bank manager from Godalming. After a brief and frankly disappointing interlude in which King Herod muses on the problems of kingship, the action returns to the tiny manger where three wise men have also arrived to offer praise. By fantastic coincidence they're also from Peterborough, Portslade and Godalming. After their visit Mary sings to the infant that she 'will watch him grow'. Hardly an earth-shattering observation, but sincerely meant, no doubt. Then it's the interval.

After the interval the family flee to Egypt, while a crowd of excited onlookers all holding flaming torches sing 'Ding Dong Merrily on High' behind them. Except the torches are actually tiny electrical bulbs with wires connecting them to batteries concealed in the handles because East Sussex Health and Safety Executive won't allow naked flames in a place of public entertainment. Which, given some of this material, I'm not sure it is, but still. The baby Jesus is blessed by a cleric called Simeon with an enormous bald domed head (his own) and a beard of biblical proportions (glued-on), who sings a solemn and impressive Nunc Dimittis over the tiny baby wrapped in swaddling clothes cradled in his arms.

Anyway, it all ends happily with everyone, even King Herod, singing that

We will make a new tomorrow,
Make a new tomorrow,
And we'll try to make it happen too-daayy.

The publicity leaflet describes it as irresistible.

The rehearsals are, on the other hand, anything but. In fact, they're a nightmare.

Not for me, I hasten to add. Not for King Herod. Apart from

my one scene musing on the problems of kingship I'm hardly involved, so I spend most of my time talking to the man at the security desk at the front door of the town hall. Meanwhile, in the chamber of commerce, it's all hands to the pumps. One of the shepherds is tone deaf and makes a noise like a seal being harpooned on the floes of Newfoundland, the innkeeper leaves his cassette tape of all his notes on the bus in from Sompting, and Buster is nearly killed in a car crash on his way to rehearsals one morning, his Volvo sliding off the carriageway and into the central barrier and back out into the fast lane where it's nearly flattened by an army truck on its way to Aldershot. He arrives at lunchtime in the passenger seat of an AA relay truck looking white and shaky, spends the afternoon insisting he's all right to practise giving frankincense to the baby Jesus despite his horrific brush with death, and then bursts into uncontrollable floods of tears the moment the cast are released for the day.

It would normally be nice to see a bank manager weeping copiously, but somehow none of us can enjoy it. We've grown fond of old Buster. A few of us take him to a nearby Wimpy bar for a cup of coffee and an omelette before putting him on the train home. We want to phone his wife to tell her what happened, but Buster doesn't want to worry her. He's afraid she'll force him to give up driving.

We decide to club together to treat him to a taxi fare. The first, and, as far as I'm aware, the only occasion of actors having a whip-round for a bank manager.

first nights

Rock Nativity. Opening night.

Opening nights are always a special time for actors. There's a buzz of adrenaline, which begins the moment you open your eyes and which increases inexorably as each hour passes until the rising of the curtain. The day is also concerned with the observance of a number of time-honoured rituals without which an opening night just wouldn't be complete: namely, your first look at the programme, the pep talk from the director, and, most crucially, your mission to purchase an entire set of good luck cards for every member of the cast without spending more than a fiver.

Let's deal with them in chronological order.

Good luck cards are obligatory at first nights. Even actors whom you've openly despised, even ones you've ended up brawling with in the green room, or whose girlfriend you're secretly sleeping with behind their back, each will expect to receive a little envelope from you on the first night containing a card: 'Best wishes for a fabulous evening and a happy run in the show, love always, Michael'. After curtain down you can resume hostilities as usual, and if the performance is going badly, even before then, but first night cards are sacrosanct. Forget them and they'll have you up before the European Court of Human Rights for emotional cruelty.

But cards are an expensive business. Take this production for instance. *Rock Nativity* has a cast of fifteen (fourteen, as you shouldn't really be buying one for yourself, unless you're desperate). But, in addition, you should also expect to buy extra ones for the director and anyone else in the building whom you deem can be useful to you later in your career. You'll still want to come in at less than a fiver: anything more is just sloppy planning.

So you're in the local branch of WH Smith on Worthing High Street, and there are some big decisions facing you: do you buy proper good luck cards, in proper vellum envelopes with illustrations of lucky horseshoes and popping champagne bottles? Or do you try to save a few bob by taking the postcard option? If postcards, do you plump for arty ones of couples kissing in Parisian side streets that look as though you've actually expended some time and brain cells in choosing them, or do you try to get away with 'Greetings From Worthing', which will set you back barely more than three quid for the lot but have the word 'cheapskate' printed in invisible ink, which only becomes apparent when exposed to sixty-watt light bulbs arranged around a mirror?

My tip is to go for the 'Greetings From Worthing' motif, but to make sure your choice appears wittily post-ironic by the insertion of some wry, gently mocking message. 'Let's hope it is', or 'Greetings? I'll settle for grudging applause!' That way you can save yourself a packet and mark yourself out as a satirist at the same time. If you're afraid the recipient won't realize your irony, just bung in a few exclamation marks at the end. They are the literary equivalent of the double-take; a sure give-away that you're trying to be funny.

What about gifts? Again, an ironic slant can work wonders. No need for the silver-plated key rings or mini photo frames, just buy a load of Marathon bars from the local confectioners and leave one on everyone's place. Actors will laugh at the connotations of an exhausting event of endless duration (particularly if the show is by Tony Hatch), and they'll appreciate the chocolate (the only professionals who have a worse diet than actors are long-distance lorry drivers).

For *Rock Nativity* I've already done some background research. I've tracked down a large selection of postcards on a revolving stand outside a rock shop on the seafront. But when I examine them close up there's an unexpected setback; they're not only rain damaged but there aren't even any 'Greetings

From Worthing'. Instead, there is a trickier variation on the same theme: 'Interesting Scenes Around Town'. Which are, if you're curious, Brooklands 'Pitch and Putt' course, the Dome cinema, the municipal Pier and the new Guildbourne shopping complex.

'Interesting Scenes Around Town.'

To which I can add ...

'Well, we've *really* arrived!!!!!'

Perfect.

I spend the lunch hour in the café, eating my fourth macaroni cheese of the week and writing, 'Well, we've *really* arrived!!!!' twenty-three times in succession. Two hours later I'm back in WH Smith buying a single embossed greetings card with a velvet tassel down the side for the director: I've just heard a rumour that he's in the running for the artistic directorship of the Thorndike Theatre, Leatherhead, and 'Interesting Scenes Around Town' will no longer suffice for him. Not if he's going places. The Virgin Mary and Joseph of Nazareth are also browsing at nearby shelves – word's obviously getting around.

The second ceremony of the day is the pep talk.

This is an important historical ritual, and often associated with the pursuit of lost causes against insuperable odds: Agincourt, the Somme, Tobruk, *Rock Nativity*. It usually takes place in the auditorium a couple of hours before the performance, and it follows a timeless tradition. Instead of mud-filled trenches we have the first row of the stalls, in which we precious few sit like greyhounds in the slips or whatever it is. It's just past 4 p.m. and all is peace. Another couple of hours and this auditorium will be full of the screams of dying actors.

The artistic director sits slightly above us in an elevated position facing the actors on the edge of the stage with his legs dangling over the orchestra pit. Ideally he should be wearing a multi-coloured sweater and be holding a mug of coffee in one hand and a spiral-bound notebook in the other, the twin symbols of directorial authority, symbolizing tenderness and command in equal measure. Instead of ciggies and tots of rum we have sandwiches and throat sweets. Talk is in hushed tones. It's suddenly all very touchy-feely down here; though I might give that a miss with the Angel Gabriel – he looks as if he might enjoy that sort of thing a bit too much.

After a few minutes' hushed banter, Nick calls everyone to order. He hasn't yet said anything to any of us about last night's solitary dress rehearsal, but his face is stern, noncommittal: it's impossible to gauge what he's going to say. So, what am I looking for in the pep talk? What can we all expect?

Well, the minimum requirement is how hard we've worked, how proud he is of all of us, how marvellous it all looks from the front, and how he just wants us to go out there tonight and enjoy ourselves. That's the minimum. If he can keep a straight face he might even try for the double-pointer, the announcement that a big West End producer has booked tickets for the performance and is hoping to make it down.

He flips open his notebook and stares balefully at some huge squiggles in swirly black ink. Some words are underlined five times in thick, angry lines. Buster, the retired rookie, has already spotted them and I can see he's worried. But I know it's all part of the ritual: Eric Morley uses the same solemn and concerned expression before announcing the winner of Miss World and it always lends the occasion some much-needed gravitas.

'OK, folks, I haven't got much to say. Of course I took some notes on last night's dress rehearsal but I gave up after a while. Because in all truth ...'

This is it. Good cop bad cop in the same moment. This guy is good.

His face slowly rewraps into a smile. A smile of blessing. He raises his coffee cup in salute.

'We have a show.'

Brilliant. We have a show. Understated, yet theatrical, almost camp. We have a show. Ivor Novello would have been proud of that one.

Apparently we've all worked hard, it's all been marvellous, he's enjoyed working with us hugely, and tonight will not only be a full house but ...

My God. He's going for it.

157

He peers confidentially over his glasses and he's not even blushing.

'We're hopeful that there are one or two London producers in.'

Absolutely brilliant. This is little short of a masterclass; no wonder the Thorndike, Leatherhead want him. I'm only glad I invested in the embossed card with the velvet tassel.

Of course there aren't any West End producers in, but that's not the point. We need to think there might be. Most actors are lured down to small seaside towns to perform in musicals by popular theme-tune writers for £130 a week on the catch-all promise that it might just be the show in a million which catches somebody's eye and rockets us from oblivion to stardom double quick. And it does happen, it really does. Think of *Oh What a Lovely War*, *The Rocky Horror Show*, *Dear Octopus*. Admittedly about once every ten years, which, given all the regional productions which occur round the country during that period, works out at around one in three thousand shows, but right now we'll settle for those percentages, because actors live on hope, and some tiny part of us has to believe that a publicity leaflet may somehow have found its way on to Cameron Mackintosh's desk.

Cut to fantasy sequence.

The world's most successful producer of musicals and seventieth richest man in Britain is sitting behind the plush, vellum-topped desk of his executive suite above the Waldorf. A publicity handout for *Rock Nativity* flutters down on to his desk.

'Hey what is this? A new musical about the slaughter of the innocents by the guy who wrote the theme tune to *Crossroads* and starring a bank manager from Godalming! And it's in Worthing, a crumbling south coast town with the highest geriatric percentage per capita in the entire country.'

He consults a large coloured road map of Great Britain pinned on the wall.

'Why, that's only a three-hour drive from here down a rain-lashed A24 through endless dreary dormitory towns gridlocked with Christmas shoppers.'

He turns to his secretary.

'Tell Stephen Sondheim I can't meet him and cancel that booking at La Caprice. *This I gotta see!*'

Miracles do happen. Water into wine. Connaught, Worthing, into Drury Lane. And that man with the festive sweater and the coffee mug with the words 'Don't ask me, I'm only the director' printed on the side (obviously a first-night gift from someone with more money than me) is our plasterboard Messiah. We know that the only chance that Cameron Mackintosh or any other impresario will enter this building tonight is if their car breaks down while they're driving past on their way to visit some aged aunt in a nursing home. But the director knows that we, the cast members, crouching hopefully in the front stalls with our prawn baps and tubes of Lockets won't call his bluff by asking for names or go poking around in the box office for booking slips, because he knows we can't bear to have our illusions shattered. He's given us enough.

And don't think all directors automatically pull the pep talk routine off as well as this. It's not as easy as it sounds. One actor I know playing the title role in *Richard III* at Crewe witnessed a pep talk at which the director sunk his head in both hands and said, 'What the fuck are we going to do?' But that was Crewe. Our man wouldn't be in contention for Leatherhead if he made basic errors like that. You only have to see his sweater and mug to know he's a pro. This is pep-talking big time; he's like an Olympic skier on his way through the giant slalom, and he's barely missing a gate ...

As we leave the auditorium to go to our dressing rooms, Buster comes up to me. His cheeks beneath his grizzled beard are flushed with excitement. 'My first show and we've got a West End producer in!' he says. 'Would you believe it! I've got to tell the wife!'

Innocence is a wonderful thing. It reminds me of when I was his age.

Two hours later I'm sitting in the corner of the male dressing room, still in my underpants but already with Herod's swirly moustache glued to my upper lip, when the familiar knock on the door comes. And so to the last and the most exciting of all the first night rituals to be played out. Your first look at the theatre programme.

The press officer, a careworn man in his mid-forties, peeks round the doorway clutching a pile of programmes. 'Anybody like a copy?' he asks. But he knows the response, and he drops one on to each of our spaces without waiting for a reply. Buster stops buttoning his jerkin, the Angel Gabriel stops cross-threading that sinister crotch device at the top of his tights, Simeon finishes gluing his beard, and within seconds we're all greedily devouring the page with our photograph and biography on it. 'Good luck, chaps,' he says as he exits, 'I saw some of the dress rehearsal last night. You should get away with it.'

But we're no longer listening. I don't know why, but there's something foolishly exciting about seeing your name in print, and it never fails to thrill. Here we are. Michael Simkins: King Herod. And the correct spelling: a good sign. 'Michael trained at Rada ...' followed by a potted resumé, written by one of my agent's office minions after consultation with me and posted to the theatre press officer along with the signed contract at the start of rehearsals.

Judging your own biography for a theatre programme is a delicate skill, requiring craft, conciseness and the ability to be economical with the truth. Ostensibly it's supposed to give the reader an idea of who you are, where you've appeared, what parts you've played, and where they might have seen you before. Hopefully it should be able to do a lot more. Ideally it should suggest you're constantly in demand, highly successful and that one job runs seamlessly into another. This is not easy, particularly as it's wedged in between adverts for local takeaways and directions to the disabled toilet. It's also usual to pop in a little something about your private life in the last sentence, just something to warm the reader, to suggest you have another life outside the confines of the crazed ego-driven existence you seem to have chosen. Perhaps something about family or hobbies, in my case: 'Michael grew up in nearby Brighton where his interests included cricket and the operas of Gilbert and Sullivan ...'

Finally: 'Michael is pleased to be making his debut at Worthing as King Herod...' Perfect. Just the right tone struck, suggesting I'm thrilled to be appearing in this small rundown south coast seaside town, but not so thrilled that I would have gnawed my left arm off. And what's more, it's modest. The one golden rule about biogs is that they should be understated. Trumpeting the actor's talent and ability is considered the height of vulgarity, particularly if you've written it yourself.

The other biogs throw up some interesting titbits. The chap from Peterborough has spent three years with the RSC. King Melchior speaks fluent Mandarin. The Bethlehem Innkeeper was born in Shanghai and is restoring an old Norton motorcycle. The Virgin Mary once trained to be a hairdresser.

Then I come to Colin's entry. Colin is playing Simeon the prophet and is sitting next to me in the dressing room scratching his crotch.

Colin's career has been a multi-faceted diamond: he is a highly skilled and versatile performer, one of the country's finest character actors and possessing a fine baritone voice. Acclaimed by many in his home town of Stoke-on-Trent as one of the greatest talents ever to have come from the area, he has given memorable performances up and down the country, as well as enjoying success in a whole range of media and TV and films ...

It goes on like this for several more lines, detailing more of his stupendous acting triumphs and moving on to 'his skills as a wind surfer and his love of home cooking'.

I stare across at this portly, balding actor in a pair of ageing boxer shorts, gluing his beard while eating a Cadbury's miniroll. If this biography is true, what the hell is he doing playing Simeon and Mayor of Munchkinland at the Connaught, Worthing, for £130 per week and no subsistence?

'Whoever came up with this must love you!' I shout across. 'Who wrote it?'

'I did,' he replies without a hint of shame.

relax

First night parties are de rigueur. Actors need to celebrate and there's usually some sort of function laid on. If you're in a hit West End show it'll be a huge do at some fashionable night-spot, complete with ice sculptures and Filipino maids moving among you with tasty canapés and refills of champagne. The festivities for *Rock Nativity* are more modest – one free drink and some dancing to a mobile disco operated by a sixteen-year-old called Adrian. Nonetheless, it's a chance to release some of the tension. My King Herod has thankfully gone without mishap, the director has bought me a drink in the bar afterwards, and to top it off I've been offered a lift back to the station by a divorced woman called Gilly who works behind the bar and who's been touching me playfully on the arm all evening …

First night parties are about letting your hair down.

The multi-faceted diamond playing Simeon has already let his down, which is why he's meeting the director tomorrow for a crisis summit over lunch. His beard fell off during the performance and the director is going to try and persuade him over a macaroni cheese to complete his contract by joining the rest of us tomorrow morning at eleven to begin rehearsals as Mayor of Munchkinland. For the moment Simeon is content to sit slumped in a corner of the bar telling Buster's wife what a fucking fucked-up profession this all is, how it takes your dreams and tramples them underfoot like they're fucking matchwood. Buster's wife is a well-mannered, kindly lady in a pleated skirt, which tells you all you need to know about her response to being pinned in a corner by a desperate munchkin who only has one adjective in his vocabulary and who, until tonight, was one of the finest actors ever to come out of Stoke-on-Trent.

The divorcee stops her car outside a small house in Heene Terrace. Thank you, Gilly. I'd love to come in for a coffee.

Simeon's evening had turned from fantasy to nightmare in the space of a couple of calamitous seconds, some time between 9.25 and 9.27 p.m. He was in the middle of his big number, the Nunc Dimittis, when his long pontiff's beard came unglued from his jaw and fluttered down on to the baby Jesus. I suppose what with the lights and the sweat and the first night nerves, it was, as they say on BBC public information films, 'an accident waiting to happen'. There has been speculation among the residents of Bethlehem that his decision to eat a Cadbury's mini-roll while undertaking this difficult gluing operation may also have contributed to his downfall. 'Unprofessional' was how the innkeeper described it to me in private. There's no more damning indictment.

Whatever the root cause for the spirit gum failing to do its job, the sight of the beard falling on to the face of Our Saviour Jesus Christ caused uproar in the rows of the audience close enough to see it, since when Simeon has been inconsolable, sitting dejectedly in his vest and pants in the dressing room long after curtain down while all around him changed into their party clothes and pursued the distant throb of disco music in the circle bar. It didn't help that the press officer popped his head round the door afterwards and said that was the worse case of alopecia he'd ever seen.

That did it. Multi-faceted diamond wants out.

There's no chance of me wanting out. Gilly has just dimmed the lights, kicked her shoes off and handed me a mountainous gin and tonic.

'There was a rumour in the bar that there might have been some West End producers in,' she says, pouring herself a Baileys the size of a small jar of salad cream. She touches my forearm playfully. 'Just imagine, you as King Herod in the West End with your name in lights.' She goes over to the music centre and puts on some Sergio Mendes before returning to the sofa. 'Do you think there might have been?'

'It's quite possible,' I assure her smoothly. 'Someone said Cameron Mackintosh was hoping to come. He's always on the lookout for stuff to transfer.'

'Goodness,' she says. 'You in the West End? How exciting! I'd have to come up and see you.'

'Well, we're not counting any chickens, but ...' I cross my fingers exaggeratedly and hold them up in the air. I only need her to think I might be on the verge of stardom and I'm home and dry. It seems to work: she giggles and touches my forearm again.

'That strong enough for you, is it?' she asks.

I don't want out.

I want in.

lion

My neighbour Ron must be in his sixties now. He fought in the jungles of Burma during the Second World War and during his time there suffered horrible atrocities at the hands of his Japanese captors. He doesn't talk about it much, but he described one evening how he was once forced to squat on all fours for nearly six weeks in a tiny prison in boiling heat, unable to go to the toilet and with no means of maintaining his personal hygiene, while his tormentors stood around laughing and jeering at his misery. He lost nearly half his body weight in sweat and still suffers from arthritis of the knees. It proved a seminal experience; in fact he still can't recall it without a shudder.

I now have some idea of what he went through.

When people hear you're about to play the Cowardly Lion, they tell you that it's 'one of those parts'.

It's a gift, virtually actor-proof. 'You'll steal the show,' they say. 'You can't go wrong. You'll get all the reviews, the kids will love you, you'll get the biggest cheer of anyone in the curtain call, best of all, you'll have the most fun you've ever had in your professional life, you lucky bastard.' They will then hold up their fists and caper round you a few times shouting, 'Put 'em up, put 'em up'.

What they won't tell you is that you'll spend nearly six weeks encased in a hairy tent made of low-quality nylon fun fur, with your face, the only part of your body open to the fresh air, smeared in thick yellow make-up. Nor that you'll be spending much of the evening on your haunches trying vainly to prevent your tail – which has been strengthened with a length of coat-hanger wire to 'provide some definition' and which consequently has a vicious point protruding through the material – from putting out the eyes of most of the inhabitants of the Emerald City.

Nor that you'll sweat nearly half a pint of bodily fluids a performance, most of which will be absorbed into the weave of the fun fur, which consequently will become a stone heavier by the final performance. Nor that any liquid not absorbed by the material will collect in the paw sections at the bottom, leading to you being the first suspected case of trench foot on the south coast since the end of the Great War. They don't say that you can't reach the fastening at the back of the costume to let yourself out, and that even if you could, you won't be able to unzip the bloody thing anyway because your hands are encased in woollen gauntlets with plastic claws stuck to the end. There are men I know who are prepared to pay handsomely for this sort of experience in the back streets of Soho, and I can only say they must be pretty desperate.

I'm sure it wasn't much fun working on the Burma Road either, but at least you didn't have to sing 'If I Were King of the Forest' at the end of it.

Things start promisingly enough. The TV actress Stacey Dorning, star of ITV's *Black Beauty*, has been contracted to play Dorothy; Barbara Morton, another well-known comic actress, is playing the Wicked Witch of the West (the fact that she lives in neighbouring Shoreham-by-Sea is entirely coincidental); and a troupe of children from a local school of dancing are contracted to play the munchkins. This is a clever trick; not only will it swell the numbers on stage (without them, the total munchkin inventory would have been three), but also the audiences, which will now be filled by mums, dads, siblings and extended family members, each of whom will take illicit flash photographs every time their youngest heaves into view. Of course the young munchkins aren't allowed to speak as that would infringe Equity regulations, but that's all right because the Angel Gabriel is essaying the role of the head of Lollipop Guild, the Nazareth innkeeper will be representing the interests of the Lullaby League, and Stoke-on-Trent's multi-faceted diamond has been persuaded to stay on to give his Mayor of Munchkinland a shot.

So I'm looking forward to it. Particularly when the director tells me he wants me to redefine the role, to take it in a different direction from the film, to get out from under the long shadow cast by Bert Lahr. 'Something more genuinely lionesque perhaps.' He also wants me to make my first entrance, the one where I surprise the party on their way to the Emerald City, by leaping on to the stage by means of a gymnastic trampette secreted in the wings. Suddenly I can't wait. They're right – it's a gift.

I should have spotted trouble ahead at the costume fitting.

Instead of the specially created animal skin, made and fitted by specialists in London using drawings and anatomical sketches of the real thing hunting in the plains of the Serengeti (the powerful thick hindquarters, the immense splaying feet, the narrow tapering ribcage), my Cowardly Lion seems to have been made from various offcuts of nylon bath matting from the local carpet warehouse. Either that or there's now a Ford Cortina somewhere in the town without any seat covers. Nonetheless, the wardrobe supervisor, a highly strung and overworked woman called Janine, tries to explain to me how I'll be able to perform in it twice nightly without collapsing from heat exhaustion. 'I'm putting in some webbing round the neck and under the armpits,' she explains. 'That will enable the costume to breathe.' I point out that I'm not worried about the costume being able to breathe, rather how I'm going to.

We try it the next day in conjunction with the headpiece, a sort of woollen diving helmet made of the same material, which rests on my shoulders and overhangs the top of the suit. It also has a hole cut in the front of it, just enough for me to peer out from and hopefully communicate an expression or two. The following morning we attempt it with full nylon whiskers sprouting from each cheek (attached with spirit gum), and a redrawn feline mouth line. While I'm examining the effect in the mirror, Stacey comes in to try on her gingham dress and ankle socks, so I ask her what she thinks of it.

'It's a gift,' she replies.

That clinches it.

Just as I'm leaving to go back into rehearsal, I remember I'm also playing the Kansas farmhand. 'Anything to try on for that?' I ask.

'No. Not yet,' replies Janine, lighting another fag. 'We'll get something ready for you. It's the Lion that counts.'

'No problem, I was just wondering if—'

'For God's sake, stop fussing,' she replies.

A bit sharply, I thought. I was only asking.

At the dress rehearsal I see the reason for her anxiety.

The opening minutes of *The Wizard of Oz* are the worst thing I've ever been involved in. But not because the performances are bad, or the script is terrible, but simply because the theatre has run out of money before it can do Kansas. Everything has gone into the Oz bit; the Emerald City, the yellow brick road, the witch's lair – and once we've got past the tornado and Dorothy has met the munchkins, it looks great; there's even a couple of impressive smoke flashes to accompany the first entrance of the weird and wonderful wizard, as well as a huge wicker basket into which we all climb at the end of the show for our return to earth. But Kansas is a shocker.

You'll know the opening scene, of course. At the end of the overture the curtain rises to reveal Dorothy's farm. It's cotton-picking time, and according to the official script, the farmhands are toiling away on the land to bring in the bales. It's a scene of rustic industry – some are bringing on an old wagon, others are pitch-forking cotton bales into it, while others are building a fence or boiling coffee on a stove. And ... enter Dorothy stage right. You know the rest.

When our curtain rises, it looks as if the show has been re-located to Ethiopia. There are no pitchforks, no wagon, no fence and no tools to build it with. There's no fire and no coffee; there are a couple of mugs to drink from, but only because they've been borrowed from the front of house bar at the last minute. Worst of all, there's no cotton; only a single bundle of wispy-looking twigs sprayed silver for the entire team of farmhands to pass between each other. One of the stage managers throws the bale on from the wings to Melchior, who passes it to the innkeeper, who passes it to me, who throws it off into the wings on the other side of the stage, where another stage manager collects it, runs round the back and returns it to his colleague, who chucks it on again. It's a landscape seemingly awaiting famine relief from the United Nations. East Sussex County Council had already forbidden us from using a real dog on stage to play Toto, and it's probably just as well; if he lived on this farm he'd have been eaten.

The scene is lent a more sinister overtone by the look of the farmhands; because there's no money for costumes either. Rumour has it that there was a crisis meeting in the theatre during production week, at which Janine informed the finance director she only had £14 of her budget left to cover the entire cost of kitting out Kansas. I can only assume she must have over-estimated. We look as if we've just arrived from some secretive gay bar in upper Manhattan; I'm kitted out in Angel Gabriel's silk open-neck shirt from *Rock Nativity*, a pair of mechanic's dungarees with a vague imprint of 'Gray's Brakes and Tyres Centre' still just visible on the back, and a pair of black patent leather dinner shoes. To cap it all I'm given a pair of bright pink socks.

When I ask if I may bring in a pair of my own black socks instead, Janine looks at me as if I've just offered to donate a kidney.

We do what we can. Someone brings in a step-ladder so that the farmhands can at least chuck the bale of cotton up as well as along. Buster provides a hammer and a pair of pliers from his garden shed. One of the munchkinette's mothers tears up an old red and white striped tablecloth into strips so we can all have a neckerchief. But the smell of death still lingers on our farm. It's a sobering start to the evening. I can hardly wait to climb into my fun fur, hit the trampette and put 'em up.

Thankfully, Stacey is lovely as Dorothy, with a sweet, pure voice that picks up well on the float mikes arranged along the front of the stage. Her rendering of 'Somewhere over the Rainbow', particularly with the addition of the rarely heard accompanying verse (and offering the audience the prospect of getting out of this stricken place) is genuinely melodic and wistful, and by the time I come on in the haunted forest things are going swimmingly.

I'm afraid there's no denyin'
I'm just a dandy-lion ...

It's a gift.

It's about a week into the run that I find other actors beginning to avoid me in the dressing room; the multi-faceted diamond of Munchkinland has even moved all his personal possessions from the space next to mine to a previously vacant berth on the other side of the room. I tell myself it's just jealousy because I was seen leaving the theatre with the divorcee, but then I find others are always leaving the windows open, despite the fact it's early January and we're only a few hundred yards off the seafront.

I'm shrinking inside here as well. The costume now resembles a small marquee, and when I turn my head to the right during the Thursday matinée the headpiece stays where it is. For the rest of the performance I face front: there's nothing for it but to keep my head still. I look as if I've broken my neck.

I'm on my way to Janine after curtain down to have some velcro fastenings inserted when I meet the director in the corridor. 'Lost a few laughs today, I thought,' he says.

The ordeal sprawls over Christmas. At the grab bag ceremony on Christmas Eve I find I've been bought a can of deodorant. I begin ticking off the days, then individual performances, then even individual acts. At the curtain call on the last night I experience a sudden overwhelming rush of euphoria: five more minutes and I can come out for ever, never again to clamber into that stinking, infested carcass. But the costume has one last fiendish trick up its sleeve for me.

In the dressing room afterwards the zip breaks. Some of the fur has become caught up in the fastening, and despite the efforts of the entire dressing room it refuses to budge. My hope to make a quick exit to the divorcee's for some more Sergio Mendes and my own music of the mountains evaporates with each passing minute. I'm eventually cut free by Janine using a pair of dressmaking scissors nearly an hour after curtain down. Buster's probably back in Godalming by now.

As I stand there in my sopping underpants, my suffering is made manifest. The mirror shows my altered physique in a mere four and a half weeks: huge hind quarters, massive splayed feet, and an entire set of ribs sticking through my upper torso. I've become the part.

Out in the car park Janine carries the remains of the outfit at arm's length to the refuse bins.

fire

By 1982 I've been acting for four years. Although I've barely kept in touch with my class from RADA, I've heard on the grapevine that nearly half have already given up, or are thinking of doing so. One is an agent, another a struggling scriptwriter, two are solicitors, while five more seem to have disappeared off the face of the earth. Despite my steady stream of regular work I'm all too aware that it has been a little provincial in its tastes. In fact it has been an exclusively small-town diet of live theatre: Canterbury, Worthing, York, Farnham, Southampton. I haven't had so much as a sniff of a camera. My agent may season his occasional pep talks with phrases about 'building solid foundations' and 'learning your craft', but despite his grand projections and cosy assurances, we both know I'm heading for oblivion unless I can make some progress. Sooner or later I've got to get my face in front of a lens. Provincial theatre is all very well, but the money is in film and TV, and the days when you could forge an international career within the length of Shaftesbury Avenue have long gone. Nowadays it's the screen that makes or breaks your reputation.

Although my agent has promised that it will happen if only I remain patient – the long game, as he described it – I was beginning to think it might never happen. But at last I'm on my way: I've got a starring role in a small independent film project – solo camera, videotape rather than film, modest production values, but it's the lead, and it's on camera. I reckon I can do something with it.

How to sum up the project?

I suppose it's a slice of urban realism, the sort of fly-on-the-wall piece you can trace in a direct line back to *Poor Cow* and *Cathy Come Home*. The character I'm playing – we never learn his name – is a middle-manager type, running a large retail outlet somewhere in Britain: the precise location is specifically never referred to. We don't know whether he's married or if he has kids, his private life is a nether world of maybes and perhaps, which never impinges into the harsh reality of his work place – the only context in which we see him. His journey is one of a common man coming to terms with technology, of struggling to surmount the endless onslaught of this increasingly industrialized world, which he can no longer ignore.

You could also describe it as a training video for Safeway Supermarkets to demonstrate the correct procedure for the use of fire extinguishers in the event of an emergency. But I reckon I've spotted hidden layers nestling beneath the ten pages of foolscap I've got to learn by Monday.

Training films, or 'corporate videos' to give them their official title, are one of the more curious backwaters of the acting game. There's a huge market for in-house educational tapes, the sort used by major companies to demonstrate to staff new customer-care procedures or safety codes in the workplace. Some actors won't touch them, but my agent assures me there's no shame, and besides, they're useful for practising your camera technique, as well as paying more in a day than a rep theatre manages in a fortnight. What's more, rumour has it the director is American, and that the film is certain to get a wide general release – in fact they're planning to show it at least once to *every employee of Safeway Supermarkets in the United Kingdom during the coming year.*

(My italics.)

I've got three nights to learn the script. I've got props to handle as well: and they're big ones. I never knew there were so many different types of extinguisher – Water, Foam, Carbon Dioxide, Dry Powder and Halon – and I've got about three hundred words on each type to get into my head in the next seventy-two hours.

Class A extinguishers will put out fires in ordinary combustibles, such as wood and paper.

This two-kilogram carbon dioxide extinguisher is for class B fires only, involving flammable liquids, flammable gases and electrical hazards.

Class C extinguishers are suitable for use on electrically energized fires, and the presence of the letter C indicates that the extinguishing agent is non-conductive.

Funny how they all seem the same after a while.

It's obvious after a day poring over the script that I'm never going to be able to learn it all. There's just too much. I call my agent to see if there might be a teleprompter available – a transparent device fixed to the camera, which enables the performer to read his lines while appearing to be talking spontaneously. Bob Hope never travelled without one. My enquiry is answered with a hollow laugh: if they could afford a teleprompter they could have also afforded Nick Ross and done the thing properly. I'm being paid to sit down and slog away at the words until I can repeat them in my sleep.

For reasons of safety it must be stored on the appropriate mounting bracket, and must be depressed and recharged after use.

A day's filming on Monday, £200 for the day, meals to be provided in the staff canteen, cameras to roll at 8 a.m. sharp in Safeway in Maidstone.

Ensure at all times that you don't keep hold of the horn while discharging.

I wonder if they'll send a car?

The train to Maidstone clatters out of Charing Cross at 6.08 a.m. I treat myself to a bacon sandwich and a cup of scalding hot tea from the station concourse, and spend the hour and a half journey time, as I've spent every previous waking minute since last Friday, feverishly repeating my lines. They go in easily enough, but if I leave them more than a couple of hours without repetition they evaporate into a foamy mush of nozzles and chemicals and this-way-ups. By the time I arrive at Safeway Maidstone I've got a splitting headache and still can't get through more than a paragraph without having to glance at the script. The security officer offers some Phensic and points me in the direction of the film crew, a knot of men grouped at the furthermost checkout surrounded by huge metal cases. They've been setting up the camera equipment since first light and are nearly ready to begin the shoot.

It's not difficult to identify the American director; he's the only person in the entire building who doesn't look as if he's been kitted out at C&A. Buzz is originally from California but has been living over here making corporates and promos since the mid-seventies. He's got a shaved head, a Zapata moustache, and perma-tan, and he forms a stark visual contrast to his film crew: Alan from Hungerford on sound, Darren from Sidcup on camera, and Dave from Bedford on lighting all look like people you'd see sitting in the audience at the Embassy world darts final. I'm invited to join them all for a running breakfast. Buzz is mixing something in a plastic container, which he tells me contains tree bark, guava juice, pumpkin seeds and a rare form of kelp found only in the Barents Sea. Dave, Alan, and Darren are tucking into a tin tray full of Cadbury's Creme Eggs they found in the stockroom.

Buzz is anxious to get on. They've decided to film the video during normal Safeway opening hours so as to capture the bustle and industry of a real supermarket and to save on having to hire hundreds of extras who will turn up looking like refugees from Dallas, insist on being fed every two hours and look straight down the camera lens at the first opportunity. I'm introduced to Miriam, the Safeway representative who's been allocated to look after my every need while I'm here.

Miriam is the supermarket health and safety officer. She looks like a Russian air stewardess but according to the lapel badge she's 'Here to Help'. She gives me a friendly Safeway smile and I follow her down past the frozen meats and poultry, along feminine hygiene, through a heavy duty plastic curtain at the rear of the store, past a gaggle of men all wearing white wellingtons and nylon trilbies cutting up sides of meat, up a concrete staircase and finally through a security door.

'This is your dressing room,' she announces reverentially.

I enter a tiny stockroom smelling of cement dust and lit by a flickering fluorescent tube. For a terrible moment it feels like I've entered a wormhole and have ended up back in the stockroom at Gamley's. The floor is littered with pages from a four-day-old copy of the *Sun* and there are tiny cardboard boxes marked Rentokil lying on the corners of the floor. Gamley's was never this chic.

'Here we are,' says Miriam, pointing behind the door frame. Hanging neatly on the peg behind the door is a complete Safeway under-manager's kit. Off-white nylon shirt, clip-on tie in company colours, shapeless navy blue blazer, sensible slacks, and black shoes with a pre-injected sheen.

'I'll leave you to it,' she continues, handing me the uniform. 'It should be all right. They're designed to fit all sizes.'

I gingerly unfurl the jacket from the hanger. The aroma of old sweat drifts up from the armpits. The shirt has a tidemark round the collar and the end of the tie appears to have once been accidentally dunked in beef fat.

There's a knock on the door.

'Are we decent?' calls Miriam.

It's difficult to answer that. I look like a Yugoslavian politician.

'Lovely,' she smiles, revealing a row of yellowing teeth.

We trail out through the staff canteen. There are paper plates and half-used sachets of butter strewn across the tables, and it smells of toast. Back down the concrete stairs, out through the nylon trilbies, and we emerge into the clean, cool, bright lines of the supermarket. Herb Alpert's 'Mexican Jumping Bean' drifts lazily out over the loudspeakers. The aisles are already filling up with shoppers.

Buzz is waiting. 'OK, Mike, this is what I want you to do. When I shout "Action", I want you to walk forwards, past the checkout towards the camera. When you hit your mark, pick up the first device, this Halon thing, and go into your speech. You have learned it, haven't you?'

'Yes, yes, it's all here,' I reply gaily, tapping the side of my head with my forefinger. What was it now? The Halon extinguisher is a heavy duty appliance for use on ... is it pan fires? Or electrical ... No, that's the multi-purpose dry powder ...

'Right then, let's have a look at this baby!' Buzz is already staring at the TV monitor attached to Darren's camera. 'Can I see the shot?'

I wander towards the camera a couple of times while Dave

adjusts his portable lamps and Alan tests my voice for sound levels. Buzz is troubled by the lack of background movement. He thinks it doesn't look like a working supermarket. A girl looking like Olive from *On the Buses* is dragged away from her other duties on the fish counter to provide some authentic background movement and is positioned at the checkout. She gets out a Puzzler book and waits for instruction.

'Do you want me to acknowledge the assistant?' I ask.

'Why not? Sure, whatever!' replies Buzz. 'The important thing is that you look friendly, authoritative, a regular guy. Know what I mean?'

Buzz is moving swiftly. He's already handing me the first of an assortment of bulky appliances bristling with nozzles and valves. When I try to lift it I feel something pull in my upper arm. Geoff Capes would struggle with this.

'You OK holding that?

'Fine.'

'Good.' Buzz flashes a brilliant smile. 'Now, before we start – it's obviously crucial we reflect the proper training procedure here. Are you familiar with how to work these things?'

I'm not. I must have missed that class at the RADA.

Luckily we've got Miriam. She's an expert in health and safety, and lifts the extinguisher as if it were a set of children's bagpipes. She shows me the correct way of gripping the frame and the method of directing the jet officially approved by the Government's Health and Safety Executive while Buzz briefs Olive on her role in this drama. Dave lays down a small squishy tube looking like a burglar's cosh on the floor. 'Start here,' he says, pointing to the sausage, 'and walk to there.' He points at another sausage, a few feet away. 'Try to hit the sausages,' he says laconically as he wanders back to the camera.

'OK, first positions,' yells Buzz. 'Nice and relaxed.'

I strike an expression somewhere between Fred Dineage and Charles Wheeler.

'And *action*!'

'We at Safeway take the issue of staff and customer safety seriously. All our outlets are fitted with state-of-the-art technology to ensure complete comfort and security for all our employees. But from time to time of course, emergencies do occur.'

As I pass Olive I give a wry, Roger Moore-type nod, just enough to suggest approachability and gentle authority in equal measure. She responds by unwrapping a grin reminiscent of Bernie Winters greeting the arrival of Schnorbitz the dog.

The experiment is abandoned. Olive has blown her one fleeting stab at stardom: she collects up her Puzzler book and trudges back to the anonymity of a lifetime doling out mackerel pâté. I return to my sausage.

'We at Safeway take the issue of staff and customer safety seriously. All our outlets are fitted with state-of-the-art technology to ensure complete comfort and security for all our employees ...' My toecaps nudge against the second sausage. Perfect. I've hit my marks.

I'm halfway through the demonstration of how to discharge the Halon-based extinguisher and have just got to the bit about remembering to grip your horn while discharging, when an elderly woman interrupts to ask me if we still do Libby's mandarin segments in syrup. She wants to know why we keep moving everything every few months, as she never knows where anything is. Given the chance I'm sure she'd also like to know why we let single-parent families shop here, why Nina Myskow is allowed to be a judge on *New Faces*, and why we had to join the Common Market. Miriam offers to show her personally to aisle three and the tinned fruits. The old woman brightens immediately and allows herself to be led off.

I hurriedly check the script. The words are already starting to seep out of my memory.

The new labelling shows a diagonal red line drawn through the picture to illustrate what type of fire—

'You're not on the sausage!' shouts Darren, squinting through the viewfinder.

'And ... *action*.'

'We at Safeway take the issue of staff and customer safety seriously. All our outlets are fitted with state-of-the-art technology to ensure complete comfort and security for—'

'A tannoy announcement alerting shoppers that there are special deals today on Safeway own-brand washing-up liquid drowns out the rest of the speech. Miriam hurries off to disable the public address system. Fifteen minutes later she's still not back.

'OK, let's break for coffee,' says Buzz.

Between coffee and lunch we try again. Take four is ruined when a youth wearing a white apron shambles into the store pushing a convoy of about a hundred and fifty complaining trolleys. Buzz yells, 'We're trying to make a goddam movie here, for Christ's sake,' and unleashes a volley of abuse at him before a put-out Miriam informs him that the person is special needs and on a workshare scheme set up in conjunction with Kent Health Authority, which the Safeway management are very proud of. Take five is accounted for when Ron has to go outside to the van to fetch a new camera battery. Take six is clean, but unusable because of a screaming baby in aisle three. Take seven is delayed by Buzz having to move his Vauxhall Astra, which apparently is blocking an access ramp in the car park.

'OK, let's get this one in the can now.' Buzz's jaw is firmly clenched.

'By contrast, this two-kilogram carbon dioxide extinguisher is for class B fires only involving flammable liquids, flammable gasses and sorry, Buzz, I'm going to have to put this down for a moment ...'

Miriam is nudging him again. She's ordered six meals for the cast and crew in the staff canteen and it's closing in ten minutes.

Over lunch Buzz stares moodily into his guava and kelp while the rest of us tuck into Safeway canteen meat pie, boiled potatoes and peas, with spotted dick and custard to follow, all washed down with a fizzy blackcurrant drink.

The aqueous film-forming foam multi-purpose must be directed at the inside edge of the container or on a nearby surface ...

My arms are so tired I can hardly lift my cutlery. I urgently need the toilet but Miriam says we mustn't use the staff facilities as there's been what's called a blowback.

Older extinguishers are labelled with coloured geometrical shapes with letter designations ...

Buzz approaches and puts his arm round me. This is always a bad sign – whenever the director does this it's a dead cert he's got some bad news to break.

He gives me a light, all-American squeeze.

'Mike, there's been a mix-up with the scripts. I'm sorry to have to do this, but you should have been sent an extra page on fire blankets. I'll leave you this to look at now, it's only a few paragraphs: I know you'll deliver for me ...'

Grip the blanket firmly by the guiding tapes and place carefully over the fire. Do not waft the flames towards you. If the blanket does not completely cover the fire the flames will not be extinguished ...

Just as I think things can't get much worse, Olive from the fish counter comes across from another table and asks for my autograph on a paper napkin. Bless her. I sign it with a flourish, and a tiny glimmer of self-respect flickers into life again.

She inspects it uncertainly for a moment, thanks me and says how much she enjoys watching me read the news.

thriller

'I've had an enquiry,' says my agent. 'You know you mentioned you'd like to get back on stage? Well, you probably don't, but do you fancy doing a thriller?'

Call me old-fashioned, but I still can't consider myself a proper actor simply because I haven't yet done a thriller. Even while I was studying at RADA, the West End and provincial theatres were full of them, with suave men-about-town criss-crossing the stage in a cravat and fawn slacks.

And while I've been distracted by Equity cards and agents and seasons at Scarborough they've disappeared off the face of the earth – the only one that's still performed is Arnold Ridley's *The Ghost Train*, which doesn't really count as it's become kind of kitsch and is always camped up in a knowing sort of way. In any case it doesn't involve a character in fawn slacks so strictly speaking isn't part of the genre.

There are of course other essential items on the thriller checklist. They are always set in country houses or smart London flats, are always advertised as 'prior to the West End' and are always written by Francis Durbridge. They star an actor off the television, Gerald Harper or Jack Watling or Richard Todd, feature a drinks trolley, an attractive wife, an unsuspecting best friend, a smouldering mistress and a stalwart detective who appears after the interval to investigate the crime. And just in case you can't follow the tangled skein of deceit and double-crossing you can always pop outside at the interval and catch up by reading the poster: 'A lonely house, a man with gambling debts, a life insurance policy, a beautiful but sick wife, and a rugged cliff top. What could be easier?'

Hardly any need to see it really. Certainly no need to fork out for a programme. So Gerald Harper has got gambling debts and has tipped his missus over the crumbling escarpment, and he's obviously celebrating her death over a glass of Scotch with his smouldering mistress; she must be the one with too much eye make-up and a beauty spot. Gerald Harper is the one in the blazer holding the insurance claim and the aeroplane tickets to Rio de Janeiro.

Telly star: To us?
Mistress (curling her long, tawny arm round his neck): To us ...

They kiss. Slow descent of curtain to a communal 'Ooohh' from the blue-rinse brigade. A rush for the Kia-Ora, and before you know it it's the second half. And the second half can only mean one thing: a knock on the door.

Mistress: Who's that?
Telly star: I don't know. You weren't expecting anyone, were you?
Mistress : No, of course not.
Telly star (fingering cravat nervously): I'd ... I'd better answer it.
Mistress: But what if ...?
Telly star: You don't want to raise suspicion, do you, you little fool?

It's the detective. He is just making a routine call and is sorry to have called at such an inconvenient time – there's just one or two questions.

This is a pivotal encounter; the detective must be a burly, square-jawed sort of bloke in a trilby and trenchcoat, who wanders around picking up knick-knacks off the set and examining them in an absent-minded sort of way while grilling the star with seemingly innocuous yet somehow alarming questions.

Detective: Nice place you've got here.

Telly star: Yes. Yes it is.

Detective: Must have cost a pretty penny?

Telly star: Excuse me, Inspector, but is that any of your damned business?

That's what I want acting to be about. I want to be Gerald Harper. I want to tug at that cravat, to hitch those fawn slacks, to smoulder with the busty mistress, to ask the detective if it's any of his damned business, to roll those ice cubes round in that tumbler of Scotch (not Scotch at all incidentally, but cold tea), which is de rigueur when your character is cornered.

Inspector: But I thought you said you weren't here last weekend?

Telly star: Did I?

Detective: Yes, sir. You did. In which case you couldn't have seen your wife at the casino. (Picks up knick-knack and studies it.) Could you?

Telly star (rolls cold tea round the ice cubes in the tumbler): I ... I must have been mistaken.

The dialogue also has to include the line: 'Just what are you driving at, Inspector?' If it doesn't, you should ask for your money back.

I've been asked to go to the Queen's Theatre, Hornchurch, to star in the best thriller of them all, the classic – *Dial M For Murder*.

I can already taste that tea.

Hornchurch is an odd location for a theatre. The town itself is a sort of displaced East End, row after row of mock Tudor thirties houses crammed with relocated Cockneys all working for Ford at their car plant in nearby Dagenham. The theatre itself is marooned on waste ground in the centre of the town, surrounded by dogshite and upturned rubbish bins. But by a vibrant policy of no-nonsense populist entertainment, rock

musicals and tributes to Roy Orbison interspersed with uproarious comedies and tense new thrillers, all prior to the West End,
it seems to be hanging on in there. Though it's a close-run thing
– you get the sense that a couple of failures and it would be
changed into a bowling alley overnight.

The journey out there by tube train from central London is
interminable; Mile End, Plaistow, Becontree, a voyage through
the uprooted humanity of post-war London. But at least it gives
me a chance to savour the script, and the signs are good. The
copy I've been sent by the theatre is even the old-fashioned
French's acting edition. Samuel French are the leading publish-
ers of playscripts in the country, and they're synonymous with
creaky old-fashioned thrillers – even the typeface is in copper-
plate, with intertwined comedy and tragedy masks on the cover
and lengthy stage directions culled directly from the prompt
copy. Sometimes there's even a grainy photograph of the original production, Brylcreemed matinée idols standing about on
cavernous West End sets in gloomy lighting. They're a visual
equivalent of a shot across your bows, just to remind you of
what's expected just in case you were thinking of stepping out of
line and updating things. What's more, French's editions do
nearly all the work for you: so long as you've got four limbs, your
own slacks and can follow a set of simple instructions, they make
acting about as complicated as building a shed:

> Sheila hands the drink to Max. She hears something out
> in the passageway, goes to the hall door and peeps out.
> Then she closes the door, crosses stage left and resumes
> her seat. Lighting a cigarette she speaks her next line with
> faint alarm ...

At the back of the copy there's a list of necessary furniture and
props, a plan diagram of how the stage should look ('occasional
table down right, containing wicker mending basket filled with
stockings and scissors') and a lighting plot.

And what's this? A brief paragraph in minuscule italics on the
inside back cover sets out how the moment in which the intruder

is stabbed with the scissors should be carried out: 'Sheila can pretend to stab him with the scissors and he will fall back in such a way that the audience can imagine the scissors are in his back.'

That's a relief. I thought we were actually going to have to kill someone. It's reassuring to have professional advice from people experienced in stagecraft.

Apart from the fact that it's not written by Francis Durbridge, *Dial M for Murder* is obviously all I could ask for. I'm giving my Tony Wendice, the smooth businessman and fulcrum of the plot ('he has an easy charm – his mind is active and he usually seems very sure of himself'). The theatre has thoughtfully also forwarded photographs of my fellow actors so we can all recognize each other in the tea bar before the read-through. There's my beautiful but brittle wife, my unsuspecting best friend Max, and when I turn to the publicity shot of the actor playing the second-half detective I want to yell with joy: he's the amalgam of every knick-knack-fondling detective – burly, square-jawed, inscrutable – he even seems to be wearing a trenchcoat.

As the train trundles through Upney and Elm Park I re-read the script for the umpteenth time. You can see why the play is a classic of the genre: Wendice decides to hire a hitman to get rid of his beautiful but brittle wife and claim the insurance, and in order to set it up he has to find a reason to duck out of a trip to the theatre with her so that he can spend the evening alone ...

Tony: The old man's flying to Brussels on Sunday, and he wants my report first thing in the morning.

Luckily his old friend Max is also going, so is persuaded to take his place as her escort.

Tony: Hey, Max!
Max: Yes?
Tony: Try to sell my ticket and have a drink on the proceeds!
Max: Thanks – we will!

As Max leaves, Wendice slowly turns to face the audience, a look of unspeakable cruelty and malevolence souring his otherwise handsome features. And ... slow descent of curtain.

The train rumbles into Hornchurch District Line after what seems to have been a three-hour trip from Victoria. A brisk walk up the High Street past car showrooms, hair salons and letting agents, and suddenly there's the theatre, an anonymous sixties complex of glass and concrete. Some kids are using the front steps as an impromptu skateboard park and an elderly man walking a dog is peering at a sandwich board positioned by the entrance doors. As I hurry up the steps I see what he's looking at; it's a poster advertising the play. The letters of the title are arranged as if numbers on a telephone. Below there's an illustration of a hand brandishing a knife, the point apparently aimed towards a suave man-about-town holding a tumbler of Scotch. The man's face looks as if it's been drawn as a likeness from my publicity photograph. And underneath that 'a callous husband, a convenient catspaw, and the whiff of blackmail. But Inspector Hubbard has spotted something ...'

I'm thrilled. My picture on a theatre billboard! How about that? Looks like I'm getting somewhere at last.

I'm just going in through the door when I notice the dog has cocked its leg against the poster and is weeing on it.

water

Actors are adept at dealing with unexpected emergencies. A live performance is a dangerous and uncertain event, and things will always go wrong from time to time. My mate Des told me once of the time he was playing the detective in Agatha Christie's *A Murder Is Announced* at Bridlington when the actor playing the chief suspect failed to turn up on stage for the vital interrogation scene. After several lone circuits of the stage picking up knick-knacks and studying them aloud ('Hmm, what's this, a handbell in the shape of a leprechaun? I might buy one for myself') Des brilliantly bought himself several minutes of extra time by announcing: 'I feel so happy today I think I'll sing a song.' He then launched into the only number he could think of – 'I'd Do Anything' from the musical *Oliver*. Apparently the old dears loved it.

This sort of crisis doesn't happen often, as the stage management will soon be alerted that something's wrong and will attempt to sort it out for you. If your fellow actor has gone AWOL they'll hunt them down (the payphone or the bar are the most common destinations) and get them on as quickly as possible: if you've forgotten your lines and request a prompt from the wings they'll offer it immediately (though another mate of mine who asked for a line three times under his breath was answered with, 'Hang on, I'm doing something ...'). If the door jams or the handle comes off in your hand trapping you on stage they'll force it open from the other side with a screwdriver. If, on the other hand, it won't close properly, forcing you to continually walk over and shut it again every ten seconds (OK in a farce but unhelpful if you're performing *A Day in the Death of Joe Egg*), they'll hold it shut for you from offstage until the theatre carpenter can be located. In other words, the stage manager is the actor's friend and guardian angel and a steel thread of absolute trust stretches between us. They are the unsung heroes of theatre, who despite terrible rates of pay, brutal hours and fetid work conditions, can be relied on absolutely.

Unless they happen to be called Vikki and have their minds on a six-foot Australian commis-chef whom they haven't seen for nearly a year.

It's around 8.27 p.m. on the evening of 8 July. About a week into the run of *Dial M for Murder.*

Let's see. Imagine, if you will, that you're hovering above the Queen's Theatre, Hornchurch, in a helicopter, and wearing a pair of special X-ray specs that enable you to see through walls. Outside your cockpit it's a balmy evening in high summer: the sun has not long set and the sky is still a beautiful dark vermilion. The air is full with the familiar smells and sounds of a summer's evening in Hornchurch – the crackle of barbecues, the smash of telephone kiosk glass, the bark of stray dogs.

Down onstage, Max and I are in the final seconds of the first act of tonight's performance of the play. I've just asked him if he'd mind escorting my wife on a trip to the theatre:

'The old man's flying to Brussels on Sunday and he wants my report first thing in the morning ...'

I amble stage left and look out of the French windows at what is supposed to be a small walled garden but what in fact is the assistant stage manager in the wings picking his nose. Then I pour myself a cold tea from a decanter on the nearby card table.

'Well, if you're sure ...'

Sitting watching us from the darkness of the auditorium are nearly three hundred people, mostly middle-aged women. And they're rapt. You could hear a pin drop if it weren't for the continual screech of brakes: some kids out in the car park are practising handbrake turns in a stolen Mini Metro.

Out in the foyer, a young boy in a nylon school shirt with a clip-on bow tie is rearranging his consignment of ice-cream tubs in his tray. Another minute or so, and it'll be time to open the pass doors and brave the stampede.

In the dressing room the hired hitman is scrutinizing a large pustule on his cheek in the long mirror on the rear of the door. He checks the clock on the wall and wonders if he'll have time for a shit during the interval, or whether to hold it in till the end of the play.

The actor playing the detective isn't here yet. In fact he's dozing on a tube train, somewhere between Whitechapel and Stepney Green. Normally actors have to be inside the building in time for the 'half', usually thirty-five minutes before curtain up, but theatre custom dictates that if your character is not on till after the interval you can ask for what's known as a late call. Missing a performance is an actor's worst nightmare, yet for the past five stops he's been fighting a losing battle against the desire to nod off and have twenty winks, courtesy of a late lunch. As his head lolls uncertainly on to the shoulder of the passenger next to him he's already falling into a fitful dream in which I'm marooned on stage having to re-invent the entire ten-page confrontation with him as a phone conversation, while he argues with London Underground ticket inspectors ten miles further on in Upminster.

Tony: 'What's that, officer? You've got some questions you'd like to ask me but can't leave the station at the moment? I'm sorry, what did you say – where was I last night between 7 and 10? Funny you should ask that because...'

What else? The actress playing my brittle wife, having already left the stage, is now making herself a cup of tea in the green room and talking to Len, the theatre fireman, who's sitting at the far end watching Liverpool versus Anderlecht on a battered television. Currently she's regaling him with tales of how the cigarette lighter wouldn't work on stage when she tried it this evening, and how she had to hunt for a box of back-up matches in the desk drawer.

'And of course there was a draught from somewhere offstage, so it was as much as I could do keep the match lit long enough to light my fag,' she says through great jerks of nervous laughter. 'It was an absolute bloody nightmare, and I thought, what the hell am

I going to do?' As she pours the boiling water into a mug with the logo of a local garden centre on the side her eyes fill with tears of mirth. 'And then I remembered the matches and I thought, Thank Christ, but I'll tell you, that was the worst few seconds of my life out there ...' She's now laughing so much she's spilling water on to the sink unit, which is the norm because actors always think that the recounting of any mishap during a performance, however trivial or footling, is always a surefire A1 uproarious anecdote. Len is laughing dutifully, and wondering privately if she's up for it.

In his tiny office above the foyer, Bill, the theatre administrator, is staring glumly at various balance sheets and account documents spread chaotically across his desk. The unexpected heatwave, the recent IRA bomb attack in Hyde Park and the lower than expected audience figures for the previous production, *Dick Terrapin, Tortoise Detective,* have thrown the theatre into a steep cash-flow liquidity crisis. He's going to have to lose another stage manager for the autumn season to claw back some of the deficit.

And finally, perched at the control board in the wings, the assistant stage manager, a large Australian girl called Vikki, is following the action of the play on a video monitor and preparing to cue the various technical departments involved in the successful docking of the first act. Vikki is looking forward to the end of the show: her boyfriend will be arriving at Heathrow from Brisbane about now and she's got a late-night supper prepared for him back at her bedsit in Plaistow.

She activates a microphone on the desk by pushing a small fluorescent button and presses her lips softly on to it. 'Stand by for curtain down on Act One. LX, sound and front of house. Stand by, please ...'

Her whispered instructions are relayed to the lighting and sound operators. As soon as Max has said his last line – '*Thanks. We will!*' – and closed the door behind him, Vikki will count to four, allowing me to turn slowly to the audience and unfurl the trademark villain smile, before pressing the various banks of coloured switches on the desk and then feeling behind her for the large iron handle that controls the curtain. A swift tug, the tabs will slowly descend, the old ladies will collectively 'Ooohh'

– and house lights up, cue interval music, everyone's happy. Vikki will even have time to phone the airport to see if the flight's landed before calling beginners for Act Two.

Max stands and shoots his cuffs. That's another good tip for thriller acting, by the way, particularly if you've forgotten your next line but don't want to request a prompt. Cuff shooting is worth at least three seconds of thinking time.

I reach into the inside pocket of my blazer.

'Here are the tickets, Max.'

He collects his overcoat from the hooks by the door while I roll the ice cubes round a couple of times. Another distant screech of brakes in the car park: there's no point hanging on for pregnant pauses with that as competition – the audience members will all be wondering if it's their car being wrecked. Best to hurry it along, let them stretch their legs, inspect the damage and phone their insurance companies.

I open the door and usher Max out. He disappears behind the door frame.

'Hey, Max!'

'Yes?'

In the dressing room, the hitman decides he can't hang on: he's already touching cloth. He walks the few yards along the corridor to the gents and starts unbuttoning his mackintosh.

In the green room the wife is now recounting the incident of the cigarette lighter to a young girl from a nearby technical college who's here on work experience. 'I was telling Reg here, the bloody cigarette lighter just wouldn't stay lit ...'

In his office Bill decides to try and cancel the booking he's recently made for the Syd Lawrence Orchestra in October: tickets haven't been sold yet and with any luck he can save a couple of thousand that way without being sued.

Back in the toilet cubicle the hitman drops his trousers and sits down on the seat: he hasn't realized that the belt of his mackintosh is trailing beneath him in the pan.

Outside in the foyer the schoolboy nudges the pass doors open and slides into the auditorium with his ice-cream tray.

On the District Line the detective jumps with a start and

leaps out on to the platform seconds before the doors close and the train leaves Hornchurch station.

And in the wings, Vikki whispers into the microphone and feels behind her for the curtain release. It's a large, rusting metal lever located against the wall: in fact it's is not unlike the one next to it, which operates the automated stage sprinkler system: but confusion is impossible – one is bare metal whereas the sprinkler handler is painted in a garish red and has the words 'Caution – Sprinkler' embossed on the side.

Her hands clasp the cool iron frame. He'll have landed by now.

'Try to sell my ticket and have a drink on the proceeds!'

This is perhaps my favourite moment as Tony Wendice: the slow turn to the audience. In some ways it's the defining moment of a thriller, the apotheosis of the genre. If comedy is measured by laughter and drama by tears, then thrillers are judged by the length of the 'Oooohh' from the audience at descent of curtain.

And I want to hear a big fat one tonight.

Max is already at the doorway.

'Thanks. We will!'

He softly closes the door behind him. I take a measured swig of the tea and turn slowly to the audience, while a few feet away Vikki dreams of the mammoth rogering she's going to get tonight and pulls the lever to operate the stage sprinkler system.

The first I'm aware of the situation is when droplets of water start spattering the surface of the tea. My initial thought is that someone's left a window open. But of course, theatres don't have windows; at least, not in the area above the stage. What they do have is complicated lighting rigs, masses of wiring and connectors, and thousands of volts of electricity. Dark blotches are appearing on the sleeves of my blazer, water droplets are bouncing off the studded leather of the Chesterfield – it's barely two seconds since the first drop spattered my cold tea, and it's already a deluge. Within moments the cigarette butts are afloat in the ashtray, the mending basket so beloved of the French's acting edition has sprung a leak, and my matinée-idol hairdo is now plastered to my head. I look like Billy Bunter waiting for a postal order.

It's funny the things that come into your mind at times like this. Perhaps if my mate Des hadn't told me of his experience in Bridlington I would have reacted differently, but faced with this current crisis the only thing I can think of is to sing a song. The trouble is, there's only one in my head – 'Come on, Eileen' by Dexy's Midnight Runners. It was playing on the radio in the green room just before the performance and is now lodged in my head, blocking out any and all other tunes and ballads I've ever heard, including all thirteen Gilbert and Sullivan operas.

Meanwhile Vikki has found the correct handle. The front curtain starts to descend, huge ropes of rain sloping off it. As my Scotch gently overflows the rim of the tumbler, I'm aware somebody is knocking on the door.

It's Max.

He opens the door and pops his head back in. He'd caught a glimpse of what happened as he was leaving a moment or two before, and after hovering offstage a moment or two the temptation has been too much to resist, his mouth already creasing into a schoolboy smirk.

'Oh, and another thing.'

I stare back at him through stinging eyelids.

'I'd get that roof fixed if I were you ...'

tour

A college professor, having just witnessed a touring production of *Hamlet*, asks the director of the piece whether he believes the Prince of Denmark actually ever consummated his relationship with Ophelia?

'Yes,' replied the director, 'I think it was during the second week in Wolverhampton.'

There are only three things certain in this lifetime: death, taxes, and actors on tour. Affairs are almost de rigueur among actors on commercial tours round the provinces, if only because there's little else to do with your time. It's a unique experience in which the triumphs and insecurities of the lifestyle, already stretched to buggery by a constant diet of indolence, rejection, euphoria and despair, are strung out to a degree whereby something has to give. Think about it; you're mixed in with a lot of strangers for months on end, in a different town each week, with money in your pocket and nothing to spend it on but clothes, booze and Marks and Spencer sandwiches. What's more, you're all bundled together in unfamiliar lodgings, often miles from anywhere. What else are you to do? There are only so many National Trust properties you can visit. A loving partner and settled home life are about as much use to you as a three-speed walking stick. That's why actors are notoriously promiscuous once they're living out of a suitcase – it isn't anything personal, they're just huddling together for warmth. Tallulah Bankhead summed it up when she said, 'Darling, if it's on tour, it ain't adultery.'

That's my hope, anyway. My next job is in a touring production of Shakespeare's *The Merchant of Venice*, kicking off at the Forum centre, Billingham-on-Tees, before embarking on a twelve-week tour including Hanwell, Poole, Llandudno, Southsea, Stevenage and Thirsk, before ending up at the Winter Gardens, Malvern.

At the very least I'm hoping for a close encounter of the Thirsk kind.

The good news is I'm playing Bassanio, one of the leading parts in the drama and a role I can really get my teeth into.

The bad news is the director has a 'concept'.

This explains why I'm standing at the costume fitting in dove-grey tights, a pair of suede bootees, a velvet miniskirt and a treacle coloured codpiece. I've also been asked to don a black, shoulder-length wig.

Let's join us at the point in the fitting where I've just put the costume on for the first time. I'm staring at myself in a full-length mirror provided for the purpose. With me is the wardrobe super-visor, a woman called Christine. She's the one in the blue jeans with the pale pink cashmere sweater draped across her shoulders. I'm the one looking like popular 1950s balladeer Alma Cogan.

'You are joking.'

'What do you mean?'

'You can't send me out on to a stage looking like this?'

'Why not?'

'Because I look like a great poof.'

'Michael, it looks fine.'

'But Christine, we're doing school matinées, for Christ's sake! What chance have I got in a dove-grey tights and suede bootees?'

'Michael, this is the authentic Jacobean style. This is what they wore in Venice in those days. It's all part of Derek's concept, he's been through it with me and this is what he wants. It's utterly authentic to the period. I have to say I don't know what you're worrying about. You certainly don't look like a great poof. As a matter of fact you look a complete knock-out ...'

'Do I?'

'Of course you do. Strangely sexy.'

'Really?'

'Yes, really. Just look at yourself. I'd go to bed with you look-ing like that.'

'Would you?'

'Of course. You look a million dollars. You actors are all the same, you always want to look like you do in the street. What the hell did you expect, jeans and a T-shirt? It's set in Renaissance Venice, for God's sake. You've got to trust me on this one, Michael. I'm working to a specific brief and I know my job. I won't send you out there looking a berk.'

I study myself once more in the mirror. I must say the quality of the fabric is astonishingly good considering it's a low-budget tour starting in Cleveland. The fabric is thick and luxuriant, the piping delicate, the various decorative touches beautifully intricate, even the corrugated cuffs are starched and crisp and pristine white. How the hell have they been able to afford it? Christine meanwhile runs her fingers through my hair before returning it to my head. It falls in a sort of bob cut just below my neck ruff.

'You see?' she says.

She's right. That rearrangement of the hair makes all the difference. She's right; I actually look more like Nana Mouskouri.

She turns me round by my shoulders so that I'm facing her. She's got a hair grip clenched in her teeth but her eyes are bright with hurt pride.

'Do you believe I'm a good designer, Michael?'

'Of course I do.'

'*Do you?*'

'Yes!'

'Well then. Give me a break. I won't let you down.'

The cast assembles in the café of a small arts centre in Deptford where we're to spend the next three weeks rehearsing. The café itself is a low-ceilinged space at the front of the building, cluttered with tables and chairs and looking out on to the street through a long row of windows. I can already see the director, Derek inside waiting for us, greeting each new arrival with an expansive bear hug and the offer of a cappuccino. He has made his name with experimental theatre in Germany: he wears a loose-fitting charcoal sweatshirt and chinos, and his hair is tied back in a ponytail. After several minutes of swapping costume

traumas with my fellow actors, Derek invites us all to sit down so
he can give a brief outline of how he sees the next few weeks.

'Let me begin by explaining my concept.'

'Here we go,' somebody mutters next to me.

'The play is a fairy tale. A romantic weaving of sanity and
madness, of masculine and feminine. We want to suggest the
exotic and oppressive climate of Renaissance Venice. Here we
have a wealthy, febrile city, a place of rich appearance, of
commerce and masques, of excess and debauchery, of sexual
ambiguity and political intrigue.'

A melancholy rendering of 'When the Saints Go Marching
In' drifts in from the street. I look out of the window; on the
opposite pavement a tramp is sitting against the wall and using a
traffic cone as a trumpet.

'The world is one of opulence, gilded and luxurious, alive
with gossip, frivolity and romance. Nothing can be taken at face
value – we want the audience to ask themselves who's good,
who's bad, who's straight, who's gay, who's fucking who …'

'He's obviously done a lot of touring,' mutters the same person.

'Let me show you the set.' Derek reaches below the table
and fishes out a detailed scale model made from cardboard. It
depicts a tiny stage area coloured in a checkerboard pattern, with
three doors at the back and a metal walkway stretching overhead.
The cast cluster round the tiny replica: there's an air of bogus
enthusiasm, yet behind the intense looks and earnest nods the
eyes are glazed and dull. The costumes are obviously preying on
minds other than just mine. I've already heard dark rumours of
bare shoulders and slashed tunics, exposing sagging forearms,
beer guts and grizzled chests.

As Lorenzo said to me over coffee: 'Alma Cogan? Count
yourself lucky.'

Derek points at the model. 'We're going to press home this
idea of fluidity, of shifting allegiances and sexual predilections
even before curtain up. My idea is a short mime sequence to
open the play: a sort of liquid dumb show. For instance …' He
turns to the model and begins flicking the tiny doors open with
a stubby forefinger. 'Bassanio strides on to gaze at Portia's

portrait here. Shylock can appear on the end of this walkway and jangle a money pouch here. Antonio walks on and scans the horizon with a telescope for his fleet of argosies out on the high seas here. Portia and Nerissa chase each other round the bottom of the gantry in an innocent game of hide and seek from here. Perhaps she sees Bassanio still standing by the pillar, perhaps she doesn't: maybe she fancies him, or she really fancies Nerissa, we just don't know ...'

One of the doors falls over.

'Hence the costumes, which I hope you're as thrilled about as we are.' He indicates Christine, who's standing at the rear of the room. She beams back confidently. Derek presses on. 'All this will be overlaid with some genuine Venetian court music played on a crumhorn and knackers.' (He pronounces them 'knaykers' and says the word quickly hoping to forestall any wisecracks.) 'It's a genuine part song lament by a pupil of Scarlatti, I found the tune in the music conservatoire at Padua while I was over there recently. So you see, we're creating sort of visual and aural tableaux with each character simultaneously miming a silent vignette of their journey through the play.'

'Why?'

That's the actor playing Salerio; I recognize his as the muttering voice. This is his first job back after playing the caretaker in seven series of *Grange Hill*, and it's obvious he's an adherent of the Bish Bash Bosh school of acting (sometimes also known as 'Get on, get on with it, get off'): he's already rolling a fag and has a torn-out square of newspaper containing today's *Times* crossword secreted in his script. A can of lager pokes out from the top of the supermarket plastic bag at his feet.

'Don't worry,' replies Derek excitedly. 'If this works they'll be hooked before you've spoken a line.'

The rehearsal process is by far the most relentless and demanding I've ever known. Not the play itself – we barely touch that – but the dumb show proves both emotionally and physically exhausting. Derek spends all but five days of the total rehearsal time on the mime, and by the time of the final run-through in the rehearsal room we've tried every possible combination that it's mathematically possible to devise of fifteen actors, four entrances and a metal walkway. The crucial casket scene (Bassanio's pivotal moment in the text and containing some of the Bard's most complex and beautiful poetry), I've been through just twice – three times if you count the word run I did with the actress playing Portia in the pub next door on Thursday night.

Derek watches the final run with a beatific smile across his face, an unused notepad and pencil and a set of Nepalese worry beads on the table in front of him. 'I haven't really taken notes – they're essentially a bourgeoisie concept, everything you've offered up today is of its own creation and therefore equally valid – but suffice to say ...' He splays his hands and holds them out inclusively. 'It works.'

'What about the dumb show?' That's Salerio. He speaks with the resigned air of a man who knows the answer.

Derek smiles smoothly back. 'You have a problem with the dumb show, Ian?'

'Yes, I do.'

'Why's that?'

'I feel like a cunt.'

'Trust me,' replies Derek.

As we leave the room for the last time before setting off for our last free weekend for two months, I glance at the notepad, still unmarked on the desk. A single sentence is scrawled on it.

'Remember to buy asparagus ...'

knackers

An out-of-work actor meets a leading theatrical producer in the street. After a few minutes customary chit-chat about the dire state of the business the actor asks the producer if he's doing anything at the moment. The producer answers that he's currently staging a production of *Goodnight, Vienna* in Walthamstow.

'How's it going?' asks the actor.

'About as well as a production of *Goodnight, Walthamstow* would be going in Vienna,' answers the producer.

I'm reminded of this chestnut as I set off for the first date on our tour of Shakespeare's *The Merchant of Venice* – Billingham-on-Tees.

Billingham-on-Tees is a large industrial town in the county of Cleveland and is famous for two things: it's the home of the chemical conglomerate ICI and of Billingham Bombers, reportedly the most violent and technically inept ice hockey team in the whole of Britain. They don't bury their dead in Billingham, they just stand them up in bus shelters. We're to be ready for a costume parade at 10.30 on the Monday morning, with a tech/dress rehearsal starting promptly at 11 a.m.

Another problem of touring is that you spend most of your days off travelling between venues as far apart as Edinburgh and Poole in unreliable cars owned by other equally impecunious actors. My first Sunday is spent on the A1 in heavy traffic and even heavier rain in the back of a Volkswagen Beetle owned by Salerio, along with the Prince of Arragon whom we have to pick up in Potters Bar. The floor of the car has a hole in it and by the time we reach Middlesbrough the rear mats are floating in an inch of water. We finally reach the outskirts of Billingham soon after 8 p.m. The town centre looks as though someone has exploded an atom bomb and caused at least fifteen pounds worth of damage. With none of us wanting to brave our digs, arranged hurriedly over the phone the previous weekend, Salerio suggests we park the car, call in briefly at the theatre for a look at the partially erected set and then go for a meal. Somewhere there'll be an All-You-Can-Eat buffet with our name on it.

The stage doorman is sitting in his little cubby hole watching *Birds of a Feather* on the telly. If anyone knows a cheap place to eat it'll be him.

'There's only one. The China Garden ...' He nods his head towards a grubby establishment with fogged-up windows just visible across the precinct.

'Thanks.'

'But it closes at nine.'

'Ah.' A glance at the clock behind him shows us it's ten past.

'Do you think they'll still serve us?'

'They're not open Sundays.'

Welcome to Billingham.

The next morning I catch the bus into the town centre. It's still drizzling and the air smells faintly of paint stripper. Nonetheless as I approach the central precinct my heart momentarily leaps – a long queue of people are waiting patiently outside the box office, snaking round the side of the theatre and out of sight. Actors are born optimists: maybe it's going to be a hit after all. But as I get nearer I see that they're all under sixteen and carrying ice skates – it's half-term and the Forum theatre shares the same complex as the local rink. Apart from our *Merchant of Venice* the only other artistic activity in the town appears to be a visit by Jake Thackray to the local folk club next month.

Derek is already in the stalls surveying the progress of the set and it doesn't look good: the walkway is only partially erected and a knot of dishevelled stagehands are standing around holding scaffolding poles and scratching their heads. Christine is beside him in the stalls and waves to me when I enter. 'They're all hanging up for you,' she informs us. 'Any problems, come and find me.'

I'd forgotten about Alma. When I enter my dressing room she's waiting quietly for me on the dress rail, looking like some terrible transvestite brother you'd hoped had lost your address. I struggle into the tights and bootees, after which the treacle codpiece has to be positioned and fastened together with a series of interlocking tapes round the waist and under the crutch. With each new addition I brace myself for the anticipated volley of abuse from my fellow actors, but it never occurs, and when I at last look up from my Elizabethan cricket box I can see why. I thought I had problems ...

The women haven't come out of it too badly – long quilted dresses, luxuriant Pre-Raphaelite tresses and delicately stitched felt slippers – but the costume parade for the men is a sinister affair. The actor playing Gratiano is in a similar miniskirt and codpiece combo to mine but with a blonde wig instead of my black: he looks like Miss Piggy. The Prince of Arragon looks like Karen Carpenter, while the actor playing the Prince of Morocco could expect to do well in a Joan Armatrading lookalike contest: his appearance made even more alarming by the fact that being a white European male he's also had to black up. The green room resembles a drag queen convention. Christine looks on implacably – in her opinion we look absolutely wonderful and why don't we just get on with it instead of standing around making smart-arsed comments?

Derek lounges in a corner, adjusting ruffs and making suggestions: the dress rehearsal is already in jeopardy because the ladders allowing the actors concealed access up to the metal walkway in the wings can be seen by the audience and the walkway itself is so high that when the actors are up there, anyone sitting in rows M to Z can only see their legs.

'We may have to tidge it a little,' he says.

For 'tidge' read 're-stage'. The afternoon is spent relocating virtually the entire play to ground level. By 4 p.m. we've still not reached halfway. Derek despatches a stage manager to the box office to inform them that some seats will have to be resold as 'restricted view' only. She returns with the news that it won't be a problem because there's only thirty-one booked.

The exercise is abandoned at 7 p.m. A pungent stench of ice-making chemicals hangs round the stage area, and worse, the general manager of Cleveland District Leisure and Entertainment has warned us that once our crumhorn has stopped we may have to put up with the sound of light orchestral favourites in the background; it's apparently the night of the Cleveland junior ice-dancing championships in the adjoining rink and the original contractors skimped on the soundproofing. It can't be helped: the stage crew have now been working without a break for thirty-one hours and the usherettes are already peeking anxiously through the rear doors. I spend the hour leading up to the off sitting gloomily in my dressing room with Joan Armatrading, Karen Carpenter and a plate of limp cheese baps.

At 7.20 we get the call to go over the top: 'full company to the stage please for the curtain up and the crumhorn tableau'. A glance through a crack in one of the scenery flats confirms the worst, around eighty people dotted about in small clumps and staring bleakly at the empty stage.

Derek has now changed into a linen suit and flutters around nervously. 'Don't forget,' he pipes, 'deception, ambiguity, who's fucking who ...'

The house lights dim. It's 7.32. The crumhorn and knackers strike up: Shylock is poised behind his door, Miss Piggy is at the top of the gantry. Joan Armatrading is across the stage – he catches my eye and raises his hands before waggling them at me and simultaneously mouthing, 'Mammy ...' If nothing else, living in Potters Bar teaches you a sense of irony.

And we're off. As the knackers swing into action I walk on with Derek's final words ringing in my ears. Deception, ambiguity ...

Who's fucking who.

I've been on stage about four seconds when I become aware that the crumhorn and knackers duet is beginning to drop in pitch.

By the time I've reached my special spotlight for my inspection of the casket it has ground to a funereal dirge: I wrestle the portrait of Portia from a pouch in my miniskirt and try to look interested in it. Surely the music should be going faster than this? Someone is tittering in the audience. I've no way of knowing whether it's my costume or the sound of the dropping knackers.

The part song lament slows to a stop. The only noise now is Miss Piggy walking along the gantry to the distant sound of a hundred rippling violins playing 'Charmaine'. We plunge on. Shylock jingles some change behind me. Antonio trudges on and surveys his argosies. Portia chases Nerissa in their lesbian love tryst round the columns. The Prince of Morocco waves a sabre. Somebody in the audience coughs. Silence.

Except of course for Mantovani and his orchestra playing 'The Westminster Waltz'.

At the post-mortem afterwards in the China Garden Derek explains what went wrong: the sound operator had inadvertently left his anorak laying against one of the spools on the tape recorder. 'If it's any help to you all he's inconsolable,' says Derek. This seems unlikely – I've never seen a theatre technician the slightest bit fussed about anything, and my suspicion is confirmed when Salerio assures me he's just seen the culprit playing darts in the pub over the road. But it's hardly worth arguing about. In any case, Derek's off. He can't even stay beyond the main course as he's got to catch an early flight next morning from Manchester airport to Utrecht where's he starts directing an all-male version of *Seven Brides for Seven Brothers*.

'Have a great week,' he says as he promenades round the table kissing each of us on the top of our head. 'Drive safely, keep it lively and remember, you're in a world of gossip, frivolity and romance! Who's fucking who!'

Five minutes after his departure we realize he hasn't left anything for his share of the bill.

As for gossip, frivolity and romance, we're barely into our dessert before the thespian hormones start kicking in. It's been a dispiriting first night, we're far from home, it's still raining hard out in the precinct and we've got another seven performances before the 200-mile journey down to Poole on Sunday for more of the same. At first it's hardly noticeable: Gratiano announces he's going now as he's feeling suddenly very tired, and offers Nerissa a lift home to her digs as they're both staying in the same part of town. A few minutes later Jessica and Lorenzo announce that they're going to get some fresh air, and as we're fetching our coats from the hatstand by the fish tank, Balthazar and the Duke of Venice discover they've both left scarves in the dressing rooms back at the theatre and are going to find them.

By the end of the meal there's only me and Salerio. I'd been sort of hoping that Christine might have joined us – in fact she'd told me to save a place for her at the table in case she managed to get through the long list of emergency costume maintenance she was staying behind to complete – but by 12.15 she's still not arrived and the entire Chinese community of Cleveland are now staring at us with their coats on. I bum a lift in the back of the Volkswagen, kneeling on the front passenger seat so as to keep my feet dry, and by 1 a.m. I'm in bed at Mrs Elsom's with a cup of Milo and a fig roll.

The *Middlesbrough Evening Gazette* speaks for an entire disappointed community the following day: 'Patches of phoney heartiness follow background sequences of feeble revelry.' It concludes: 'Michael Simkins's Bassanio is a thoroughly unsympathetic little squirt ...'

christine

Twelve weeks and ninety-six shows later it's all over. Twelve long weeks, nearly three thousand miles criss-crossing the country in Ian's leaking Volkswagen, much of it without functioning wind-screen wipers, stays in country cottages, university campuses, flats and bedsits, and a diet of pop and chips, interspersed with the occasional curry and all washed down with vats of booze. Some of the places we've visited have liked Derek's production of *The Merchant of Venice*. Most have not. Certainly none have been overwhelmed. Whelmed would be the best we could say for it. In fact it has been the schools matinées that have provoked the most comment: we've done two each week, and each and every time I've strode onstage in the bootees and tights I've had to wait for up to thirty seconds for the laughter to subside. I've tried to remember Christine's mantra: 'Strangely sexy ... strangely sexy ...' But it hasn't made any difference. Ken Dodd would have struggled to achieve the response I achieved one afternoon in Stevenage.

But that's onstage. Offstage it's been like the final days of Caligula. Virtually no week has gone by without some sexual experiment: with each new venue the tour has spiralled into depravity, which has progressively sucked in stage management, lighting and sound, then usherettes and bar staff, as well as the clientele of nightclubs and discotheques up and down the M1 corridor. There have been many striking feats, but the winner by a mile has been the actor playing Solanio, an ex-PE teacher from Belfast called Sean who has broken even his own previous best by notching up seventeen one-night stands, three two-night stands and a pregnancy scare – and this was before he broke his foot in an impromptu game of football, which left him doing the part on crutches from Poole onwards and which at least partially curtailed his sexual progress.

There have been other travails. The actor playing Antonio got pissed and abusive in a curry house in Hanwell and ended up spending the night in a police cell. You can understand it. Twenty years ago he was one of the leads in *Zulu*, his name above the title on the posters, alongside Stanley Baker and Michael Caine, he modelled pullovers in women's magazines and had an E-type jag. Now he's standing in satin culottes at the Winter Gardens, Malvern, scanning the horizon for his argosies with a child's telescope with no glass in it. I reckon I'd become pissed and abusive if that had happened to me.

And me? I've made remarkably little headway. Somehow my heart hasn't been in it. It may be the curse of Alma, but I just haven't had the appetite for prowling the dancefloors of provincial nightclubs after curtain down. Or perhaps it's more to do with Christine. I've got to know her well over the last couple of months, and nearly got to know her a great deal better in her Triumph Herald after a night out at a pizza place in Bury St Edmunds. But she's got a partner who runs his own business in Uxbridge and they've bought a house together and are trying for a baby and they've already got back together once after a painful split, so …

It's now August, and a warm summer's evening in downtown Malvern. Again I'm sitting in Christine's Triumph Herald in the car park of the Winter Gardens. A few yards in front of us, lit only by the sickly light of the overspill from the theatre building, a giant pantechnicon is being loaded with the disassembled sections of what until an hour ago was the febrile city of Venice, complete with Meccano walkway. The set will be transported to a warehouse in Bermondsey where it will be recycled or trashed in the next few weeks. Next to it a smaller transit van is loaded to the gunnels with giant wicker skips containing a full set of Renaissance costumes, each one neatly folded and cellophaned. The lids are firmly buckled down with thick leather straps. Alma Cogan can't hurt me any more.

Christine's hand reaches across the gear stick and takes mine. Her hands are cold. She's only just finished the packing.

'Are you going back tonight?' I ask.

'Eventually. I've got more stuff to sort yet. What about you?'

'Ian's dropping me at Hendon, if we make it that far. I'd better go too, he'll be wondering where the hell I am ...'

'Come on then. Take care of yourself.' She kisses me on the cheek and reaches for the door handle.

'Christine.'

'Yes?'

'Can I ask you something?'

'I don't know.'

We stare ahead out of the windscreen, not daring to look at each other.

'How the hell did you make all those sumptuous costumes on your piffling budget?'

She sighs and explains.

Christine only got the job of wardrobe supervisor because she had a contact in BBC costume department and assured Derek she could get whatever he required at a snip. The BBC had just received back all the outfits from their 1981 ten-parter sixteenth-century Italian drama *The Borgias*, one of the most expensive television co-productions projects ever, sucking in vast quantities of both the BBC's and TV Italia's drama budgets, and starring an international cast including Adolpho Celi and Oliver Cotton. Hundreds of hand-sewn outfits in only the finest materials and textures and made to specific Venetian period design, and she'd be able to get hold of them for less than five hundred quid the lot.

'So you see you had to wear them. All of you. If I hadn't persuaded you I'd have lost my job and you'd have been walking round in smocks and tights.'

She squeezes my hand gently.

'Anyway, count yourself lucky. At least you got Oliver Cotton's.'

And suddenly I realize why I like her. Why my gentle infatuation with her over the past four months has blotted out all other possibilities. Because she would have persuaded me to wear that treacle-coloured codpiece and velvet bootees even if they'd been Billy Cotton's. You can't help but admire her in a way. She did what she had to do and tried to make everyone feel as good about it as she could manage. It's rather an attractive trait when you think about it. And somehow, strangely sexy ...

'So what did I really look like in it?'

There's a long pause. Too long.

'You looked like a great poof.'

leaving

There may be fifty ways to leave your lover, but there are only two ways to leave your agent: and they both stink.

The right and proper method of telling your agent that you're moving on to somebody new is the most hotly debated subject at theatrical dinner parties. I've been paying a lot of attention to the experiences of my peers recently and, so far as I can see, nobody has come up with an elegant and painless way of putting the knife in. It's simply a matter of naming your poison.

Method one. Arrange to see your agent personally.

What happens is this. You call them up and ask to see them in their place of work: probably at the start of the lunch hour or at close of play. Upon arriving you announce your decision in a mature and businesslike way, maintaining civility throughout and taking care to thank them and their staff personally for all their hard work during your time together.

They burst into tears and call you an ungrateful cunt.

Your agent won't have been expecting the assassination, so will have welcomed you into the office as an honoured client and friend, particularly as they'll be feeling bad they haven't called you for the past three months. They'll have arranged for some minion to fetch you a drink and shown you to a comfy seat, enquired about the health of your parents and loved ones, showed you their holiday snaps and told you how excited they are about the big ideas they've got lined up for you. Your subsequent public repudiation of them in front of their staff will only add to the bile and invective you're certain to get spat back at you, and they will certainly ask why you didn't just write them a letter and have done with it, so at least they needn't waste their precious free time being ritually humiliated like this.

Under no circumstances be persuaded to take them out for a meal in order to do it away from their business environment. A mate of mine tried that recently and ended up with a mixed grill over his head.

So. It must be Method Two. Write a letter.

What happens is this. You frame a carefully worded epistle, announcing clearly your decision in a mature and businesslike way, maintaining civility throughout and taking care to thank them and their staff personally for all their hard work during your time there.

They will read it and call you an ungrateful cunt. They will then phone you, and in a frosty, bruised and overly polite manner will assure you that they too were thinking it was time to part company, that they wish you all good luck for the future but that frankly they are surprised you didn't have the good grace to come in and tell them personally: they would have thought it was the least courtesy they could expect after all they've done for you, but it seems their faith was misguided in that regard as well.

The problem with relying on the Royal Mail to do your dirty work for you is obvious: you can't ever be certain when it'll arrive, so you'll spend an uncomfortable day or two cowering behind the sofa every time the phone rings. If you do answer it you can be sure it'll be them calling out of the blue and still in all innocence, to tell you they've arranged some stupendous audition for you to meet Franco Zefferelli. It always happens.

In either case you may be assured they will express their shock and dismay that you could be so disloyal as to secretly negotiate to move on to a rival agent before telling them, and that their successor in your affections obviously has no scruples either if he's prepared to poach you in such an underhand and thoroughly unprofessional manner. They've never heard of such dishonest and weaselly way of going about things and in their opinion you both deserve each other.

So. Choose your poison. Method One or Two.

A word of encouragement. Whichever route you plump for, five minutes after you've left them, probably less, they'll be getting a call from some actor wishing to move to them. 'I haven't told my current one yet that I'm looking to leave but I'm wondering if I could come and discuss things with you?' will be the plea. If your ex-agent can smell dollars in the idea, they'll have them round quicker than you can say *Brief Encounter*.

Does that make you feel better? It did me.

The reason for my dissatisfaction was simple. I've recently been hanging about with a bloke called Rob. Rob has been an actor some years less than me, but he's got into adverts. You may not know of Rob, but if you live in Yorkshire and I was to mention Bertie Bottlebank you'll have him at once. He's the giant tin can on legs that wanders around the streets of Doncaster persuading the good folk to recycle their glass and aluminium. This is only one of his recent incarnations. Over the last couple of years he's done commercials for Domestos, Campbell's soups, the RAC, Sylvanian families, Alton Towers, Carling Black Label, Kingdom of Leather as well as a series of local ones in the Tyne Tees area advertising a clinic specializing in the treatment of leg ulcers.

Consequently Rob earns between eighty and a hundred grand a year. He has a house in Leeds and a flat in Crouch End, a vintage Triumph Herald, a Harley Davidson and a succession of busty girlfriends to occupy the pillion seat. He goes on holiday three times a year and has an interest in a timeshare in Marbella. He has no mortgage and a string of pension plans for when he retires, which, at his current rate of earning, will be before he's thirty. Rob likes me and finds my interest in live theatre rather quaint, but he assures me it's for the birds. If my agent can't get me some advert interviews I should wise up and change to one who can.

I decided to follow his advice and asked my agent to try and get me some auditions. 'It's an area I'm interested in moving into,' I told him. He assured me he'd get on the case at once. In fact the only subsequent interview in the following three months was for a new musical set in the Wild West called *Yee-Ha*. Starting at Colchester.

So I've gone to Rob's agent. She's confident she can get me some big multi-national gigs and lots of repeat cheques. It's just a matter of time and a couple of grand on having my teeth straightened. 'Think of it as an investment,' she assures me. Frankly I'm thrilled to bits. I think we're going to really go places together, and I'm going into her office now with my photos and recent press clippings so we can formulate a press release and a plan of campaign.

Just as soon as I've told my ex I'm leaving.

chicken

There's an old theatrical maxim that says that changing your agent is a bit like swapping deck chairs on the *Titanic*; move to a different one if you like, but don't expect it to make any difference to your ultimate fate. But this time it's going to be different. Where Bertie Bottlebank leads, I follow.

The thing about adverts is that you only need to get one to make the equivalent of a year's money in a couple of days. There are no special Equity Lows if you get the latest Coke campaign or the new Ford Sierra – you'll be lighting cigars with fivers. Because of this, advert interviews are notoriously brutal affairs, involving loss of dignity, collapse of self-respect, with a healthy dose of humiliation heaped on for good measure. My new agent says that getting ads is a 'knack' and that once I get one I'll get a lot more: until then I'll probably have to go up for hundreds before I crack it, and I'm not to become disillusioned if I get a lot of initial rejections.

'Just think of the repeat cheques', she says.

'I will.'

'Now, before I start putting you up for things, are there any products you wouldn't want to be seen for?'

The question hadn't occurred to me. What could I possibly object to?

'Well, for instance, some actors won't advertise certain products because of their beliefs. Anything plugging the Conservative Party, for instance. Don't forget there's a general election coming up, and Major's fighting for his life, so they're sure to be giving it all they've got. I'm certain to get a call to provide some man-in-the-street vox-pop types ...'

'No problem. They're only trying to save their jobs. I'll do that.'

'Fur products?'

'Fur's fine. People need to keep warm.'

'What about cosmetics? Aftershave and deodorant, that sort of thing? Some of them may have been tested on animals.'

'That's OK. Women have got to look nice, haven't they?'

'High street clothing retailers? Some actors feel they exploit poorly paid workers in third world countries – sweatshops and child labour and so on?'

'No problem. At least they're not having to go into prostitution.'

'Admiral car insurance?'

'I don't follow. Do they invest in politically corrupt countries or something?'

'No, darling, I was thinking more of the fact that you'll get known as that prat who stands in a crowded office dressed as Lord Nelson.'

'Think of the repeat cheques.' I try to remember this during my first audition a few days later. For Chicken Tonight.

The interview is in an attic room at on the top floor of a shabby building off Carnaby Street – I'm to learn they're always in shabby attic rooms off Carnaby Street – the other bell on the door is for a model called Gloria who specializes in re-caning seats. I walk up the narrow staircase and find myself in a tiny waiting area full of blokes all my age and each dressed as a friendly dad.

A young girl is swivelling back and forth on an office chair behind a desk and carrying on a conversation with someone called Kevin whose behaviour she seems keen to stress is 'out of order'. She breaks off from her litany of complaint and glances surlily up at me.

'Name?'

'Michael Simkins.'

'Here for?'

'Um ... Chicken Tonight ...' I whisper it, just in case I've come to the wrong place and these are the auditions for the RSC. I wouldn't want Terry Hands to know I'm here.

She runs a finger down a list of names; eventually she locates mine and highlights it with a fluorescent marker. 'You're 11.20, forms to fill in over there, they're running late ...' She waves airily at a sheaf of photocopied papers and a holder full of biros, before turning her dazzling wit back to Kevin. I find a seat in the corner and start to fill in the paperwork – age, hair colour, waist size, shoe size, bust size (women only), am I prepared to allow my image to be used on billboards, and have I recently appeared in any advertisements for products that might compete with Hot 'n' Spicy Chicken Tonight . I haven't, but I recognize a bloke opposite me from a telly advert for Cuprinol Wood Preservative and I can see he could be a bit stuck.

There's also a brief outline of the advert, including a story-board – a series of tiny boxed-in drawings depicting the different shots to be filmed. Most of them seem to feature a large rooster careering round a kitchen. I gaze glumly at the various boxes for a minute or two before sitting back to savour the atmosphere: most of my rivals are still form-filling or reading their news-papers, but one or two seem to know one another and are discussing their latest skiing holiday or comparing boarding school fees. A couple have even met this morning already at a casting for Coffee Mate. The receptionist finishes her conversa-tion, positions me against the door frame and takes a Polaroid of me before ripping it from the camera and waving it distractedly around in her fingers. As she staples it to my completed forms I catch a glance, and it's horrendous – I know Polaroids are notori-ously unflattering but the man in that photo looks like someone wanted for assaults on children in the Thames Ditton area. You certainly wouldn't let him loose at a family mealtime.

I can't think about that now. I've got other worries ahead, judging by the noise coming from the interview room. Somebody is impersonating a rooster.

A moment later the door opens and a dad walks out, red-faced and panting, looking like a client of Gloria's who's wandered into the wrong room. He retrieves his briefcase hurriedly from a nearby chair and bustles out without speaking. He's followed by Sylvie, the casting director, whose job it is to compile the assortment of actors for the interview. Like most casting directors she's female, struggling with her weight, and has a fondness for brown rollneck pullovers. She gives a hurried smile before ushering another dad into the interview room. Ten minutes later it's my turn.

Most actors I know have the wrong idea about casting directors. We mistakenly believe that their job is to get people in for interviews, and that by currying favour with them we're likely to improve our chances of getting through the door. I'm here to tell you it's a waste of time. Any project is so hopelessly oversubscribed that there's never a shortage of interview fodder – in fact the reverse is true – and thus we come to the job of the casting director. They're there to keep you out, to prevent all but the best few from getting their foot in the door, so don't waste your time toadying up to them. It doesn't work.

'This is Michael Simkins, everyone!' The room is bare apart from a teenager perched behind a video camera on a tripod and some shadowy figures at the far end. 'This is Darren, our operator.' The youth at the camera makes a movement with the left side of his face, which I think is intended to be a friendly smile.

Compared with the people behind him, his welcome is positively garrulous; two girls and a man, each dressed from head to toe in business suits, seated on a sofa. On a rectangular pine table in front of them are a selection of fresh muffins, a substantial fruit bowl and a cafetière of piping, freshly ground coffee. All three clients are looking at the floor.

'Michael, these are the representatives from Chicken Tonight,' says Sylvie hopefully. I give them a breezy grin. Nothing. I suppose I can't blame them. They've learned the hard way that if they actually make eye contact with actors we'll assume we've got the job and will start wading into the muffins.

'Stand here, please, Michael, that's lovely ...' Sylvie indicates a spot on the floor marked with gaffer tape. 'Sorry the director can't be here, he's on Marmite all this week, but it's quite straightforward, we'll have a lot of fun! Have you seen any of the adverts?'

I nod enthusiastically.

'Good, so you'll know it's a bit off the wall. You don't mind making a bit of a fool of yourself, do you?'

Think of the repeat cheque. Three-day shoot – £250 per day plus guaranteed £7,000 repeat fees, extra if my image is used on billboard and poster campaigns.

'If we could just do the usual?' she says.

Darren turns on the camera and adjusts the focus. I announce my name and representation, briefly turn to show left and right profiles, and hold up both palms to the lens. 'It's just a precaution,' my agent has explained. 'They like to know you've got a full set of fingers. Particularly if you're handling food.'

Sylvie seems pleased. 'Marvellous. So it's teatime, you're sitting here at this table waiting for your wife to put your tea down in front of you, and you're pretty bored, you're expecting meat pie or beans on toast or something. And then she gives you this ...'

She indicates a paper plate lying on a table beside me, with a plastic knife and fork next to it. The fork is covered with dried spittle.

'Imagine this is a big piping hot dish of delicious chicken wings, covered in new Hot 'n' Spicy Chicken Tonight. So you take a forkful, you're pretty suspicious, it's not what you were expecting, you're not sure you're going to like it, and then you put it in your mouth and *pow!*'

She throws an expression suggestive of lunatic delight. Behind her the executives are looking on in quiet distaste. Darren on the video camera has picked up a copy of *Viz* and is reading the latest vicissitudes of Buster Gonad and his unfeasibly large testicles.

'Now the fun bit,' says Sylvie, warming to her task. 'I want you to do whatever comes into your head, so long as it looks like a cockerel. This meal is the most fantastic thing you've ever tasted and you want to be a great big chicken yourself, flap your wings, scratch the floor, whatever you like, just try to make us laugh ... All right?'

Make them laugh? Those people on the sofa? I'd have more chance with the judging panel at the Nuremberg trials.

'Please sing the theme song if that helps. Do you know it?' She warbles a couple of bars of 'I Feel Like Chicken Tonight' in a trembling soprano.

Just think of the repeat cheque. I decide to give it everything I've got.

My agent calls me that evening.

'Congratulations, darling, they absolutely loved you. Looks like you've taken to it like a duck to water.'

'You mean I've got it?' An image of me on a beach in Hawaii is already calling me.

'Not quite. You've got a pencil.'

'Sorry?'

'Chicken Tonight have given you a pencil.'

'What's that?'

'Well, it means they want you to leave the shoot dates free and under no circumstances accept any other work without informing them first.'

'So I've got the job?'

'Not exactly.'

'I haven't got the job?'

'Certainly not. You're on a pencil. That means you're one of a few. In my experience it usually means that they're waiting for the managing director to have a look at the tapes and select his final preference. It should happen within a couple of days ...'

'How many's a few?'

'Um ... hang on.' She consults her notes. 'Well, they've told me it's a heavy pencil. Good sign. That probably means you're down to the last three or four ... So – great news! Well done!'

So. The company has chosen me to do the job, they want me to leave the dates of the shoot entirely free of other work, and barring calamities, the contract will be in the post just as soon as somebody in the office gets round to typing one up. In effect it means I'm now one of five or six roosters in various parts of

London who now have their careers and bank balance in temporary suspended animation until the boss gets back from his golfing break in South Africa.

Three weeks later I call my agent.

'I was just wondering what's happened to my pencil?'

'Was it a light one or a heavy one?' she asks distractedly.

'I think it was a heavy.'

'What was it for again?'

'Chicken Tonight.'

'Oh yes, Chicken Tonight. I'll get on to it. They should have made their decision by now. I'll find out and call you back.'

She rings me that afternoon. 'I've got an answer out of them at last,' she says. 'There was just some office girl on the phone, she didn't seem to know anything, silly cow. I explained we've been waiting nearly a month for a decision and she agreed it was out of order. Anyway, she says she's sorry, she made some enquiries and it looks as if the pencil is going in another direction.'

'Which means what?'

'It means that they shot the ad last Friday.'

pickle

Over the following six months I screen-test for Lassie Meaty Chunks, B&Q, Buitoni Ravioli, Blue Stratos, Curry Motors, Burger King, and an alarming product called Cobblers. They're a type of biscuit only produced in the United States, which explains why the ad executives couldn't understand the difficulty the English actors were all having in keeping a straight face at the interview.

'Have you tried one of my cobblers?'

'I didn't know you had any.'

'Try them. I think you'll like them.'

The casting director, Katrina, attempts to explain what's required.

'You're a bit of a nerd and you've invited your mate over to view your stamp collection. He offers you a biscuit and you're not really interested in it, it's not what you're used to, but when you bite on it you have the most fantastic taste sensation. Hundreds of tiny cobblers cascade out of your ears and whirl around your head. One of them lands on your shoulder and turns into a little elf-like creature who kisses you on the ear. It tickles you and you laugh uncontrollably and suddenly you're throwing all your stamps up into the air like a maniac and they're raining down on you like confetti, it's the most fun you've had for years – and then you wake up to find your friend staring at you with a worried expression on his face. Can you show us that?'

She hands me a piece of badly folded cardboard. 'If you could pretend that's the cobbler,' she says. 'We haven't been able to get the real things shipped over in time for the auditions, and we don't want to use a rival product as a stand-in, do we?' She laughs nervously.

I don't get it. I also don't get Lunn Poly, Hedex, Cockburn's sherry, Whiskas, and a new product for dealing with trapped wind. Then I get an interview for Branston Pickle. It's scheduled for 12.30 p.m., but at 12.35 I'm still stuck in a stifling carriage a few metres outside Oxford Circus tube station. I eventually reach the shabby attic room just off Carnaby Street at a few minutes past one, the smell of vomit from a panic-stricken passenger in the next seat still clinging about me. I consider popping into the lav for a wash and brush up, but I'm already over half an hour late. They may already have gone. I'll have to brave it out.

The waiting room is empty.

'Hello?' I shout hopefully. A door opens and the casting director, Yvonne, comes out. She wears a rollneck pullover: a pair of spectacles on a chain hangs round her bosom.

'Ah, Michael, we were wondering where you were, we thought you'd forgotten to come.'

'So sorry, Yvonne. Have I missed it?'

'Nearly dear, we've got to be out of here in ten minutes, it's being used for a casting for Pampers this afternoon. We've been pairing boys and girls up all morning for this one – we had an actress left over when you didn't show up and I was just about to stand in for you for the screen test. She's in there now, she'll be very relieved you're here, I'm sure. Are you happy to come straight through?'

I follow her through into an airless studio, which is bare except for the obligatory spotty video operative and sofa full of stony-faced clients ...

And Lucy.

Lucy is the girl who claimed to have been discovered in a compromising position by my landlord ten years previously. The last I heard she was living in Barnes with an ex-*Blue Peter* presenter. She's still looks much the same: fine auburn hair, freckles, perhaps a little more drawn than I remember her ...

'Lucy, we've found your partner for you. Michael, this is Lucy.'

Not a flicker. She stands up and extends her hand but says nothing.

'Hello, Lucy. Pleased to meet you.'

'And you ...'

'It's Michael,' interrupts Yvonne, helpfully.

'Pleased to meet you, Michael.'

'Now, darlings, we'll get on as we're running late. You can fill out the forms and do the Polaroid afterwards.' Yvonne puts down her clipboard. 'The story is about a couple who are going out with each other, love's young dream, but the thing is, they can't agree about anything except the wonderful fruity taste of Branston. That's the idea anyway – whatever disagreements we have with one another, we all love Branston. But the main part of the ad shows our love's young dream constantly quarrelling. So what I'd like you both to do is to improvise an argument, a real belter, no holds barred, it doesn't matter what it's about, just as long as you really tear into each other... Do you think you could have a go at that?' she adds, anxiously.

I turn to Lucy. She smiles crisply back at me.

'No problem,' she says. 'Looking forward to it.'

Yvonne is delighted. 'Good. Would you like a practice go?'

'No,' replies Lucy. 'I think we'll be all right.'

'Marvellous,' says Yvonne. 'We'll roll the tape, and in your own time ...'

We stare at each other for a moment.

'So?' she says eventually.

'OK. Springbank Crescent, Scarborough, 3 a.m., nineteen seventy-nine ...'

'Eighty,' she corrects.

hamlet

Another call.

'I've got an appointment for you on Friday at ten, darling. It's only for another advert I'm afraid but—'

'I don't think I've got any more in me.'

'Course you have, you've just had a couple of bad experiences ... You need a bit of luck, that's all. In fact I think you'd have got that last one for Kwik-Fit if you hadn't strained your back at the audition. You're starting to care too much, that's your trouble.'

'Well—'

'Anyway, it's up to you,' she goes on (agents rarely have more than a few seconds worth of sympathy at their disposal), 'do you want to go for this or not?'

'What's it for?'

'Hamlet cigars. Cinema campaign only. I told them you smoked. You can learn by Friday, can't you?'

Actually it's quite appropriate. A man accepts the slings and arrows of outrageous fortune with equanimity by lighting up moments after some embarrassing setback. The setting is a spoof *Antiques Roadshow* set on a lawn of a country house. It begins with a slow tracking shot along a line of people of all ages and shapes, each clutching some family artefact and queuing patiently for a valuation: suits of armour, teddy bears, moose heads, you get the idea. At last we reach the front, where a woman is standing horror-struck next to the expert, who is holding two ceramic handles, one in each hand. At his feet, in a million pieces, lies a priceless antique vase.

Cue Jacques Loussier.

I am that expert. Or at least I shall be if the audition goes well.

I'm in the interview, wearing a bow tie and a chalk-stripe suit I've borrowed for the day off a friend who works in insurance. This time there are no clients: just me, the director and the pock-marked operative. The director hands me a ceramic vase.

'So when I say "action", Michael, say a few words about this beautiful ornament, blah blah, doesn't matter what, we only need a few seconds, and then drop it out of shot, and then let's see your reaction. Understood?' He moves briskly back to his stool next to the video camera. 'And ...roll videotape.'

I raise my hand apologetically. 'Sorry, before we film, could I just ask? Do you actually want me to drop this vase?'

'Yeah, drop the vase out of shot and then react. And ... roll.'

I raise my hand again. I can see he's already got me marked out as troublemaker: don't I realize he's got another thirty guys just like me in cheap suits and badly knotted bow ties to get through before he can get out of this crummy joint? But he digs deep and manages to retain a patina of civility.

'Is there something you don't understand, Michael?' He has to glance down at my name on his audition list before he says it.

'I'm so sorry to be so dense, just to clarify – you actually want me to drop the vase?'

'Yes, drop the vase out of shot.'

'I understand that, but do I literally drop it, or do you just want me to pretend to drop it until it's out of shot, but really to keep hold of it?' Troublemaker is already giving way to pedant: but it's an important distinction – pretending to drop something is very different from actually dropping it. Isn't it?

Tell me it's different.

He speaks slowly and sweetly, as if I'm care-in-the-community. 'Yes, I want you to drop it.'

'On to the floor?'

'Yes, Michael, on to the floor. Don't worry, it won't break.'

'You're sure?'

'It had better not, we've only got the one for the whole morning.' He laughs mechanically, turning to the pockmarked youth for a supportive smile. 'All right?

I nod uncertainly.

'No more questions?'

'No. Sorry ...'

'Good. And roll video.'

The red light above the lens begins to blink. Right. What did he say he wanted? Something about improvising on a theme of *Antiques Roadshow* or something. My mind's suddenly gone blank. I can't remember what the programme is like. The only one I can recall is *Going for a Song*, which I last saw an episode of when I was six. Who was the presenter? It was that show-jumping commentator. Dorian somebody. He'll have to do. I lurch into some terrible cod analysis of the vase, mentioning the words Ming and dynasty about five times in quick succession. After a few seconds of this bogus antique speak I manage a little phoney fumble and let go.

The vase hits the carpet with the noise of a pistol shot, shattering into a million pieces and filling the room with clay dust. It must have been full of talcum powder or somebody's granny. Whatever it was the contents are now smothering the room in a choking pall. Through the haze I hear the youth say, 'Fuckin' hell' before launching into a coughing fit.

Slowly the air clears. The youth is now laughing uncontrollably but trying to make it look like still coughing so the director won't turn round and ask what was so goddam funny. After a moment, the door to the waiting room opens and the casting director, Janet, sticks her head in nervously. Behind her I can see a room full of men in bow ties. 'Is everything all right? she asks. 'I thought I heard a gun.'

'Uh, can you go out and buy a vase?' says the director. 'And tell the next guy we'll be a little while.'

Three weeks later I film the ad in the gardens of a country house near Uxbridge. I have my own trailer and a car to take me to the shoot: and now I know the secret of happiness. And it's not a cigar called Hamlet. True happiness is a repeat cheque dropping through your letterbox every few weeks for the next year and a half.

Which is just as well. I'm going to be needing some spare cash. Because six weeks after the Hamlet advert, I meet Julia.

act three

julia

My liaison with Julia begins with a call in the summer of 1984 from Mark Piper, artistic director of the theatre at Harrogate. He rings out of the blue to offer me the lead role in the musical, *They're Playing Our Song*. The show is the centre point of his season, he's scheduled it especially with me in mind, there's nobody else who could play it, and can I start on Monday morning at ten?

The show – book by Neil Simon, music by Marvin Hamlisch and lyrics by Carole Bayer Sager – is virtually a two-hander, and tells the story of the love affair between Vernon, a composer, and Sonia, a kooky but gifted lyricist. With brilliant dialogue by one of America's funniest writers and a fair smattering of popular hits including 'I Still Believe in Love' and 'Fill in the Words', it would be my first musical. Sonia is being played by an actress who has just had success in a David Puttnam film, *Mr Love*. I even recall reading about her recently in the *Daily Mail* in an article entitled 'Next Stop Hollywood'. Mark is in no doubt it'll only be a matter of weeks before the inevitable transatlantic call whisks her stateside for ever, so if I want to work with the next major movie star …

I'm not so sure. The allure of rep is beginning to fade now I'm approaching thirty. But it's only a seven-week contract, it's the lead part, and it's in the middle of high summer when sod all else is casting. I decide to give it a go: a last hurrah.

The moment I meet her at the read-through I realize I'm genetically doomed to wasting all of the next two months making myself irresistibly attractive to her. Stick thin, tanned legs up to her armpits, a mane of long auburn hair and an ability with one-liners that would run Neil Simon himself pretty close, Julia spends the period of the rehearsals viewing my fumbling attempts at courtship with a detached amusement. Nothing seems to work: each witticism is effortlessly topped, each new purchase from what seem to me to be Harrogate's trendiest clothes shops viewed with the sort of beneficent pity usually associated with Penelope Keith peering over the fence in any number of BBC sit-coms.

The first sign that I might be making some progress is the Saturday evening just before production week. I persuade her to accompany me for a drive over to Scarborough, just for a walk on the sands, a look at the theatre and a drink with some of my old mates there. My evil designs have largely withered through lack of nourishment, but my luck is about to change: while walking along the beach, a wild kick from a teenager during a nearby game of football sends the ball cannoning into the side of my face from about ten yards while I'm pontificating on the peculiarities of acting in-the-round. The incident does more in a split second to melt her than all my best gags had achieved in nearly a month. It may not be much, but it's a start.

A week later it's August Bank Holiday. We've got the evening off – Harrogate can't afford the overtime – and are sitting in a field somewhere in south Yorkshire, the remains of a substantial picnic spread out before us on a rug. It's a peerless English summer's afternoon, and from somewhere over a nearby hill the fragmentary snatches of a village fête are wafting across on the breeze: children's laughing, smatterings of applause, loudspeaker announcements about cake-weighing contests. It's about as romantic a setting as I'm likely to get.

Julia pours herself another glass of wine.

'So what do you do when you're not acting?' I ask casually.

'I'm a Buddhist.'

'Oh yes?' It's all I can think of. I'm trying to recall the name of that hotel in nearby Ripon. It's only a few miles away, and the task now is to get us both there, preferably in the same room.

'Do you know anything about Buddhism?' she asks.

A brass band is striking up in the distance. The tune is 'Abide with Me'. It's perfect.

'No, but I'd like to. Tell me about it.'

Three hours later – three of the longest hours I've ever spent, but it seems to have paid off – we drive into the car park of the Swan at Ripon. A doorman outside wishes us good afternoon and casts the customary doorman's cynical glance at our pitiful amount of luggage – a straw holdall filled with empty wine bottles. His attitude is mirrored at the reception desk. Now's the time to assure Julia of my credentials as an experienced lover.

'Would it be one room or two?'

'Just the one please,' I reply smoothly.

'En suite?'

'Yes, please.'

'That would be £19 including breakfast ...'

Jesus, that's a bit more than I'd expected. This place has obviously gone upmarket. I turn to Julia.

'What do you think?'

spotlight

The Harrogate experience may be over, but Julia and I continue to see one another, and within weeks our fragile confederacy has blossomed and deepened into a steady relationship, one based on love, trust, and my need for a base in London. Even in this respect it's reciprocal, with her gaining a weekend place by the sea in return. It's a perfect marriage of convenience: I spend two or three nights a week up in her stylish and pristinely maintained pad off the Kilburn High Road, while she catches the train down to the coast on Friday nights. Her studio flat and my bedsit sum up our differing lifestyles perfectly. It's difficult to imagine two people more ill-suited to spend time together. When not acting, her main recreation seems to be wiping down surfaces. Yet she seems to find my squalid bachelor lifestyle (complete with baby Belling two-ring cooker) quaintly bohemian. So long as I don't try to duplicate it in NW2.

The fact is we have nothing in common. She loves sunbathing and fresh air; I love sitting in a darkened room all day watching cricket on the television. She likes beautiful food; I prefer straight out of the can. She likes tranquillity; I like brass bands. She likes early nights; I prefer 3 a.m. reruns of *The High Chaparral*. She likes ceramics; I like fairground organs. Her reading interests include books on ancient eastern philosophy. I prefer biographies of famous murderers. In fact, apart from a love of Chinese take-aways, it's difficult to uncover any shared interests.

It's her twice-daily Buddhist practice that causes the most problems. Each morning and evening she kneels in front of a tiny shrine erected on a chest of drawers in the corner of the room and recites a section of something she assures me is called a

Lotus Sutra followed by an endlessly repeated mantra, all delivered at full volume in a sonorous, nasal twang. This rarely takes less than an hour, and even when she comes for the weekend there's no let-up as she brings the shrine with her on the train in a small wooden box resembling a dartboard cabinet.

In Brighton the noise she produces during these twice daily devotions is just about bearable – at least in the summer she can wedge herself out on to the tiny balcony overlooking the street while I can simply burrow further down into the bedclothes. But in her studio flat in London escape is impossible. Each morning and evening a noise resembling a blend of a dentist's drill and a Peter O'Sullivan racing commentary pierces the air. Her morning supplications rarely begin later than 7 a.m., while her evening ceremony can usually be relied upon to coincide exactly with *Coronation Street*. There's nothing for it but to crouch so near to the TV speaker that I can no longer focus on the picture, or to go out to the pub. I tried reading some more murder biographies but it was giving me ideas.

'You can always join in,' she says. 'You seemed so interested in it all that afternoon in Ripon.'

That's what I like about Julia. There is an innocence about her.

A shared love of crispy aromatic duck may not be the broadest of bases on which to base a lifetime together, yet we manage to find a way through, and with each successive week Julia inveigles me into a world of lifestyle possibilities I'd only previously glimpsed in the pages of glossy magazines. Strange and exotic concepts such as aftershave, clean towels, bath scourers. She's obviously encouraged by my response to these new-fangled ways, because after a couple of months of discreet liaisons she announces one night that my solitary confinement is over. We're coming out.

We've been invited to a dinner party being thrown by her mate Joanna in South Hampstead. Joanna is a thirty-something actress with all the trappings of one of the successful 10 per cent: a roof terrace, a garlic crusher and more than one bottle of wine in the fridge. Julia isn't sure which of her culinary treasures her friend is going to unveil ('it'll be either fish in cloth or steak in coffee'), but assures me it won't arrive by way of a Chinaman on a moped.

This is a major development. Until now I haven't been allowed to meet the inner sanctum of her social world. In fact Julia freely admits that she's tried to ensure that 'I stay on my paper' as she graphically describes it, just in case she realizes it's all a terrible mistake. The notion of a bespoke meal and social interaction is a new and exciting concept but it's no free lunch. Julia refuses point-blank to allow me to turn up in my customary trademark V-neck jumper, flared jeans and monkey boots, and insists I get kitted out in something more elegant. A trip to a designer outlet in Covent Garden results in an account-crippling Martinique casual windcheater with trendy Velcro fastenings, a pair of black jeans, powder-blue T-shirt and trainers. When Joanna opens the door of her flat to welcome us in I feel like Eliza Doolittle arriving at Ascot.

As we troop up the stairs to the doorway of Joanna's top-floor apartment, Julia momentarily restrains me to whisper in my ear.

'Don't drink too much and don't overstay our welcome,' she hisses.

I soon see the reason for Julia's insistence on the makeover. Joanna, dressed in a simple yet exquisite black linen dress, shepherds us out on to an elegant, pebble-strewn rooftop balcony where tiny candles are fluttering in glass domes. Her boyfriend Roger is already out there dressed in a flowing linen shirt, a glass of white wine in one hand and a bowl of olives stuffed with anchovies in the other. He sits me down in a white canvas deckchair while he perches on the railings opposite talking about his time at film school and pointing out Michael Palin's house, which can be glimpsed obliquely through the shimmering trees.

It's already 8.30 p.m. One by one the other guests arrive. A huge, jovial man called Des, who seems to know Julia from a previous incarnation at Swansea Rep, is having an evening off from one-night gigs touring Britain with *Rupert and the Outlaws*. I spend some minutes trying to equate this jolly Welshman with the notion of a rock group, until he explains it's a play for children about Rupert Bear in which he's playing Edward the elephant.

Another ring at the doorbell heralds the arrival of an actress with tumbling black locks called Geraldine. She's carrying a raspberry pavlova over which ash from a cigarette clamped between her teeth threatens to cascade at any moment. Roger has already let slip that he'd asked her to be here for seven because she was sure to arrive two hours late and be in a foul mood when she finally did so. She hasn't been able to find anywhere to park so has left her car in front of a single barrier further up the road marked 'Do not obstruct, access for emergency vehicles needed at all times' with a note on the windscreen telling any passing ambulance driver where they can find her.

The final guests are the neighbours from the flat below. Steve and Sandra both work in social services; this is their first trip out since the birth of their first baby, and they arrive with a bottle of champagne and a box of pistachio-flavoured Turkish Delight. With each new arrival Roger erects more canvas chairs, while Joanna moves between us with salmon roulades and bowls of rice crackers, making occasional discreet forays back into the kitchen. The conversation on the crowded balcony falls smoothly into a diet of breezy chit-chat, while below us, the gardens of Gospel Oak fade from view in the gathering dusk. In nearby houses, vignettes of other dinner parties are framed in lighted windows. A fabulous aroma of cooking wafts from all directions on the breeze.

Just before nine, Roger invites anyone who wants to join in with the evening prayer ceremony before eating. Julia, Joanna and Geraldine follow him into the dining room. The common mortals left outside hand round the olives and talk about work and its relationship to spiritual well-being. Steve explains about Camden's policies of care for the aged, Sandra speaks passionately on the rewards of teaching children with special needs, and Des holds forth for twenty minutes on the problems of working onstage with a paper-mâché trunk.

At last we're ready to eat. Roger guides us into the dining room where Joanna is serving fresh whitebait with Italian bread.

It's already ten but nobody seems to mind, or asks if they can have it on their laps while they put on *Match of the Day*. Julia stops me from cramming a handful of whitebait between two chunks of bread and eating it like a chip sandwich.

As the meal progresses, the conversation continues relentlessly on the subject of acting. Every so often Joanna breaks off from their latest anecdote to explain to Steve and Sandra the streams of impenetrable jargon – corpsing, cheating, drying, flies, wings, fluffing – without which our gabbled gossip must sound to them faintly like pornography. They nod and try to laugh in the right places. Roger opens another bottle of wine. Geraldine rolls a joint. Joanna puts on a tape of Himalayan folk music.

Before I know it it's midnight and Julia is looking at her watch. We're driving up to Lincolnshire the following morning for lunch with her parents and it'll be an early start. Roger has suggested we move through into the lounge for a brandy, and I take the opportunity quietly to ask Julia how I'm doing.

'Fine,' she says. 'They think you're lovely. Joanna said how stylish you looked. Don't drink any more, we're going in five minutes.' I stagger happily into the lounge where Roger is pouring coffee. Stylish. Julia's South Hampstead friends think I'm stylish.

And then, just as I think I'm about to drink my coffee, I notice a copy of *Spotlight* lying on one of Joanna's bookshelves.

Spotlight is the actors' directory, published each year since before the Second World War, and contains a photograph of every professional actor. Flicking through even a single volume can become hypnotic – page after page of wannabe Hamlets and Ophelias, Len Fairdoughs and Bet Lynches. If Alec Guinness ever decides to pass on *Star Wars*, there are 300 pages of replacement Obi-Wan Kenobis in the 'Character Actors' section alone.

When I announce that it's the 1963 edition, the squeal of delight from Des and Geraldine can be heard up on Hampstead Heath. Actors love looking through old *Spotlights* and 1963 should be a belter.

Within seconds I've retrieved it and sat back heavily on the sofa. Des repositions a nearby desk lamp while the others swarm round me to inspect the yellowing tome. The pages throw up the pungent, damp aroma of old bookshops. And it doesn't disappoint. Page after page of actors, all clad in the styles of the early sixties. Actors in suits, actors in coats, actors smoking cigarettes or draped sulkily against ornamental railings, actors in yachting caps, actors with contrasting serious and comedy poses to demonstrate their versatility to potential employers, actors so famous they don't even bother to include a photo, actors who can only afford a sixth of a page, the ultimate ignominy. Two thousand pages, from Frederick Abbott to Ahmed Zulkiflee.

Joanna suddenly notices Steve and Sandra. We'd forgotten them in all our excitement. They're looking forlornly across from the opposite settee. Joanna moves over to encourage them, but the gulf between us is widening with each turn of the page: this is very much a private ritual, and even with the help of Joanna's simultaneous translation we're no longer speaking the same language. Sandra offers to wash up while Steve pours the coffee. The Turkish Delight remains unopened in its decorative cellophane. Who wants Turkish Delight? We've found Warren Mitchell when he still had hair.

Julia is tugging at my arm. Her eyes are drooping and she wants to go. I shake her off brusquely and pour myself another glass of wine. 'Just ten more minutes,' I assure her.

Forty minutes later we're approaching the end of the volume and the atmosphere becomes marginally more sober. It's Roger who first voices what we're all silently thinking; namely, how many are entirely unknown to him. Remarkably few of the thousands of entries are household names twenty years on. In fact, most of them seem to have disappeared. Their faces peer out at us, blithely locked in a moment of time, naive to their fates. We hardly notice Steve and Sandra standing in the doorway saying goodnight. Des points out a newsreader from Harlech Television, Geraldine finds her current agent in the juvenile Character section, and I spot a recent victim of a brutal homosexual murder in Hammersmith. Julia nudges me. She's driving, and is the only one in the room still sober. We've got to be up in six hours.

But before she can protest further, Joanna reappears clutching another volume. 'Got it,' she proclaims in triumph. 'This one's a scream.' Geraldine's offering me one of her cigarettes, Roger is opening the brandy, Des has found the Turkish Delight. Joanna puts the volume down between us on the settee. 'Here we are. Actors N to Z, nineteen seventy-eight. You've never seen so many terrible sideburns.'

My graduation year from RADA. Time to go. Julia's right, it's much later than I thought and we've got a long trip up to Lincolnshire in the morning.

I lurch from the settee, upsetting a glass of red wine over my Velcro fastenings and Roger's linen shirt. He tells me not to worry about it and hurries off for some kitchen roll. I offer to pay for the dry cleaning and begin fumbling in my ash-smudged jeans for any loose change, but Julia tugs me away. Thanks, Joanna, thanks Roger, don't worry, we'll find our coats, you must come down to Brighton some time. Joanna is at the doorway, still as immaculate as my first sight of her five hours earlier. She kisses me on the cheek and thanks me for coming. Behind her the others remain transfixed, oblivious to our departure, the only sound the swishing of pages and the occasional bark of drunken laughter. I can tell Julia is furious that I've ruined Roger's shirt and possibly one of those cream sofa cushions. I can be sure she'll express her views on the way home. But that can wait. The first thing is to get out. She has her car keys in her hand. We're nearly out of the door.

'Hey, Michael, you're in this!'

Geraldine is shouting gleefully from the lounge. She's noticed my name in the index and is sheafing towards the appropriate page as quickly as her sozzled fingers can manage. My first *Spotlight* entry, half-page, name and contact number only, photograph taken by the movement teacher June Kemp in the canteen.

I smile weakly at Joanna and set off past Julia down the stairs. But Julia is hurrying back into the flat to rejoin them on the sofa. I follow her in miserably. A few more page flicks, and finally the explosion of laughter announces they've found my entry.

Nothing is more risible than the recently dated. Julia's shout is the loudest of all.

There I am. Rounded adolescent features encased in a beige sweater with an embroidered neck, my newly washed hair neatly parted down one side, my head resting on my folded arms astride a kitchen chair. I'm still barely twenty, yet somehow manage to look like an advert for pipe tobacco, my unctuous smile suggesting someone who's just experienced that Condor moment. My carefully managed Martinique image has been exposed in a single moment.

At last Des speaks. 'Can you talk us through the Christine Keeler motif?' he says through his tears.

We're finally outside by her car. It's nearly 3 a.m. and the laughter provoked by page 701 is still ringing in my ears. Julia stares at me across the roof of her Fiat. It's dark, and difficult to gauge her expression. Particularly as her image is swimming gently in front of me. Is it sympathy or contempt? Has page 701 endeared me to her further, or persuaded her that I should follow the beige sweater to the Oxfam Shop? I'm too drunk to tell.

Stylish. Who was I kidding? I stare down at my designer windcheater. Blotches of red wine now decorate the front, and the Velcro fastenings are caked with meringue crumbs and fag ash. 'Look at my new jacket,' I mouth drunkenly. 'It cost me a bloody fortune. What are we going to do?'

'I'll chant about it,' she says, and climbs into the car.

game boy

Whatever her qualifications as a domestic goddess, Julia's chant-
ing immediately proves talismanic for my commercial prospects.
Suddenly I can do no wrong: over the next six months I get
adverts for Harvester Restaurants, Tandy Computers, Ford
Thames, and a new type of orange juice called Valencina, which
is notable for the fact that it has bits in. None of them are huge
earners, but suddenly it's just as my agent predicted: I've got the
knack. One designer jacket with Velcro fastenings becomes two,
then three. My ageing Renault Six is swapped for a moderately
new Ford Fiesta, and I'm able to take my first foreign holiday, a
week-long break to Tunisia. Even the clients on the sofas are
starting to return my smiles. All I need now is one big pay-off, a
Pepsi or a McDonald's, one huge, multi-media, all-region block-
buster, and I too can have that beach villa on the Costas.

Then I go up for the Christmas ad campaign for the new
Nintendo Game Boy.

And I get it.

'This is a biggie,' says my agent with barely suppressed glee.
She's calling me to explain the contract and her voice suddenly
has a breathy quality, which is rather sexy and which can only
indicate the prospect of serious money. 'It's only a day's filming,
which will be £250 and no overtime, but Nintendo are staking
their sales figures on this one. We're talking a nationwide
campaign, every ad break on ITV and Channel 4 for six weeks
up to Christmas Day: it's difficult to estimate what the repeat
fees will be but is there any lifetime holiday destination you've
always wanted to visit?'

'Well, yes. I've always wanted to visit Captain Scott's polar hut from his nineteen twelve expedition on the Ross Iceshelf in Antarctica.'

'Oh yes?' I can tell my agent's wishing she hadn't asked.

'You can get all-inclusive polar cruises now which take you all round the region, and it even stops off briefly at the site itself; they featured it recently on *Wish You Were Here*. Mind you, I don't think you get much change out of £20,000 ...'

'Why not order a brochure?' she says smoothly.

The advert is set in a TV studio and stars Rik Mayall. I play a presenter, a quasi-Jeremy Paxman, interviewing Mayall about the new Nintendo console. As he describes the product the TV studio around us becomes like the game itself, with colossal explosions, stunning special effects and general mayhem, and ends up with my disembodied head laying on the studio floor still trying to carry on the interview. Mayall picks my head up off the floor, stuffs it under his jumper and runs off with it. End of ad.

The day's filming itself proves to be both a laborious and uncomfortable process. It takes place in a huge sound stage at Shepperton on one of the coldest days of the year. A false studio floor, five feet high, has to be built literally round my disembodied head. For nearly five hours I stand motionless while a small army of carpenters and joiners assemble it with millimetre precision around my neck. I'm advised not to drink too much as once installed, it will prove a cumbersome and time-consuming job to disengage me for any visit to the toilet. 'Either that or Penny here will gladly fit you with a catheter,' says the director gaily.

Finally, some time mid-afternoon – I've lost track of time by now – the false floor is completed and we're ready to roll. There then follows a period of a further hour while the assorted footwear of technicians and special effects experts walk back and forth with ladders and racks of lighting equipment. Several times I'm nearly trodden on. And after six hours enduring freezing temperatures my nose is running. Just as I'm wondering if I dare ask Penny if she'd mind wiping it for me, the door at the far end of the studio opens and a woman in overalls enters pushing a loaded tea trolley. The entire cast and crew immediately scurry off to fill up on cakes and sandwiches, leaving my head marooned on the set pleading for somebody to fetch me a piece of Battenberg and a teaspoon of water to help it go down.

Those hours are among the most miserable of my professional life. Stuck down below eye level with only my clamped head on show, I suddenly know how paraplegics must feel. I resolve to send a substantial cheque to a relevant charity when I get my first repeat fee.

Ah, the repeats. I comfort myself during those long hours with thoughts of all those repeats, and what the advert might do for my profile; invites to appear on *Celebrity Squares* and *This Morning*, plus the occasional guest appearance opening a supermarket. Not to mention my double banquette with sea view on the *Polar Venturer*. I can sniff a little longer.

A week later I come home to find a message on my answerphone from the director – the only time this has ever happened – to congratulate me on my contribution. 'Mike, the ad looks fantastic,' he says. 'Just great. The guys at Nintendo UK laughed like drains and are chuffed to bits.' He goes on to confirm that the illusion of my bodiless head prattling away is genuinely startling and hilarious, and he's hopeful there might be follow-up ads in the pipeline. He ends by thanking me for my patience and wishes me a happy Christmas.

He needn't worry on that score.

Never believe it till you see it on your own TV. Even as I'm flicking through Teletext for the details of the travel firm, a rough cut of the advert is being screened for the managing directors of Nintendo Worldwide at their head office in Tokyo. Their reaction is immediate.

The script is fantastic. Rik Mayall is hilarious. The special effects are awesome. But the bodiless head on floor? It's too reminiscent of Japanese atrocities in the Second World War. Nintendo mustn't on any account be seen to be confirming the stereotype of the cruel Jap burying poor Englishman up to his head. Particularly at Christmas. They'll have to think again. A week later the ad is rewritten, reshot and re-edited, still with

Mayall but no longer with me. And no appearance means no repeat fee.

I never get to Antarctica; but with the £250 fee for my one day's filming I do manage to take Julia for a long weekend in Cardiff.

reconstruction

The next couple of years are spent trolling round theatres and telly studios playing an assortment of stalwarts and best friends. Then in the spring of 1987 I'm called to the offices of LWT on the south bank of the Thames for a telly interview. It's for their true crime reconstruction programme *Crime Monthly*.

The project is an interesting one. A year or so ago, the notorious criminal Freddie the Fox was finally apprehended in a daring police operation after months of detailed surveillance. The man who had terrorized most of Essex for nearly two decades, who had been involved in every known criminal activity from extortion scams and protection rackets to blackmail, gambling and prostitution, was arrested as he stepped blinking into the sunshine from the public bar of the Freemason's Arms in Ilford. A squad of special officers led by Detective Inspector Brian Wiggins wrestled the Fox to the ground and bundled him into a police van before he could make his escape. The raid had to be planned with split-second timing – Freddie was a popular character in the area, and any delay in getting him into a vehicle and away from the scene would almost certainly have led to a violent reaction from the gang of friends and hangers-on who rarely left his side, and whose own reputation for extreme violence was scarcely less fearsome than his own. It was a dramatic event. So dramatic that the whole story is being reconstructed on film. And they want me to give my Wiggins of the Yard.

I've been selected after my agent sent my photograph to the programme's casting department. (Their required description was: early thirties, careworn, a face etched from years of dour struggle, must have own notebook.) In the days leading up to the shoot I hear nothing: and then the evening before I'm due to turn up I get a call from the director. Her name is Samantha and my name suddenly seems to be 'babe'.

'Hi, babe, I'm just ringing to see you're all right for the shoot tomorrow ... You're our Wiggins, right?'

I tell her I am but I'm concerned that I haven't been asked to go in yet for a costume fitting.

'Sorry, babe, didn't they tell you? We usually we ask our artistes to bring their own outfit. Have you got a dark suit?'

Yes, I have.

'Well could you bring that in, babe? And a pair of shoes?'

I've got several pairs of shoes. But they're all casual. The only formal pair in my possession are brown. Would a man like Wiggins wear brown shoes with a black suit? I'd have to make him an Irishman. Best to mention it now rather than on set.

'Don't worry, babe, we won't really see your feet, you'll be at a desk most of the time, that'll be great. Could you bring a couple of shirts as well?'

No problem.

'And do you have a couple of ties, babe?'

Crime Monthly has struck lucky. As it happens, I do have a couple of ties, though one of them is a Christmas present from my Aunt Gladys in Hurstpierpoint and is decorated with veteran cars. Perhaps I could suggest that my Brian Wiggins is a keen motorist in his spare time when not wrestling with violent criminals or making trips home to Dublin to see his old mammy. But Samantha seems unconcerned about these details.

'That's great, so long as there are no stripes on it, they make the screen go all fuzzy. Gotta go, my pager's bleeping. See you tomorrow. Bye, babe.'

The LWT studios are situated in an impressive location by the Thames. The studio in which we're filming the interiors has been set up to resemble a crime incident room, and the set designers have done a thorough job. All the paraphernalia of a busy police office are there: mugshots of wanted criminals stare back at us from the walls, a map of London with tiny coloured drawing pins covers most of one end of the room, polystyrene cups of tepid coffee litter the desks, and piles of mock-up crime reports lay stacked on every available surface. Every police drama series has to have piles of reports stacked on the desks, and they're worth looking inside if you get a chance – I don't know where the props buyers get them from, but they always seem to be top secret government memos or confidential company files with 'To Be Read By Authorized Personnel Only' stamped in red ink on every page, and which have somehow ended up as set dressing for popular low-budget TV drama series where they can be viewed by all and sundry.

With the film crew still preparing for the opening shot (Wiggins staring contemplatively out of the window at the mighty Thames) I take a few minutes to look through them. LWT have excelled themselves this time: they seem to have got hold of a job lot of confidential casepapers for a NHS practice on the outskirts of Warrington in the late seventies. I never knew the citizens of east Cheshire were so poorly. Varicose veins, bronchial complaints, bowel cancer requiring immediate hospitalisation ... I pass several intriguing minutes studying them before I'm called to rehearse. I wonder to this day if Mrs Mercer ever did find a cure for her dry vagina during intercourse.

The filming follows the usual formulaic routine. We've got five scenes to do in the office, all of them in silence to be overlaid with a punchy commentary later on from the programme's presenter, Paul Ross. After Mighty Thames, we shoot the scene where I stand in front of the flip chart and explain to my fellow officers how we're going to set about locating Freddie. Then we do the scene where we're pretending to be making important phone calls. Then the one with us all staring wearily at our computer screens ('loosen your ties for this one please, babes'); and finally the scene where one of us bursts in with a piece of paper and says, 'Guv, I think we've got something.' We're through by twelve-thirty.

Over lunch ('Can you wear these napkins, babes? We don't want apple crumble down your suit ...') Samantha explains what's going to happen next. We're to be bussed out to Ilford, Essex, for the big action scene; the arrest of Freddie the Fox on the pavement outside the pub. Samantha has decided to shoot the whole denouement from a fifteenth-floor window of a block of flats on the opposite side of the road, giving it a gritty, over-looked by accident sort of feel. 'And we're filming outside the actual pub where he was arrested. Isn't that wonderful?'

This is the scene where I have my big moment. I have to shout, '*Go-go-go*' into a walkie-talkie when Freddie the Fox appears in the doorway of the Freemason's Arms before running full pelt towards the pub for the lightning arrest. The actors follow the camera crew out into the foyer of the sleek office block that forms the LWT building. I've spent many happy hours here waiting to be seen for job interviews: the sofas are plush, there's free coffee in the corner, ITV on tap courtesy of a large television screen set into the wall, and a selection of news-papers are spread across the side tables. While we wait for the minibus to arrive I compare careers with my fellow flying squad-ders. Colin tells me this is his first day's acting work this year: he's making ends met by delivering sandwiches in the Clapham Common area. The others have a similar story to tell: Geoff does painting and decorating; Billy works as a relief sauce operative for Heinz in Wigan; and Helen, playing the token female, has recently finished work as a grotto assistant in Santa's Kingdom at the Harlequin Centre, Watford. Apparently her duties included taking the entrance money and operating an illusion machine.

'OK, babes, we're off.' Samantha hurries in from outside to tell us the transport is here. We follow her out through the revolving doors and on to the pavement: as we climb in I notice a figure sitting wrapped in a car coat in the front seat.

Samantha does the introductions. 'This is our Freddie,' she says proudly, indicating a man who looks like Charles Hawtrey's younger brother. 'Sorry, babe, what's your name again?'

'Wilfred,' quavers the man uncertainly. One by one we lean over and shake hands. His grasp is flaccid and he has long deli-cate fingernails: it's not how I imagined the most dangerous man in Britain to look, but I suppose some people would say that they didn't envisage Brian Wiggins in black trousers with brown shoes and a tie with veteran cars on it. People still talk about how Freddie once threw a rival gangster down a set of concrete steps, breaking the miscreant's spine in the process. Wilfred looks as if he'd need a Stannah stair lift to even get up there in the first place.

Samantha slots into the driver's seat and we're off, edging through heavy traffic along Waterloo, over Southwark Bridge and towards Whitechapel. Wilfred turns round and asks if it would be all right to open a window: he's not a very good traveller. After several minutes of laboured breathing he seems to perk up. 'How's it been going?' he asks.

'They've been great, babe,' answers Samantha, accelerating down a bus lane. 'We've knocked all the interiors off in the office, so we've just got the action scene to do with you and we can all go home.'

'Yes, I was going to ask about that.' Wilfred explains that this is his first dip back into acting after a long lay-off due to what he refers to as 'problems with his waterworks'. 'I haven't really handled any pressure for some years,' he confides. 'I hope I won't let everybody down.'

'I'm sure you won't.' Colin, the one who sells sandwiches on Clapham Common, smiles reassuringly back at him and offers him a Polo. Wilfred accepts it with a troubled smile and stares unhappily ahead.

We arrive in a desolate precinct in deepest Ilford soon after two. The Freemason's Arms is a mock-Tudor structure with peeling timbers and discoloured pebbledash walls set back from the pavement between a betting shop and a double-glazing company with a life-sized cardboard cut-out of Ted Moult in the window. The pub itself looks distinctly unwelcoming: the doorway is covered with a frayed coconut-matting rug, and there's a scrawled notice on fluorescent card advertising lunchtime stripping every Saturday. From inside Wham's 'Careless Whisper' pumps out, mingling with a steady insistent bleep suggesting a formidable array of fruit machines. The crew unload the equipment while Samantha explains what's going to happen next.

'OK, babes, we're going to leave you down here while we go up there.' She points to a forbidding block of flats opposite. 'We'll leave you a walkie-talkie so we can communicate, just sit tight, make yourselves comfy, as soon as we're set up I'll tell you what to do.' She hands me the walkie-talkie and explains it will be doubling as my personal prop for my 'Go-go-go' moment.

The crew troop off, leaving Scotland Yard's finest huddled conspicuously in the back of the minibus. Silence descends. A few yards away the doors of the Freemason's Arms remain still: nobody goes in and nobody comes out. A group of teenagers study us from some nearby railings outside a sweetshop. Colin suggests making a dash for more Polos but just as he's about to go, the walkie-talkie crackles into life.

It's Samantha through a fuzz of static. 'Sorry we were so long, the lifts were vandalized, we had to carry everything up by hand. Wilfred, babe, can you hear me?'

Wilfred, who has been inhaling deeply from an asthma throat spray, peers out through the windscreen and waves hopefully in the general direction of the flats.

'Lovely, babe. Now what I want you to do is to go to the pub and just wait inside the door for a minute or two while the other boys take up positions nearby. When we've rolled the tape up to speed, I want you to stride out as if you've just had a few drinks with your mates and a bloody good lunch, you're cock of the walk, and then Mike and the boys will run towards you and grapple you to the ground. You're not expecting it, all right, so look plenty surprised and then put up a bit of a struggle. Is that all right, babe?'

Wilfred looks anxiously towards the Freemason's Arms. 'Have you agreed this with the publican?' he shouts into the walkie-talkie.

'Only quick as you can or we'll lose the light, babe,' crackles the reply. Our walkie-talkie only seems able to receive but not transmit.

Wilfred turns to me and grips my wrist. 'Can you go easy on the grappling? My knees aren't so good these days.' He tries to open the side passenger door and one of his nails breaks. Helen the grotto assistant leans over and slides it open. He eases out gingerly and totters off towards the pub.

It's difficult to see how he got the part. Perhaps he was the only one with a car coat.

'Ok, babes, now I'd like you to find somewhere near the pub and hide yourselves. Mike, babe, you stay by the van.' One by one we clamber out. Helen hides in the doorway of the betting shop. Colin bobs down below the parapet of a low brick wall. Billy crouches by a rubbish bin near Ted Moult. I hover uncertainly behind the wheel arch of the minibus, now doubling as an anonymous police surveillance car, all too aware that my behaviour is attracting the interest of the teenagers.

At last we're ready.

'OK, babes, videotape running, as soon as you see him, off you go ...'

The seconds tick by. Nothing. Perhaps Wilfred has had a recurrence with his waterworks. And then just as I'm starting to feel the first ominous signs of cramp in my leg, the doors swing open. It's our signal to move. I leap clumsily to my feet, push the walkie-talkie to my lips and start running.

'Go-go-go ...'

To the sound of ironic cheering from the teenagers, unemployed thespians are suddenly converging on the Freemason's Arms from all directions. As I approach the threshold Freddie the Fox is walking out but with his hands held high above his head in surrender: it's hardly the image of a confident gangster doing cock-of-the-walk acting. From my coat pocket I hear Samantha shouting, 'Cut, what the fuck is he doing?'

Wilfred has stopped. Behind him are four men with a combined weight of about seventy stone and biceps the sides of hams. One of them wears a bomber jacket. A second has a deep scar running down one side of his face. The third is carrying an empty pint glass. Another has a mastiff on a lead.

Before I can speak Samantha's voice blares out from my jacket pocket. 'For fuck's sake, can somebody ask those fat blokes to get out the bloody way, we're trying to shoot a film here ...'

Wilfred is breathing rapidly and clutching his heart. 'There's been a little misunderstanding,' he simpers. 'These gentlemen claim that no permission has been sought.'

The man with the eye patch breaks in. 'Have you got agreement to film here?' Then he sees me. 'Are you playing that fucker Wiggins?' he asks.

I nod. I know it's odd, but although I'm about to get my teeth knocked down my throat I can't help a slight surge of pride. The brown shoes and veteran car motif weren't far off after all: it's nice to know my instincts were right. But there's no time to savour the moment.

'Well, I'm Freddie's brother.' He is close enough for me to see the gold fillings in his mouth.

Wilfred breaks in. 'This gentleman has been explaining that he's believes a miscarriage of justice has occurred—'

'What I said was if any of you so much as fuckin' step over this fuckin' doorstep I'll fuckin' have you for breakfast ...' He jabs his finger into my breastbone. The man behind him with the mastiff is undoing the beast's muzzle. It's obviously time to set the record straight.

'We're not real policemen, we're just actors doing a dramatic recreation.' I'm suddenly aware of sounding like John Gielgud. 'Only ... like we're jus' doin' our job, mate.' It's worse. I now seem to have stepped through a black hole into Dick Van Dyke.

'Why don't you shut the fuck up?' suggests Freddie's brother.

Wilfred has a suggestion. 'If you'd care to take it up with our director, she'll be very pleased—' he stutters.

'What fuckin' director?' says the man with the mastiff.

Then I remember where she is – fifteen floors up on the other side of the road.

No wonder Samantha took up directing. She doesn't know anyone's name, she transmits but doesn't receive, and when the shit hits the fan she's safely located fifteen floors up on the other side of the road.

The girl's a natural.

lights

An actor returns home to find his wife crying on the sofa. When he asks her what's wrong she replies that while he was out his agent came round to the house and raped her. The husband looks troubled:

'Did he say if I was up for anything?'

Actors have to be self-obsessed, if only to make up for everyone else's passionate disinterest, so having your name in lights is the ultimate accolade. It's an immutable emblem that you've arrived. (Electricity can be fickle, however. Legend has it that a play named *I Killed the Count*, which ran for a while on Shaftesbury Avenue in the 1950s, lost the 'o' for several days when a bulb fused, thus transforming it from an elegant period drama set in eighteenth-century France to a play seemingly located on a sheep-shearing station in the Australian outback. No wonder Diana Dors changed her surname from Fluck: she obviously took advice from an electrician.)

It's December 1990. The pantos are all cast, the television studios have closed for their festivities, and Julia has flown out to Australia to see her sister who lives in the suburbs of Sydney. I'm happy enough to hang around in London for a while as I'm joining her out there as soon as I can get my mum's Christmas pudding down my throat: and in any case I've had invites to several parties and hope to blag my way into several more.

But just as I'm settling down with the double issue of *Radio Times* I get an interview for a new play by Michael Frayn; he of *Clouds*, *Noises Off* and *Benefactors*. What's more, the dates fit in perfectly – first rehearsal would be fifteen hours after I touched back down at Heathrow. In fact it would be a dream job – not only is Frayn one of our most celebrated playwrights, but the production is going straight in to London's Aldwych Theatre for a year's run, with a fail-safe of three weeks of previews beforehand in which to iron out all the glitches before releasing it to the scrutiny of the critics. And if it goes well, who knows? Brian Rix once did five years in a farce at the Whitehall – it may be a custom worth reviving.

The news is good. I get the job. I even briefly contemplate an upgrade to business class. As it is I'm in euphoric mood for the twenty-two-hour flight, although my inexperience of international travel is revealed when the pilot of the Qantas 747 announces that we're just crossing the northern coastline of Australia and I stand up to my retrieve my coat; three hours later and we're still only over Ayers Rock.

Nonetheless, it's a fantastic trip, enhanced for both of us by the prospect of a West End play and almost certainly a year's employment to look forward to. We touch back down on a freezing cold January afternoon at Heathrow, and by ten the next morning I'm in a church hall in Kennington meeting the actors who, with any luck, will be my companions for the next fifty-two weeks.

A few weeks later and with rehearsals well under way, I decide it's time to treat myself to a look at the front of the theatre. The director, Mike Ockrent, has told me the board is already wired up outside the theatre in preparation for the forthcoming opening night. Just at the point where the Strand curves round past the Waldorf Hotel and up towards Kingsway I see it. There it is, Michael Frayn's latest play, *Look Look*, picked out in bright red light bulbs on a huge sign above the entrance: and there below it, in between the names of Gabrielle Drake and Robin Bailey, are the two most beautiful words in the English language, blinking away night and day above the London buses and teeming crowds of commuters: Michael Simkins.

A new play by one of our greatest living dramatists, a year's contract, a star-studded cast, billing on the poster and my name in lights.

This time it can't go wrong. So long as Frayn has written yet another in a long list of winners, I'm home and dry.

If he hasn't, I'll kill the count.

joe's

Six weeks later I'm standing in Joe Allen's.

Joe Allen's is where actors go after curtain down in the West End. A cavernous restaurant set in a large subterranean basement just off the Strand in the heart of London's theatreland, it's become synonymous with actors unwinding after giving their all – we come here to meet friends, enjoy a discreet meal away from the glare of the spotlight, and savour a little late-night anonymity in the hope that somebody will spot us and come over to tell us how wonderful we are.

It's a bustling place, full of nervous energy and raucous laughter. The walls are covered in theatre posters: waiters in starched linen aprons weave between the closely packed tables with trays of drinks and bowls of extra large chips, and an air of brittle celebration hangs in the air. For this reason it isn't a place to tell your wife you're leaving her, because all the while you'll be talking she'll be looking over your shoulder to see which famous people are sitting at nearby tables. Not that you'll notice her not noticing because you'll be too busy looking over hers. In fact it's just the place for celebrating being in a smash hit.

Which is why I'm standing at the front desk. Because I'm in a smash hit myself. Or at least, I was when I booked the table.

We got our notice for *Look Look* earlier this evening, at a specially convened meeting in the auditorium. Our producer, Michael Codron, a crisp and urbane gentleman who has known success and failure in equal measure over the past thirty years, entered with a face reminiscent of Neville Chamberlain having had no reassurance from the German Chancellor, and said he was extremely sorry but in the face of withering reviews and subsequently disappointing box-office takings, he was left with no alternative but to close the show a week Saturday and that we may therefore take this announcement to be our official two weeks' notice. We'd done just over forty performances including previews.

Frayn then apologized that the play hadn't worked in the way he'd envisaged, going on to thank us for our enormous hard work and energy, and expressing the hope that we would all work on something else with him again in the not too distant future.

He finished: 'The play might have been a turkey, but at least it was free range.'

Good line.

Nonetheless, a major new comedy that I had expected to keep me in work for fifty-two weeks has got the chop after only five. And word seems to have got around of our imminent demise even in the three hours since we heard the news, because I suddenly can't get a table. All I've done since the announcement from Codron is to do the Monday night performance, have a shower and stroll the hundred yards or so from the Aldwych Theatre to Joe's. Yet they now have no knowledge of my booking.

'When did you make it, sir?' says the maitre d'.

'Last Thursday, from the Aldwych.'

'Isn't that where *Look Look* is playing?'

'Yes, it is.'

'I hear it's coming off.'

'Yes. Look, can you just consult your list again.'

I crane anxiously over his shoulder while he runs his eye down rows of names scrawled in thick pencil in a huge ledger.

'I'm sorry sir, we have no record of a Mr Simkins ...'

Christopher Biggins pushes past me on the way in.

Perhaps I should cut my losses here and just walk out. I could choose to leave the cigarette smoke and the gingham tablecloths and the prickly buzz of sophisticated late-night chit-chat, and catch the bus back to my flat in north London. I'm not in a West End hit any more, I'm in a flop leaking money from every pore and limping its way through sixteen more agonizing performances before it can be put out of its misery. My place is no longer alongside honey-roast Barbary duck with sautéed red cabbage, poached pear and blood orange dressing: my place is in my local kebab shop.

But I can't leave because Julia hasn't arrived yet. She's gone to see a friend in a pub show at the King's Head and we've agreed to rendezvous here afterwards. In fact, I was looking forward to greeting her at the bar with a martini and twist before a little bang-bang chicken and some choice observations on the burdens of fame. Instead I have to stand here while the great, the good and the still-employed push past me on their way to their tables.

There's Derek Jacobi ordering the Tuscan bean soup. There's Simon Callow with the pan-fried Cajun chicken livers. There's the actor who always play high court judges. I worked with him last year and he insisted on swapping telephone numbers in the car park afterwards. He only recently sent me a Christmas card and just looked away when he thought I'd caught his eye.

Fucker.

The demise of *Look Look* has come as a shock. It read fine on the page, rehearsals were a hoot, and yet when we unwrapped it to the paying public at the first preview it was as if we were doing a piece on child pornography. It just didn't work. Frayn gallantly tried to fix the second act on the hoof during the previews, working into the wee small hours before delivering the rewrites the following lunchtime for the cast to learn and assimilate into the show before the curtain up at 7.30. But it failed to gel – nobody's fault, it's just all in this business we call show. *The Times* called it 'fraught and overloaded', the *Observer* 'a lost opportunity', the *Daily Mail* 'fragile and bewildering'.

Speaking of fragile and bewildering, there's Lorraine Chase talking to Jim Davidson.

I need to get out of this restaurant. An actor who always gets my parts and who runs a particularly good line in oily and entirely bogus green room camaraderie has seen me and is now loping over between the tables with an expression of a lion spotting an injured wildebeest. He must have heard the news.

'Mike, how ya' doin'?' He flashes a brimming smile. 'Working at the moment?'

I answer his question with a rictus grin. 'I'm in *Look Look*.'

'Is that the one that's closing?' he interrupts before I've even finished my reply. He may be all ingenuous looks and wide-eyed innocence but there are curds of saliva collecting at the corners of his mouth. He's loving it. They're all loving it. Gore Vidal was right when he said, 'It is not enough to succeed. Others must fail.' There are probably theatre troupes in the forests of New Guinea who are celebrating the closure of *Look Look* as we speak.

Someone better known is coming down the stairs, and from the braying laugh I can hear behind me it sounds as if it's the actor Keith Baron. My rival can't decide whether to try to catch the eye of the star of ITV's hit comedy *Duty Free*, or to stay here and squeeze a little more blood from my fly-blown carcass. 'I'm so sorry,' he says, already peering past my shoulder. 'That must be a tough one ...'

I select savoir faire from my extensive visual portfolio. 'Oh well, it may have been a turkey, but at least it was free—'

'Keith, lovely to see you!' He hasn't even waited around for my best line. I can take a hint. Julia will have to take her chances: there'll be no shortage of people anxious to break the bad news.

I turn to find myself staring straight at Juliet Stephenson.

Juliet has entered with a couple of men in tow, and is still furling a damp umbrella. She may be one of the country's leading actresses and star of *Truly Madly Deeply*, but she's also a mate, and although we don't see much of each other she always greets me warmly on the rare occasions we bump into one another. We exchange a hug and a few seconds of pleasantries before it turns nasty.

'You're in *Look Look*, aren't you?' she says. She can't have heard. She's not like that.

She hasn't. She looks genuinely shocked at the news of the show's demise. I start to make my excuses when a man with steely grey hair appears over her shoulder. 'Did you say you were closing next Saturday?' he asks in a cultured West Coast voice. His grasp is moist and warm. 'I know your work,' he adds.

Knows my work? *Dial M For Murder* at Hornchurch? *The Merchant of Venice* at Billingham-on-Tees? Wiggins of the Yard?

His name's Robert Allan Ackerman. He's directing a play in London at the moment with Juliet and John Malkovich. 'We've just this afternoon lost a cast member who's had to pull out through ill-health and we've come here tonight to talk about who we should ask to take over the role first thing tomorrow morning.'

The pianist has swung into an up-tempo version of 'Cock-Eyed Optimist'. Ackerman is still speaking but I can barely hear him. The maitre d' seems to be having some problems catching it all too.

'... And so, if you're saying that you're free, I think you would be ideal for the part. You'd be playing a screenwriter, Juliet's fiancé, in his early thirties. We open at the Hampstead Theatre Club in three weeks' time.'

His other hand grips the top of mine and presses it gently.

'Would you be interested in starting tomorrow morning?'

It's late, and the air is thick with cigarette smoke. If I weren't feeling so seedy I'd have thought I was being asked if I'd be interested in taking over in a play starring John Malkovich. I must be hallucinating – over Ackerman's shoulder I could swear that was Captain Bird's Eye walking into the restaurant.

What's his name? John something. I think it begins with an R.

'If we could get you a copy of the play, would you be able to read it tonight and meet us at ten tomorrow morning?'

Or is it an L? Lester? Lever? It can't be John Lever, he opens the bowling for Essex. Hewer. That's it, John Hewer. I've seen him in the flesh somewhere before. Where was it?

As Captain Bird's Eye pushes past us, Ackerman is turning to another, younger man in sneakers and a baseball shirt standing next to him. He indicates me with an elegant forefinger and utters a line I never thought I'd actually hear:

'Get this guy a script.'

Thirty seconds later I'm buttoning my anorak and walking up the stairs to the door. In my hand I'm carrying a script of *Burn This* by Lanford Wilson.

'Sir?'

The maitre d' is standing at the foot of the staircase.

'Yes?'

'We unexpectedly have a table free, so if you'd still like to ...'

In the minicab on the way back to Julia's, I peer at the sheaf of curling foolscap in the light from passing street lamps. The vehicle jolts along Oxford Street, charging red lights and scaring pedestrians: the flag of Uganda stands on the dashboard on a tiny pole, and the driver, Tunji, has LBC blaring out on the car radio. It's a phone-in with Robbie Vincent and Anna Raeburn about sexual and emotional problems.

'And I found this pile of magazines at the bottom of his wardrobe and he says he's looking after them for a friend but the point is, Anna, I don't believe him ...'

Julia, having failed to find me at Joe's, arrives home at midnight to find me sitting in the bathroom practising my American accent. I'm at Hampstead by 9.30 the next morning, having had two hours' sleep, twelve cups of coffee and fourteen cigarettes. Julia is doing double extra mantra duty for me back at the dartboard. Ackerman arrives and takes me up to the rehearsal room.

'Juliet, you know, of course. And Lou you met briefly last night.' He indicates the guy who got me the script. 'Come and meet John.'

A bald man in his late thirties is sitting in a faded Chinese tunic, sewing flower patterns on to a needlework frame. I've never seen a Malkovich movie, but this must be him; there's no one else left. I smile uncertainly.

'John, this is our new Burton, Michael Simkins.'

He turns to look at me, very slowly, like he's doing a complicated tai chi manoeuvre.

'Nice to have you aboard, Michael,' he says in a sibilant rasp. 'I hope you'll be happy with us.' His voice is menacing and yet strangely tender – he sounds like Liberace trying to persuade someone down from a window ledge.

And suddenly it comes to me, the way things do, at the oddest possible times. I remember now where I've seen him before.

He was in Puss in Boots at Swindon in 1988.

Captain Bird's Eye, that is. Not John Malkovich.

shoot

In his *Actor's Handbook*, Stanislavsky writes: 'True acting can absorb an audience, making it not only understand but participate emotionally in all that is transpiring on the stage, thus being enriched by the inner experience which will not be erased by time ...'

He obviously never had to perform during a World Cup penalty shoot-out.

Burn This is a smash. Queues for returns snake round the outside of the Hampstead Theatre Club from early afternoon, with people waiting for hours on end in the blazing summer sunshine in the desperate hope of acquiring access to the evening performance. Heavily coiffured women from Golders Green reading the *Jewish Chronicle* perched on camping stools mingle happily with students dozing on the pavement. If you happen to have a couple of seats going spare you can make yourself a hundred quid on the black market – more if it's a pair together. Ticket touts in belted mackintoshes and Italian-made shoes who are normally only seen outside Les Miserables or the Wimbledon finals hover round the foyer from early evening, flashing bundles of fivers and menacing smiles in the direction of anyone with something to sell. Touts are the ultimate status symbol: for these few precious weeks I'm in the hottest ticket in town.

But tonight they're nowhere to be seen. Tonight they're relaxing in their Hacienda-style mansions in Billericay with a glass or two of vintage champagne, their mackintoshes neatly hung up in the walk-in wardrobes or stored in the boot of their Porsches. Tonight there will be no call for extra tickets for *Burn This*. Because England have progressed to the semi-finals of Italia

'90 and are playing their nemesis, West Germany, for a place in the finals. There are few attractions that could upstage the prospect of a head to head between Juliet Stephenson and John Malkovich. Lineker in Turin with only the German keeper to beat is one.

Nobody who'd booked seats all those weeks ago could have possibly known that events would collide so spectacularly. When they gave their credit card details back in May and June, Italia '90 was just an irritating little trail on the telly and 'Nessun Dorma' the name of a Japanese hatchback. But over the last few weeks everyone has been caught up in the frenzy of the World Cup. Husbands who rashly agreed in the spring to accompany their loved ones to see 'that bloke who was in *The Killing Fields*' are now cursing their folly for not scrutinizing the fixture list more closely. Couldn't they exchange it for another performance? No – all other nights are sold out, and they'll only get their money back if tonight's tickets can be resold. But there are no takers: everybody is watching TV.

Including cast and crew.

We're all huddled round a portable television set balanced precariously on a worktop in the communal male dressing room. Wardrobe, Wigs, the theatre fireman, the stage doorkeeper – everyone's here, glued to the fluttering figures moving uncertainly round the tiny screen. In Hampstead it's the end of the interval: in Turin it's England 1 West Germany 1 after extra time. Juliet and I, who open the second half of the play with a fifteen-minute duologue prior to another explosive entry from Malkovich, have already been summoned to the wings for the resumption.

Several times.

Juliet's already down there. I, on the other hand, swept up in the drama like everyone else, am trying to find any reason I can to delay my departure from the football, because we're down to a penalty shoot-out – sudden death – and Lineker's just lining up the first spot kick. I won't be a minute, my shoelace has broken, my zip's jammed, I've spilt tea on my jacket, my other shoelace has broken, for Christ's sake, kick the bloody thing.

'Mr Simkins to the stage immediately, please, Mr Simkins to the stage. Thank you.'

The only person who doesn't seem concerned is Malkovich. He's sitting quietly in the corner brewing tea and listening to Bruce Springsteen on a Walkman. Once we transfer to the West End all this mucking in together will change, of course. He'll have the executive suite combining reception room, single bed, refrigerator, personal phone line and en suite bathroom, while the rest of us are stuffed into rooms further and further up the stairs according to status. But not here – Hampstead is an egalitarian theatre, we're all equal: on the same money, in the same dressing room, sharing the same bog, box of Kleenex, set of mirror lights and washbasin. I've even used his toothpaste.

I can see now what all the fuss is about with Malkovich. His dramatic technique appears seamless – it's often difficult to know at which point he stops acting and reverts to being himself, so subtle is the transition. During a run-through of the play in the rehearsal room a few weeks ago he wandered across to the prop table at the side of the room in the middle of a scene and picked up a vital letter, which the stage manager had forgotten to place on the set. For a moment the shabby paint-flecked table and the bloke sitting at it, a stagehand called Simon, seemed to be part of the world of the play. Just for a second I wondered if this was some extra scene I'd somehow missed. That takes some doing.

'Mr Simkins to the stage immediately, please, Mr Simkins to the stage immediately ...'

I can't delay my departure any longer. The interval has already lasted nearly half an hour as it is, what with husbands calling up mates for the latest score from the payphone or nipping across the Finchley Road to gaze longingly into the window of Radio Rentals. Even now there's a restless, distracted air in the auditorium, with most of the audience just listening for the tell-tale roar of delight or wail of despair from the surrounding streets. The men are really suffering: you can see them out there in the dark, misery and resentment etched deep in their faces. Particularly the four detectives from Scotland Yard.

You can only feel sorry for them. They're only here because

they're providing official protection for HRH the Duchess of York, who for some insane reason has chosen tonight to attend the show. The one night when they'd want to be down the station with their mates, shouting, 'Go On, My Son' every time we score, they've got to sit in a sweltering theatre being forced to watch a load of pooftas jawing on about hetero- and homo-sexual love in New York just because Fergie fancied seeing her old school chum Juliet in performance. You sense if they could just get the cast out into the alleyway outside they'd only need five minutes to persuade us not to continue.

Mind you, Lou might quite like that. He's the fourth member of the cast, the one in the sneakers who fetched 'this guy' a script. He's standing next to me now in check shirt, white vest and chinos, staring at Paul Ince's rippling stomach muscles as he wipes his forehead with his England shirt.

'*Great* six-pack ...'

Lineker runs up and slots home the first goal. It's jubilation in Turin, joy in the streets of north-west London, and mayhem in the men's dressing room. The wig mistress hugs the dresser, the theatre fireman hugs the literary manager. Lou even allows me to dance a jig with him in the centre of the room before returning his gaze to the prostrate figure of the German keeper. Lineker trots back, his eyes bright with tension and relief, as John Motson wheels out the superlatives.

'Nice arse!'

That's Lou, not John Motson.

'Mr Simkins to the stage immediately, please, we have front of house clearance, Mr Simkins to the stage immediately.'

Malkovich removes the headphones, switches off the Walkman and looks up at me with a look of amused pity.

'Michael, I think you have to go now. I think you're going to have to miss the rest of the shoot-out. The people of Hampstead are waiting for you.' Malkovich is very laid-back: apart from a Bruce Springsteen track, it's difficult to imagine him getting excited about anything.

Shilton wipes his gloves on his jersey and assumes a crouch.

Brehme lines up the ball on the spot. Shilton waits. The

wings are only a few yards through a couple of sets of doors and I can be there in five seconds once I put my mind to it. I'll just see their first spot-kick.

'You mustn't disappoint your public, Michael.' Malkovich's grin extends another couple of millimetres.

The ball thunders past Shilton and into the net. I'll be reported in the book if I don't go now, the theatrical equivalent of a yellow card.

I'll just see one more.

'Michael, I want to help you. I don't like to see you suffering in this way. I'm finding your anxiety upsetting so I'll tell you what I'm going to do ...'

'Mr Simkins, we are waiting to continue ...'

I've learned to be cautious about offers of help from Malkovich, particularly if accompanied by his assassin's smile. Rumours abound of his warped sense of humour. In the original production on Broadway last year the author asked him to take out several references to 'motherfucker' for a particular matinée performance because his aged mother was going to be watching. 'She wouldn't understand,' he'd said by way of explanation in the dressing room beforehand. Malkovich turned to him with a malevolent grin and replied, 'Lanford, you shouldn't have said that ...'

At that afternoon's performance he inserted a further forty-seven 'motherfuckers' into the script in addition to the five already extant. It was definitely forty-seven because the author counted them, even though he didn't actually see them because he had his coat over his head.

Beardsley runs up and cannons the ball past Illgner. More jubilation. They must have heard that in the stalls. If we don't get a move on they'll be making a break for the bar again.

'I don't come on for a further ten minutes,' continues John, pouring a stream of Lapsang Souchong into a cup with infinite precision. His manner is almost coquettish. 'If you like, I'll tell you the result when I come onstage. Would you like that, Michael? Would you like me to do that for you?'

He makes it sound like he's offering to walk across my naked body in stilettos.

Matthaeus thumps the ball past Shilton's despairing dive. Two penalties each.

'If I come through the door and say my opening words, "You Arsehole" as in the script, that means England will have won. But if I change it tonight to "Butthole", that means your boys have blown it.' He grasps the cup in both hands and blows on it. 'Of course it's up to you.' He sips delicately.

'What was that? Arsehole means who's won?'

'England.'

'And what is it if Germany's won?'

Simon the overweight stage manager appears at the doorway. 'Mike, you've got to come, we can't hold 'em much longer and Juliet's getting fucked off down there ...' He glances at the screen. 'What's the score?'

Platt blasts the ball low into the bottom left-hand corner and smiles with relief. A cry of ecstasy echoes from every open window in Britain.

'I'm coming.' I turn to Malkovich. 'Arsehole England, Butthole Germany, right?'

Malkovich returns my anxious request for clarification with an inscrutable smile.

Down in the wings Juliet is in the middle of stretching exercises. 'I heard a scream,' she says. 'Everything all right?'

'Fine.'

'*Both* your shoelaces broke?' From anyone else I would interpret that as a slice of withering sarcasm but Juliet seems to have accepted it at face value. 'Poor you,' she says, squeezing my arm. The house lights are already dimming; a winking cue light taped to the floor changes from red to green, our signal to walk on and take our positions. As we pad on in the dark I can sense the audience shifting uneasily in their—

Was that a roar?

I think it was, but it's impossible to tell. The introductory music, cool jazz piano, is already swelling through the speakers and obliterating out all other sounds. And the stage lights are rising. God knows who Robson has got lined up for the next penalties. Waddell has got to be a contender. Presumably Ince will be taking one. Who then? Pearce? Gascoigne? He'd be a fool to use Gazza, he's emotionally incontinent since his double yellow, better to have somebody—

I'm suddenly aware of an ugly silence.

Juliet's staring at me. I think I'm supposed to be saying something.

Twelve minutes later Malkovich bursts through the door. His facial expression may not be able to convey the subtle nuance that Chris Waddell has just blasted it over the crossbar, but he doesn't need to. Underneath, Malkovich is a kind bloke, and there's something lurking in his eyes that suggests a man who knows he's got to shoot a puppy. Before he's even framed the words I know what he's going to say.

Tonight I'm a Butthole.

screen test

All actors want to do movies. We may pretend that theatre is our first love, that we can't survive without the nightly heartbeat which only a live audience responding to our craft can provide, but frankly it's bollocks. We want to do movies, to live in Monaco, to have affairs with vapid, big-breasted wannabees and to acquire a virulent coke habit. This suggests genuine class, a career that has moved above and beyond the other denizens of the glittering swamp. Real actors only do movies.

The problem is, there aren't any to do. The British film industry in the last twenty years has virtually collapsed. Can you name me ten great British movies between 1970 and 1990? *Kes*? *Chariots of Fire*? *Bugsy Malone*? After that you're struggling, admit it. While America has come up with *Apocalypse Now* and *Star Wars* we've been busy making *Confessions of a Plumber's Mate* and *Holiday on the Buses*. In the fifteen years since I stepped out of Gower Street and into the business I've not been up for a single proper film audition, and it's got to the stage now where I no longer think about it. It's just a distant pipe-dream, something to be fantasized about on the tube journey home.

Be careful what you wish for.

The starting point is encouraging enough. In the autumn of 1991 I get an interview for a feature film, and as my agent explains, it's even got a major international star in the leading role ...

'What, *the* Anthony Perkins?'

'Yes, Norman Bates Anthony Perkins.'

'I thought he was dead.'

'Apparently not.'

'Where's it filming?'

'Hackney, Dalston Junction and Maida Vale. That'd be handy for you, wouldn't it?'

It would: Maida Vale is a stone's throw from Julia's studio flat. I could almost pop home for lunch.

'You'd be going up for the part of Jonathan Dean. Let's see what it says about him ...' The familiar scuffling sound as she searches for the cast breakdown.

'Here we are. Jonathan Dean. Early thirties, scruffy low-life poet with a fondness for whiskey. Lives across the hall from the Perkins character who, unbeknown to him, is a crazed killer. Ah ...'

She tails off. When my agent says, 'Ah' that usually means there's a snag.

'What?'

'Well, only that it says here he's a native Dubliner. Can you do Irish? They're very keen to see you. They saw your photo in *Spotlight* and think you look perfect for the part ...'

'Who are they?'

'As a matter of fact they're Germans. The director's called Petra, apparently her husband is financing the movie from his business empire. He's big in plastics in the Frankfurt area and is funding the project as an anniversary gift to her or something.'

'It's a waste of time. I can't do the accent.'

'Well, it's up to you, of course. They'd be offering a grand.'

'What, for the entire job?'

'No, a day ...'

The screen test, far from taking place on the main sound stage at Pinewood, is happening above a pub in Camden Town. There are already a couple of other actors waiting to be seen, staring hopefully at the dog-eared scripts they've been issued and muttering the lines under their breath. It's impossible to tell if they're Irish or not. I sit as far away from them as I can without leaving the waiting room and scan the pages for a sign of Jonathan Dean.

Scene 73
Exterior: Front steps of house. Tony approaches with bag
of groceries. Jonathan Dean is sitting on the steps; his
eyes are moist and he looks as if he hasn't slept. His voice
breaks as he relays the news to his neighbour ...
Jonathan Dean: She's been murdered, Tony ... strangled.

It's no good: I can't do Irish. I failed the accent test at RADA,
and I'm no better now. Doing accents is a knack, and you've
either got it or you haven't. My Geordie sounds Pakistani, my
West Country sounds like Adge Cutler and my Irish sounds as if
I've been kicked in the mouth.

I mutter the line again, trying not to draw attention to
myself. 'She's bin moherdded, Tohni ... st'hhhanglehed ...'

A pretty young assistant comes out of a room and asks the
man sitting opposite me if he's had enough time to study it.

'Yes, I'm grand, thanks,' he replies, with a voice like a
pound of Kerrygold butter. He follows her through into the
interview room.

'She's bin moherdded, Tohni ... st'hhhanglehed.'

I only seem to be able to do it if I wedge my tongue out of
the right side of my mouth as I speak. It seems to help, I don't
know why. As soon as I try to do it without the tongue wedge
my voice immediately straggles all over Europe, with walkabout
to the Australian outback and Scandinavia thrown in for good
measure. But I wedge my tongue out the side of my mouth
again and the accent marginally returns. I'm not claiming Ireland
itself but the Isle of Man at least.

The assistant pokes her head out of the door.

'Petra will see you now, Michael.'

Petra, a pinched woman in her early thirties, stands behind the
ubiquitous video camera while her assistant sits opposite me with
a script. She finds scene seventy-three and, with a nod to Petra,
launches into an explanation.

'We thought we'd try the scene in which your character tells

Tony that your missing flatmate has been found murdered ...'

'Strangled,' adds Petra in a strong German accent.

'OK, Michael,' continues the assistant, 'I'll take it from the speech before yours. I'll read in the part of Tony. Ready?'

The last comment is directed back at Petra, who's still fumbling with the tripod. She nods uncertainly and settles down to watch.

The assistant clears her throat and begins.

'Scene seventy-three. Exterior. Front steps of house. Tony approaches with bag of groceries. Jonathan Dean is sitting on the steps ...'

I feel my tongue forcing its way out through clenched teeth.

'She's been moherdded, Tohni ... St'hhhanglehed ...'

The phone is already ringing as I walk in to Julia's flat. She stops hoovering the skirting boards and picks up the receiver. 'It's your agent,' she says.

You can tell if you've got a job or not by your agent's opening greeting. This time her 'Hullo, darling' sounds warm and vibrant. 'It's an offer,' she continues. 'They've just rung. Petra loved your reading and, so far as she's concerned, the part is yours. It'll be five to six days' shooting in East London later this month: they'll be ringing you about arranging a costume fitting tomorrow. Congratulations.'

Five to six days' shooting on a grand a day. I've never before been offered a job before I've even got back indoors and it's for a thousand pounds a day.

'That's wonderful. I can't quite believe they've given it to me ...'

'Petra was very impressed with your portrayal. She says that speech impediment you gave the character was a lovely touch, it gave the role a bathetic quality, which she thinks will be very useful ...'

The full script arrives the day following the interview, with a brief note – 'Delighted to have you aboard, love Petra' – attached by a paper clip to the cover. I take the phone off the hook, open a bottle of wine and sit down to read it from cover to cover. God knows I need this to be a little beauty, one of the finds of the year, the sort of small-scale picture that utterly captivates the critics and achieves a snowball effect which carries it right up to the Oscars, hopefully with me still aboard as Jonathan Dean. God knows I'd like to contemplate the big night in Los Angeles giving conveyer belt interviews to *Empire* and *Vogue* about how I achieved such heart-breaking pathos through my inspired speech defect idea, before swanning off to Sardi's in a stretch limo for supper with Goldie and Jack.

The film is called *A Demon in My View*. And stop me if any of this sounds familiar, but Anthony Perkins plays Tony, a loner, an oddball, a man living in a decrepit house who has never got over the death of his overbearing mother and who now leads a tormented existence on the fringes of the real world. From time to time innocent women stumble into his orbit, whereupon he becomes psychotic, dresses up and attacks them with a knife, stabbing them again and again in a frenzy of deranged violence. He then has to dispose of their bodies and pretend to be shocked when the occupants of the other flats in the building come to tell him about the latest brutal killing ...

'She's bihn moherdded, Tohni ... st'hhhanglehed.'

The script is terrible. Utterly, completely terrible. It makes *Psycho* look like *Brief Encounter*. A cheap hack 'n' slash flick, a cynical exploitation of the female form as horror-fodder for the purpose of cheap titillation. God knows what Perkins is doing getting involved in it. But that's his problem: the fact is, if I have an ounce of integrity I shouldn't touch this project with a bargepole.

Thankfully, I'm past integrity.

A large shiny Mercedes arrives on my first day's filming to drive me in silky luxury the seven miles to the location in Dalston. The driver is called Reg. He wears a smart suit, calls me 'sir' and even gets out to open the passenger door for me. The inside of the car is immaculate, as if it's only just been driven out of the showroom. Reg likes to talk, and spends most of the journey telling me about the time he spent as Robert Redford's personal driver during a recent film project. 'I told him, I said,

"If you want to smoke that cigar you can get out of this fuckin' motor, you cunt ...'"

The scenario would seem unlikely if it weren't for the fact that Reg carries an aura of potential and terrible violence about him. By the end of the journey I'm only marvelling that the star of such classics as *The Sting* and *All the President's Men* didn't end up in bin bags in Epping Forest. It's a relief when we arrive at the base unit. The cast and crew have already broken for lunch, and I'm taken down to a large marquee erected in a squalid car park, which is serving as the dining area. Somewhere inside is Anthony Perkins.

A film unit is very much like real life except everything happens at a tenth of the speed. Anyone who has visited a film set will have marvelled at the unspeakable tedium that forms 90 per cent of each day: hours of hanging about while blokes in polar fleeces and baseball caps stand around talking in impenetrable jargon to one another. No wonder shoots are notorious for piling on the weight – most of the time there's nothing else to do except hang around the sandwich trolley.

The moment I enter the marquee I see him: he's the one wrapped in an overcoat and stabbing nervously at a veal escalope with a fork. Even if it weren't for the fact that he looks like Norman Bates's grandfather I'd recognize him anywhere – the edgy voice, the darting eyes, the twitchy politeness, and I notice at one point a curious compulsive habit he has of continually turning his right ankle over while he's talking to you, even while he's sitting down. I've seen them all before at the Bates Motel. He welcomes me with a fragile handshake before turning back to Petra who's seated next to him and staring glumly at a bowl of fruit salad. They seem to be discussing the morning just gone.

'So, are you going to cover that last scene with a reverse after lunch, Petra?'

Petra is poking at something that might or might not be a lychee: location catering can be a dodgy affair. 'No, I think not, Anthony. We move on now to next set-up.'

'OK, Petra, only ...' He smiles wanly. 'Only I think you'll find you'll need a reverse on that one ...'

'You think so?'

'Yes, I have a feeling you won't be able to cut it together afterwards unless you cover yourself, but I don't want to interfere, it's ... er ... just a thought ...' He gives her an embarrassed smile and fingers his cutlery awkwardly before turning to ask me how my journey was.

And Petra is thinking: Anthony Perkins has had one of the great Hollywood careers. He's appeared with Orson Welles, Jeanne Moreau and Spencer Tracey. He's been nominated for an Oscar for his performance in William Wyler's *Friendly Persuasion*, and has also directed movies including *Lucky Stiff* and *Psycho 3*. I, on the other hand, have never directed so much as a home video, apart from a twenty-minute documentary on the German plastics and reinforced heavy duty laminates industry.

I'm just telling Perkins about trouble the Mercedes had in negotiating the Stamford Hill one-way gyratory system when Petra breaks in.

'Excuse me, Michael. Anthony, you really think a reverse would be useful?'

'Just a thought, Petra. I can't quite see how you'll match it up otherwise.'

'OK. I inform the crew.'

The afternoon passes slowly. Petra's decision to film the reverse angles has put the schedule even further behind than it was to start with. To make matters worse it's now raining, making it impossible to match the new stuff with that filmed before lunch in bright sunshine. Three hours later I'm dozing in the tiny Portakabin that doubles as my trailer when a knock on the door wakes me out of a fitful sleep. A fan heater has been on full blast in the tiny space and I've now got a head like the inside of a cement mixer. It's the Third Assistant Director: they're ready for me.

The set is the exterior of a crumbling tenement in a cul-de-sac off Homerton High Street, which has been cordoned off for the duration. The First Assistant Director, a leathery Scotsman called Ian, explains the procedure – we've got to do four set-ups, a master shot, a close two-shot, a single of Perkins looking down disapprovingly as he passes me on the steps, with a brief cutaway to me for: 'She's been murdered, Tony ... strangled.'

The cameraman – a jolly Bavarian called Bruno with a handlebar moustache and a colossal beer belly straining out over blue jeans – positions me on the second to bottom step while the crew attempt to rig round me. It's now a bitterly cold February afternoon and the light is fading fast. Petra and the other heads of department huddle swathed in designer windcheaters, passing hand warmers and cups of soup to one another and periodically stamping their feet. Perkins is back in his trailer thawing out, so they aim to do my close-up first, with Ian standing in for him behind the camera to deliver my cue and provide me with an eye line. Even so, it's another forty minutes before they're ready to roll, extra lighting rigs arriving with each new delay.

At last we're ready.

'She's bihn moherdded, Tohni ... st'hhhanglehed.'

Petra looks to Bruno who replies with a thumbs-up. 'Good for me, boss,' he says happily. She turns to the sound operator. 'Was that OK for you?'

The operator has a puzzled expression on his face. He removes his headphones slowly.

'Sorry, Petra, what did you say?'

'Was Michael's line good for you?'

He seems nonplussed. 'I ... er ... You're happy with it, are you?'

Petra nods.

'Well then, fine. We certainly got it. No probs.'

We finish just after 7 p.m. It would have been earlier but the master shot had to be redone after someone spotted one of the catering staff lounging in a picnic chair reading a motorcycle magazine in the corner of the picture.

On the way home Reg regales me with stories about the time he told Sylvester Stallone to take his feet of the dashboard. He flashes a mirthless smile at me in his rear-view mirror. 'You've never seen a pair of shoes move so fast, sir ...'

masterclass

No wonder film stars lose touch with reality.

In addition to my six specified days on *A Demon in My View* as laid out in the contract, I've been hired on a daily basis for a further seven. On each specified day I've been picked up by Reg at 6 a.m. and transported in air-conditioned comfort to the set, during which I've been privy to an inventory of how Reg has nearly come to blows with a long list of celebrities who wouldn't mind their manners, including Larry Hagman, Ian Rush, Russell Grant and, incredibly, Judith Chalmers. The only one who seems to come out with any credit is apparently Anneka Rice, who, according to Reg, is a 'fuckin' proper lady'. She also has 'stonking tits'.

Once at location I've been decanted into my personal trailer while a shivering Third Assistant Director has fetched me a full English breakfast, including fried bread, fried mushrooms, fried tomatoes, fried egg and black pudding. I've then dozed till lunch, whereupon she's returned offering a choice of swordfish steak or chicken chasseur with three types of vegetables, followed by apple crumble and custard all mopped up by cheese and biscuits. Then another forty winks before I'm woken for high tea, at which point she apologizes that they won't now get to my scene today so Reg will take me home as soon as I've finished that Viennese Whirl. A day, all told, for which I've pocketed a further thousand pounds.

I could get used to this ...

The last day of the shoot is notable for it also being Jonathan Dean's big moment. In fact, his only moment. The schedule has fallen so badly behind that hundreds of scenes have been butchered in order to ensure we finish before the money runs out, resulting in Jonathan Dean having little involvement other than the 'She's Bihn Mohderred' bit and the scene I'm about to do now – the wedding toast. This time tomorrow it'll all be over and Perkins will be winging his way back to Los Angeles. In fact if he's not, the penalty clauses in his contract are so swingeing that they could bring down the entire plastics industry of lower Saxony at a stroke.

The wedding toast is what I suppose could be termed my 'money shot'. The moment in a movie when an actor has the opportunity to show the manifold acting skills by conveying in no more than a flicker of an eyebrow or a tightening of the lower lip all the myriad emotions inwardly felt by the character. Only now do the great screen actors show why they're worth their huge fees: we're talking an image nearly forty foot wide on cinema screens across the length and breadth of Europe. So it's N.A.R. – No Acting Required. Just feel the emotion in your eyes, and a decent lighting cameraman will do the rest. Gary Cooper got by on nothing but N.A.R. and he didn't do so bad.

The story so far: two of the other occupants of the grotty tenement have got married at the local registry office. They have repaired to a nearby pub afterwards with their fellow residents for a knees-up, dragging the unfortunate Perkins with them after passing him on a pelican crossing. He's sitting here in the pub, surrounded by rapidly inebriating revellers, and wondering what he can give the bride as an impromptu wedding present. Luckily, an axe he's carrying in his shopping bag fits the bill.

But I'm jumping ahead of myself. In this scene, my money shot, all is happiness and confetti: the party is gathered in a corner of the snug with Perkins wedged unhappily between the bride's mother and an Irishman with a speech impediment. Everywhere he looks his gaze is returned by happy, boozy faces – there's no escape.

With only this set-up to complete there's a slightly crazed, end-of-term feel about the film unit. Everything else is in the can, or as in the can as it's ever likely to be with the wife of a plastics magnate at the helm. We filmed the scene on the pelican crossing in Islington at 6 a.m. this morning, the subsequent brutal bludgeoning of the bride was in fact filmed last week, so we've just got to nail the wedding toast and it'll be a wrap. The inside of the pub in Primrose Hill is knee-deep in camera equipment, bulky lamps and coils of cable, and the tables around which we're sitting have all the emblems necessary to denote a good time – overflowing ashtrays, half-full glasses, screwed-up crisp packets.

I've fallen in love with Anthony Perkins. I've witnessed him endure the ignominy of back-breaking hours and endless delays, often in biting conditions, while a well-meaning but ill-equipped director fumbles with the Janet and John book of *How to Direct a Movie*. Here is one of the great post-war movie actors, a performer who struck his defining role almost at the start of his career, and who seems to have been fighting a losing battle to top it ever since. He shouldn't be sitting in a grotty pub in Primrose Hill, he should be at his well-appointed home in California waiting for a special achievement award. Yet he has borne the humiliation of this car crash of a film – a ham-fisted parody of his magnum opus – with quiet dignity. I've never heard him complain, nor talk about the old days, nor throw his weight around. On the contrary, he's given each scene his best effort, remaining scrupulously polite and courteous at all times. All he asks in return is that nobody tells him how wonderful he was in *Psycho*. It may be an unspoken request but it's there in every line of his wracked features. The ghost of Norman Bates seems to hang over him like a shroud. Keeping our traps shut about burnt-out triumphs seems the least we can do in return for his grace and fortitude.

It's late afternoon. Progress has been dismayingly slow since lunch (salmon en croûte, sticky toffee pudding), but we're nearly there. Petra has been explaining what is required. She wants me to tap a butter knife lying conveniently on the table in front of me against a wine glass to attract the attention of my fellow revellers, stagger uncertainly to my feet and raise my glass to the happy couple. Simple enough. All I've got to do is to stand at the right moment and deliver the lines in the right order and we can all go home.

We rehearse it a couple of times. Petra seems satisfied. After a further delay while the camera is repositioned and the lighting tweaked, we're ready to go. A boy from the props department nips between us, topping up the foam on the beer glasses from a plastic jug and rescrunching the crisp packets, while Petra hovers with her perpetually furrowed brow.

'All right, Michael, we film, I think.' She settles down on a metal equipment box and stares at the monitor. 'Final checks now, please ...'

A gaggle of make-up and costume supervisors hurry among us. It's like a furnace in here now and everyone is wilting: the bride's mother has got a sheen of perspiration on her forehead that needs drying with powder, Perkins needs the collar of his overcoat smoothed down, one of the wedding guests has a biscuit crumb on his top lip ...

Another delay: an aircraft is flying overhead. We'll have to wait till it's passed.

'Michael, could I have a word?'

Perkins leans across. Please God he's not going to bring up my accent – not now. If he tells me not to stick my tongue out I won't be able to deliver, money shot or no money shot.

'Just a thought. I've noticed that you're looking down to find the knife before picking it up to clink the glass.' He smiles gently. 'Just a word of warning ... if you drop your eyes like that, Petra will cut away from you. Probably to me. Once the camera loses your eyes you're no use to it any more, believe me. This is your big moment, so could I suggest you practise finding the knife with your fingers without having to look down for it? Then she'll stay on you throughout.'

He sits back. 'Hope you don't think I'm interfering ...'

The girls from make-up are still fussing around one of the wedding guests, a young Japanese girl in a bright pink miniskirt with a rose in her hair. Petra is looking at her watch. I've just time to try it.

I fumble for the knife: it's too far away and I nearly knock the wine glass over scrabbling for it. I reposition the knife closer to the edge of the table.

'Quick as we can, please, everyone ...' Make-up are already scurrying away from the table. A final try. This time my fingers instinctively find the cool bone of the handle and pick it up in one smooth continuous motion.

'Roll camera. Scene two three four, take one ...' The clapperboard snaps shut.

I allow my gaze to sweep around the wedding guests as I stand. Meanwhile my fingers find the knife. The knife finds the glass. The eyes stay on the guests. The camera stays on me.

'And ... *cut*.' Petra claps her hands and smiles for the first time in five weeks. 'That is good for me. Thank you, everyone, if the gate is clear that is a wrap ...' An ironic cheer goes up from the film crew. Outside on the pavement someone is already pouring cheap champagne into hundreds of plastic cups lined up on a rickety table.

Bruno's assistant is peering down the lens with a mini torch. 'Gate clear, boss,' he says.

'Wonderful. Thank you, Michael, that was good.'

I glance over at Perkins, who smiles back and nods. The other actors are already congratulating each other and starting to remove their sweat-soaked costumes. Perkins is unwinding his scarf. Another few moments and he'll be gone. I lean across. 'Anthony, thank—'

'Excuse me, Mr Perkins.' The actress playing the bride's mother grips his hand and pumps it furiously. She fumbles on the seat between her legs and produces a small rectangular book and pen. 'I wonder if I could possibly just have your autograph before you go ...'

'Certainly.' Perkins takes the pen and begins scrawling his name on a fresh page.

'It's to Phyllis,' says the bride's mother. He finishes signing and hands it back. She inspects it uncertainly before returning it to his grasp.

'I wonder if you could put "Norman Bates" in brackets. That'd be smashing ...'

showreel

The overtime from the film provides me with the deposit for my first flat in London; a small, one-bedroom, ground-floor flat in a leafy street in NW3. In fact it's about a hundred yards from Julia's place. We nearly considered pooling our resources and purchasing together but decided that would be rushing things, so instead we're neatly positioned a mere stone's throw from one another, close enough to pop home for a clean pair of pants but far enough away to provide some distance in the event of a particularly spectacular row. It seems to be working.

A few months after moving in, I'm sunning myself on my tiny patio when my neighbour Ian, a fitter for North Thames Gas Board and a keen film buff, looks over the fence. He has the ground-floor flat below mine, which includes a substantial garden, and is returning from the end of season clearout at our local Argos with a garden swing for his kids. We rarely bump into each other, but it's a beautiful morning and neither of us is in a particular hurry, so we fall into conversation.

'Did you see Anthony Perkins has died?' he says.

I hadn't. Ian dumps the swing in his hall and returns with that morning's *Daily Mail*. He spends the next couple of minutes reading the obit. The news is vaguely shocking, though somehow the information that he had been suffering from AIDS for some years isn't. In fact it makes sense of a lot of things surrounding *A Demon in My View*.

'Great actor,' says Ian. 'One of my favourites.'

It seems an appropriate moment to mention I'd quite recently worked with him.

'What, *the* Anthony Perkins?'

'Yes, Norman Bates Anthony Perkins.' I give Ian a detailed summary of the film and of Jonathan Dean's pivotal role in it. 'I suppose you'd describe it as a cameo,' I explain. And I can see he's impressed.

'Christ, I can't believe it. What was it called again?'

'*A Demon in My View.*'

'I can't think how we missed it. When was it on?'

It wasn't. It never got a release. I explain there were so many vital shots that hadn't been covered in the initial shoot that it proved impossible to edit together into a cohesive movie. It went straight to the video rental market, and solely in mainland Europe. So as far as I know, *A Demon in My View* has never made it across the Channel. I know all this because my agent has been trying to locate a copy to use in my showreel.

Showreels are now becoming de rigueur. In fact, without one you're just not taken seriously. They're four- or five-minute compilation tapes of your recent film and TV performances, edited on to one user-friendly tape. The benefit to potential employers is that they can see what you're like without having to go to through the disagreeable and time-wasting business of actually meeting you. Instead they can sit in the comfort of their executive office with a zapper in one hand and cappuccino (or whatever else takes their fancy) in the other and decide in minutes if you're what they're looking for.

At present my personal showreel is a bit lightweight, consisting of my Safeway manager demonstrating fire extinguishers in Maidstone and my Detective Inspector Brian Wiggins stirring a cup of tea at a desk. All right in its own way but unlikely to tip the balance in a straight competition with Gary Oldman for the next Scorsese film. The addition of my Jonathan Dean would beef up my showreel nicely, not only displaying my acting skills in feature films but also intimating that I'm no stranger to major movie stars.

But, as I'm able to explain to my now-drooling neighbour, my agent's enquiries about *A Demon in My View* had been met with blank faces and shrugged shoulders. The film seemed to have been airbrushed out of existence.

Ian's a nice bloke and I can see I'm spoiling his day. He's got a wife, Lynn, and three teenage kids, and the salary of a North Thames gas fitter doesn't go far. A trip to the local Blockbusters had been fermenting in his mind for his Saturday evening, watching his favourite movie star and the bloke from next door over a pizza and a few beers. Now I was dashing his hopes.

'So you've not even seen it?' he asks in bewilderment.

Well, yes, I have. In fact, I have a tape of it upstairs in Julia's lounge. My agent eventually tracked down a film editor in Hamburg who'd managed to get hold of a bootlegged copy – it's the only one in the country, and the quality is so grainy as to render it virtually unwatchable. In any case, most of it consists merely of Perkins shambling up and down dark alleyways in pursuit of student nurses, interspersed with close-ups of blood-spattered daggers. Still – it's the only evidence I have of ever having done the job, and I guard it with my life. It would be virtually impossible to get another copy.

'I'd love to have a look at it,' he says coyly.

'Well ...'

I'd never normally let it out of my sight. But Ian's only downstairs, and I'll be back later today after my cricket match. And he's already helped me out with a damaged sparking mechanism on my Coalight in the lounge. I owe him one.

'The picture isn't much good. And there are German subtitles.'

'It doesn't matter—'

'And the sound quality is terrible. You may not even be able to understand what I'm saying—'

'Christ, Mike, we'd still love to see it. It'd be great. Lynn would be chuffed to bits. We'll guard it with our lives.'

I hurry upstairs and retrieve it from the shelves. Julia was about to wipe them down anyway. I hand over the copy of *Ein Teufel im Sicht* and five minutes later I hear Ian calling to Lynn in excitement.

The cricket match doesn't go well. I drop a sitter at cover point and get run out for three. The ground is on a horrible council playing field covered in broken glass, and the pitch is so uneven that you take your teeth in your hands every time you face a ball. But it's fresh air and Julia turns up afterwards at the pub, so that when I arrive back in Kilburn it's past 9 p.m. and nearly dark. In the moonlight I can see the figure of Ian, standing in his porch. And he's swaying.

As I pull my Ford Fiesta up to the kerb he totters forward. He's got a beer can in his hand and his flies are undone. Perhaps Lynn has left him. Now I think of it she comes from Limerick – inflicting my accent on her could have led to ugly scenes.

'Ian, what is it?'

He slumps uncertainly against the front wall. I prop him up and sit next to him, cradling his slumped head in my arms. He lets the empty can fall from his grasp and on to the pavement.

He peers up at me uncertainly through his glasses. 'We had a great time, Mike ... Lynn loved it, we thought you were great ... and then we fell asleep, Mike, and ...'

Slowly, over the next five minutes, I'm able to piece together the reason for his despairing condition. While they were dozing, he left the tape in the video and one of his kids has recorded a double episode of *You've Been Framed* over it. Most of my Jonathan Dean is now buried under footage of blokes walking into glass windows.

Somehow I can't get upset. On the day that Anthony Perkins's death was announced, it seems entirely appropriate.

trial

I spend the latter part of 1995 filming a new television series. A twice-weekly BBC flagship drama set round a family who run a building supplies business in suburban London. I'm playing Philip, eldest son and heir to the family fortune. The scripts arriving daily through the letterbox suggest it's aimed somewhere between *The Brothers* and *Coronation Street*, and intended for the more discerning soap opera addict, the sort that watch them religiously but who don't like all that violence and bad manners. Like my mum.

The contract is initially for a twenty-four episode series, to be screened on Mondays and Thursdays, but kicking off with a double-length, one-hour starter episode just to get potential viewers up and running. If all goes well I'm on an option for another series next year, and of course there's always the chance that it might become a rolling contract. But that's all in the future. For now the Beeb has to get it successfully launched and lodged into the nation's psyche; and it'll be no mean feat. Because the family tree has more oddballs and social misfits than the House of Windsor. Brothers, sisters, wives, husbands, children, ex-partners and lovers, all mired in their own domestic maelstrom. The *Radio Times* even prints a small chart for viewers to refer to during the crucial opening episodes, a cut-out-and-keep guide to who the fuck's doing what to whom.

The film studios at Elstree in leafy Hertfordshire where we're to spend the next four months cater for all manner of corporation output, from *Top of the Pops* to *EastEnders*. In the canteen one day I find myself queuing up behind Martyn Lewis and Pat Butcher.

Elstree's a curious town, comfortably off but with little sense of permanence, and caught in a time warp somewhere around the early sixties, full of ironmonger's shops and stores like Woolworths; you almost expect to see Leslie Philips drive past in an MG wearing suede driving gloves. I drive there three or four days a week, through the High Street to the studio gates, where knots of bedraggled teenagers all crane into my elderly Ford Fiesta to see if might be Robbie Williams; and finally into the car park of Studio 4, which houses the specially built interiors for the various siblings.

The scenes involving my own immediate family all involve parental crises, and take part almost exclusively round the kitchen table, usually while having breakfast. Our daughter is being bullied at school, our younger son is dabbling with under-age sex, and just as I get all that sorted out, the eldest son declares he wants to become a priest. By the end of the shoot I can't look at a box of cornflakes without shouting, 'Do you realize how worried we've been?'

The series finishes filming just before Christmas. Some months later an informal letter from the producer informs me that the opening hour-long special, on which much of the success of the venture will hang, is scheduled for the forthcoming spring bank holiday Monday.

The first transmission is always a crucial factor in determining the success or otherwise of a television series. If you can hook a large potential audience early on, before the story has become too advanced or the characters too entwined, then the chances are they'll stay with it till the end. Which probably means a second commission. Ratings are the yardstick by which it will be gauged, and the BBC press office has been generating a lot of column inches in the preceding weeks, with profiles in the dailies and prime-time trailers to whet the appetite. It's even made the front of *Woman's Realm*.

On the day of transmission Julia and I spend the afternoon sunbathing in our local park. It's a peerless early summer's day; the sunshine is glorious, and the whole of the country is gently baking. We even take a picnic. The park teems with happy families, lolling dogs and couples playing frisbee. By 5 p.m. we're back in the flat and waiting for the off, but with fifteen minutes to go my nerve fails and I decide to nip to the off licence for a bottle of wine. It's still as hot as hell and everyone is out in their gardens – as I hurry down the road the aroma of sausages sizzling on barbecues hangs in the air and the chatter of conversation from hundreds of happy couples bubbles over from every garden fence. Nobody is watching TV.

No, a few are. Every hundred yards or so I can hear the odd television set blaring from open windows. The trouble is, it's Kiri Te Kanawa singing the Rugby Union World Cup theme. England has reached the quarter-finals, and the crucial do-or-die game is being screened live on ITV any minute now. In fact kick-off will coincide exactly with our opening theme tune.

An hour later the crucial opening episode is over. And it's not bad. A bit slow perhaps, a few too many characters for comfort, but room for optimism. Outside the sun still beams mercilessly from a powder-blue sky. I decide to do a quick ring round to canvas opinion from selected mates who promised to tune in.

Each and every call is met by recorded answer-phone messages. Everyone's out.

Julia decides the bathroom floor could do with a clean. 'Phone your mum,' she says. 'She'll have seen it.' I decide to take her advice. By now I'm happy for anything I can get; if I can't rely on my mates then what hope have we for the rest of the nation's viewers? Mum is just the sort of person the series is aimed at. She'll know what to say.

She answers from her lounge up in Brighton. Her voice sounds sluggish. 'Hello, Mum, what did you think?' I ask plaintively.

'Yes, dear, I'm enjoying it.' Her voice betrays some anxiety.

'It's just finished. Didn't you see it?'

'Yes, dear, I did, sorry, only ...'

'Well?'

'I'm so sorry. It's so hot here, I must have dropped off ...'

plea

Nevertheless, I'm now a TV star. I think. Perhaps not A-list yet, but my face is on page 31 of the current *TV Quick*. The *Daily Express* want to know what would be my ultimate luxury purchase for their Thursday 'Celebrity Money Matters' column. And I'm now recognized in shops and supermarkets.

The last may be a slight overstatement. The woman who serves in MacGowan's the chemists knew me, but it turns out she remembered me as a police constable on an old episode of *The Detectives* she saw on UK Gold.

But still. Twice-weekly exposure can only lead one way. It can't just be coincidence that I've had a letter from my bank asking if I'd like to become a premiere account holder. It's the shape of things to come. Look at Dirty Den. He's only on the box twice a week himself and he's everywhere; I've even seen his face as the opening clue in Mum's jumbo crossword book.

I wonder how much he gets for that?

Every scintilla of accepted showbiz wisdom suggests that mass exposure only leads to more of the same. Once you're on a roll it can only be a matter of time before *Blankety Blank* and, the ultimate accolade, an invitation on to *This Morning* with Richard and Judy to talk about my career and my efforts to cope with the pressures of fame. Perhaps I'll even make it to be the special guest expert on *Countdown*. Richard Stilgoe has to have a holiday some time.

In the meantime I've got to be ready to follow my career wherever it leads, Los Angeles, Cannes, Rio de Janeiro. A friend has fast-tracked my membership of the Groucho Club. Another has hired a private box for the Lord's test match where I've spent the day drinking champagne and watching the Test. While I'm there I'm introduced to Rafaella.

Rafaella is half Italian and stunning. Her parents own a house on the shores of Lake Garda and she's over here for a couple of years living in a flat in Holland Park while she brushes up on her languages. I think that's what she says; her English isn't so good. She works in media and publishing and her brother is apparently a great friend of Mike Newell, the film director.

I wonder if Mike's caught my series?

She hardly speaks during the long hours in the VIP box, but there's something in that intense way she looks at me whenever I smile that somehow suggests a profound empathy. After the match we end up at a wine bar in St John's Wood High Street and I must have told her my entire life story because we don't leave until nearly midnight.

Rafaella stays in the memory. There's a maturity to her, a poise I haven't encountered before. She's not scrabbling on the same ghastly treadmill as the rest of us. She likes modern art, particularly Modigliani. She goes to Sunday morning concerts at the Wigmore Hall. She can speak fluent Russian. I agree she might be a bit short on one-liners but she more than makes up for it by an encyclo-paedic knowledge of current affairs and European politics. It's just so refreshing to talk to a woman who recognizes my wide range of interests and passions beyond what the autumn season might be at the Salisbury Playhouse. Not that we need to talk; when in repose she just stares implacably at me with those dark hazel eyes as if she's laying bare my every thought. She even makes me feel I've actually got something worth laying bare.

I meet up with her a couple of times for a martini at the Groucho and she gives me her phone number and suggests I might like to join a group of her friends who are flying over to her parents' house for a long weekend next month.

Suddenly my daily life with Julia seems so … domesticated. Julia's idea of a good evening is watching *Animal Hospital* over a plate of cheese on toast. She likes listening to Joni Mitchell and James Taylor. She likes tidying things. It's lovely, of course it is, but …

I begin to rationalize like a car salesman closing a deal. The point is, it's essential I travel light. And Julia is working as much as me just now, what with a new comedy series for the Beeb and another one in the offing for Granada; with us only seeing one another in the evenings the strain is starting to show. I admit I've become uncommunicative, snappy, restless, but she's hardly putting herself out to find out what's wrong, is she? It's appalling that she hasn't asked me what's up. Perhaps it'll even be a relief when I tell her. Thank God we didn't buy a place together. It would have made all this far more complicated.

I break the news gently to Julia late one evening that I think it's best we take a rain check on the whole thing. I remind her of how badly we've been getting on recently. That I just need some space to sort things out for a while. It's nothing personal. We'll both be all right. She must have been expecting something like this.

But no. Surprisingly, my announcement takes her completely unawares. She's making a late-night toastie and for some minutes she stands frozen, the Kitchen Devil still in her hand, a slice of Wensleydale still clinging to the blade as if glued by some secret force. I plunge on about actors and genes and lifestyle options until I finally grind to a halt and say how sorry I am.

She puts down the knife and replies quietly that she'd thought we were getting on wonderfully, that she'd rarely been happier, and only the other night had been thinking how lucky we both were to have so much good fortune.

The subsequent explanations, breast-beatings, frank exchange of views, bloody recriminations and staring at the wall for minutes on end to the sound of mutual sniffing bleeds on into the night and to the next morning. I finally put on my coat at seven, and even then I'm not out of the door until nearly ten. When I walk back into my own home a few minutes later the light on the answer-phone is unblinking. I've been away for nearly twenty-four hours and nobody has phoned.

The relationship takes a while to die. Several tortured evenings in wine bars, and a particularly wretched tea-time rendezvous in an Italian café at the back of Regent Street ensue before the life is stamped out of it once and for all. Julia is now flinty, sad, pitying. She's got nearly six months of TV work lined up herself, yet she thinks I'm making a big mistake, that I'm a bloody idiot, that I've been completely suckered into thinking I'm a bigshot just because of a couple of footling moments on the box, and that by the time I realize what a complete shite-house the whole thing is it'll be too late and I'll just be another has-been who never was, boring the arse off anybody who'll buy me a drink about how I could have become a contender before going home alone, to my lonely flat, empty apart from a pile of yellowing press cuttings and a bottle of Grecian 2000.

I understand. I've hurt her deeply and she's still smarting. But I have to be strong enough for both of us. I'm gently adamant. It's the best thing. It would never have worked. She'll see one day. Good luck and stay happy. I can't talk about it any longer or I'll start crying again.

And anyway, I'm meeting Rafaella at the Groucho. She's got the flight tickets for the weekend and I need to check out the sale at Paul Smith for a jacket suitable for a summer's evening in Italy.

verdict

They say the gods don't throw thunderbolts but custard pies. My big break doesn't go to a second series. In fact, it barely makes it through the first; after twelve of the scheduled twenty-four episodes it suddenly gets moved from weekday evenings to a Sunday tea-time, a sure sign it's in the shit. The cast only learns of its demise when the production office stops returning our phone calls.

The relationship with Rafaella finishes a month or so later. I find myself on the doorstep of her Holland Park flat one Friday night waiting for her to open the door and writing down on a scrap of paper a list of possible topics we can talk about that night. I realize then that it's doomed.

The following weekend I blurt out to her that I don't want to go on with it any more, even before I've taken my coat off for what was supposed to be a long romantic weekend. She's impossibly gracious about the whole thing, insisting on cooking me the meal she'd been planning. I end up drinking so much to dull my feeling of wretchedness that I can't drive home. She even lends me the money for the cab fare.

Part of me had always dreamt of being the kind of person that ran with the beautiful set. In my mind's eye I could easily picture it. But once I was there, deep down, I knew it wasn't me. I tried to deny it and lose myself in those hazel eyes. But I couldn't. I felt homesick for me. I need to be with people who remember the names of the Trumpton fire brigade, who like car boot fairs and pet shops, and know who Bert Weedon is.

I stop going to the Groucho in the following weeks because I don't want to bump into her, and in any case I can no longer afford the investment required to buy a round of drinks. Not that there's anyone else there I know anyway. The phone doesn't ring. Even the woman from MacGowan's stops asking me how I learn all those lines. The nights draw in.

Three weeks after learning of the devastating legacy of Will Carling and Michael Fish on my chances of fame, I'm touring the Midlands in a rented Ford Mondeo with an actor called Neil performing drama role-play workshops with employees of a large company specializing in the treatment of sewage.

Even as I sign for the hire car I'm aware that with each successive mile I'll merely be running away from a private life which is disintegrating underneath me. But anything's better than sitting staring at the phone, and in any case there's no time to dwell on my personal travails with a week of sewage issues to deal with.

Our job as drama facilitators is to demonstrate to the workforce, many of whom have been with the company for years, how the new policy of working practices in waste disposal will benefit them if only they are prepared to embrace it. And there's a lot to learn. Not least the fact that we must never refer to the raw product by its popular name. 'We take something the consistency of tomato sauce and turn it into something more resembling chocolate cake,' says the MD at our initial briefing. 'And we prefer not to use the "s" word. You can say anything else – sewage, faeces, waste, waste products, excreta, ordure, sludge – personally I quite like "mixed liquor" – but try not to use the "s" word if you can help it. We find it has a depressing effect on our workforce.'

I throw myself into the project. So to speak. The daily workshop, performed on five successive days at treatment plants throughout the West Midlands, each time to a different audience of thirty or so blokes in overalls, wellingtons and knitted socks, allows the workforce the chance to talk freely about what's bothering them without the conferences descending into eyeball to eyeball slanging matches between operatives and bosses. It also gives them a morning off work: the management even throw in a basic buffet lunch for them afterwards, egg sandwiches, bowls of hula hoops and jam tarts, most of which will eventually end up thirty yards away in the sludge tanks. They're a good bunch of blokes, and most days I find myself sharing a cup of tea and a fag with them all afterwards out in the car park. Besides, it stops me having to sit and think about the wreckage that is my personal life.

On my second morning I meet Roy.

Roy has been a de-sludger for as long as he can recall – in fact he was born on a sewage works, his dad having worked in the industry before him. We're enjoying some post-buffet nicotine in early spring sunshine at Derby north pumping station: a steady stream of tankers rumbles past us in the compound, and the smell of rotten eggs hangs in the air. Roy's fascinated to know I'm an actor: he doesn't meet many in his line of work, and wants to know if I've worked with anyone famous.

Well, yes I have. Roy presses for names. A couple of his mates are already wandering over to listen, and I can feel the weight of their expectation bearing down on me. Luckily a quick trawl through the mental archives soon throws up some responses that should do the trick.

'Well, let's see now – I know Tim Spall, Alan Ayckbourn, Rik Mayall, and Juliet Stephenson. I was at drama school with her, I know her very well. I suppose I'd call her a friend ...'

Roy shakes his head. 'Haven't come across them, I'm afraid,' he says disappointedly. I'm already losing my audience; the other workers are drifting back to the comparative glamour of the ordure separation tanks. After all the good work of this morning my reputation is gently crumbling away out here in the watery sunshine and rich aroma of the car park. But I'm underestimating Roy. He has faith in me. He lights another fag and presses on hopefully. 'What about Tosh Lines, have you met him?'

He's in luck. I have met Tosh Lines, aka the actor Kevin Lloyd. He's the one in ITV's *The Bill*, the one with the grubby raincoat and straggly moustache. A girlfriend of mine appeared as Dandini to his Buttons in Cinderella some years back at the Bristol Old Vic, and I spent several evenings with him in the pub afterwards.

Roy's face brightens immediately: 'Bloody hell, my missus is cracked on him,' he says delightedly. 'Absolutely bloody cracked. You just wait till I tell her I've met someone who knows Tosh Lines. She'll be that bloody pleased.' He nearly does a little jog around the Mondeo.

It's time to go; news is filtering back that one of the compactors had failed on site, and the guys have an afternoon's manual de-sludging to get back to. I, on the other hand, have a long drive to a Travelodge in Leamington Spa in preparation for the following day.

I'm just getting into the car when Roy hurries across. 'Sorry to bother you, Mike,' he says, peering in through the driver's window, 'I've been trying to think where I've seen you before. Were you in that series last autumn, that one about that family where everybody was having affairs and ripping each other off?'

I recognise it immediately.

'Yes, I was.'

'You had the son who was a poof, didn't you?'

'A priest, actually.'

Roy is jubilant. He punches the air: 'I knew it. We watched it for a few weeks. What happened to it?'

'I'm afraid they pulled it. It didn't do very well.'

'I'm not surprised,' replies Roy amiably. 'I thought it was shite.'

judgement

The evening of 1 May 1997 is momentous. Even before the polls have closed, the whole nation seems to sense that everything is about to change. I watch the General Election unfolding on the BBC with my mates Gilly and Steve, on their special 24-inch widescreen in the lounge of their semi-detached in north London. By the time I've arrived from Greenwich where I've been all evening the first result is already in, but there's plenty more where that came from. One by spectacular one the Tory heavyweights go down – Mellor, Lamont, Rifkind – until the images on the screen are so so utterly engrossing that I barely notice when Pierce Brosnan slumps into the sofa next to me. Pierce is a close personal friend of Steve, and sits transfixed for nearly an hour along with the rest of us. I'm sharing Cheese 'n' Chives Pringles with James Bond and I'm hardly aware of him. That's the sort of evening it is.

For me the night is doubly anticipatory. As well as polling day, it's also been the press night of a production of *Absent Friends* at the Greenwich Theatre, which I've directed. After twenty-odd years of acting I've crossed the footlights to find out if I can do better myself, and for the past four weeks (and a lot longer if you count the process of auditioning, casting, meeting designers, and all the other myriad preparatory tasks prior to the first rehearsal) I've been preparing the cast of six for the first of their scheduled forty-six performances and the scrutiny of the national press.

But then John Major calls an election and instead of the packed house of expectant theatre-goers we were hoping for, the auditorium contains a mere smattering of second-string critics and middle-aged women chewing toffees. In a few hours' time the morning papers will be passing judgement on John Major, Tony Blair and my London directorial debut. Tony is guaranteed reviews to die for. I'm studying Portillo's face on the tiny wooden stage at Epping Town Hall and I'm very nervous.

'Portillo, Michael Denzil Xavier ...'

Raucous laughter greets the announcement of his middle names. Funny, I can't recall the audience laughing that much at anything tonight at Greenwich. Portillo looks as if he's been hit over the head with a spade even though his result hasn't even been formally announced. I know how he feels.

Directing isn't as easy as it sounds. I've striven to replicate all the strengths and avoid all the pitfalls I've observed in the hundreds of theatre directors I've worked with or witnessed over the years, and with a tried and tested play by Alan Ayckbourn as my raw material you'd have thought little could go wrong. Yet it's proved a difficult ride. Helping to meld a roomful of disparate acting talents and complex sensibilities into a cohesive whole is like trying to catch eels with your bare hands. Some of the cast just want to be left alone, while others require intense psychotherapy on every word and move. I've done everything in my power to get it right, and yet somehow every time I've tried to take hold of the play and the performances, one or all have squirted out through my clenching fingers in a direction utterly opposite from the one intended. And if things can go this wrong for David Mellor, then nobody is safe.

Mind you. 'Up Your Hacienda, Jimmy?' At least I had a decent script.

Portillo is turned over soon after 3 a.m. James Bond leaves soon afterwards. I hold on a little longer, but it's been an emotionally draining night, sitting in a near-deserted Greenwich auditorium watching my carefully prepared creation slowly deflate, and I'm exhausted. By 4 a.m. I'm in my own bed, peering out into the blackness and wondering what tomorrow's papers will bring.

When I wake three hours later it's a beautiful early summer morning. Even Cricklewood seems to have a spring in its step.

People are leaning over fences and talking to their neighbours about the events of the night before. As I pass the allotments on my way to Shah's, the local newsagent, I see Bert, an elderly West Indian neighbour, swapping an early morning celebratory can of lager with Graham and Pedro, the gay couple at number fifteen.

The shop is knee-deep in reports of the victory, with each newspaper swollen to two or three times its normal size. From every page Tony and Cherie are beaming out at me. I buy the *Telegraph*, *The Times*, the *Independent* and the *Guardian*, and nearly put my shoulder out lugging them back to my flat.

The reviews for Labour are raves. For *Absent Friends* at the Greenwich Theatre, on the other hand ...

One or two don't like the play; a couple don't think the acting served it well. But they are all unanimous on the directing: staid, predictable, uninspired. Perhaps the first edition of the *Evening Standard* will be better? After all, it's London's local paper – a good mention in that is as important as all the others combined. The critic was sitting just in front of me and I'm sure I saw him smile once or twice. With any luck ...

Soon after midday I'm on my way back to Shah's. This time I can't even wait till I've got it home: instead I stand at the counter riffling through the pages in desperation. Eventually I locate it. My eye falls at random upon the judgement of Nick Curtis ...

'One can only wonder how Simkins, a trusted Ayckbourn lieutenant ...'

He hated me. I return the paper to the counter and leave without purchasing it. For much of the afternoon I sit indoors, surrounded by the debris of hundreds of pages of newsprint. Nobody rings. I turn on the TV, but even here there's no distraction. *Home and Away*, *TeleTubbies*, re-runs of *The Jerry Springer Show* – everything has been swept aside for live coverage of Tony and Cherie's triumphal cortege towards 10 Downing Street. But I'm not part of this brave new world. My place is with Major and Mellor and Goldsmith. Down among the dead men. I draw the curtains and fall into a troubled sleep.

Soon after 3 p.m. there's a ring on the doorbell. I rise clumsily and lumber out to the front door. Julia is standing in the porch. It's nearly a year since I saw her, despite our proximity. She's wearing a simple cotton frock and her hair has been revamped. She looks lovely. In her hand she carries a wicker shopping basket, from which a loaf of bread and a bottle of Jif are peeking out of the top. In her other hand she's carrying a copy of today's *Standard*.

'You all right?' she asks simply.

'Um. Yes. Fine.'

We stare uncertainly at each other for a moment.

'Would you like to come in?'

'Just for a minute.'

She steps inside and peers around warily as I throw back the heavy drapes. I realize I've nothing to offer her, not even a cup of tea. Somehow I haven't felt like eating much recently, and my larder now contains nothing more than a packet of dried pasta and a tin of Heinz London Grill. I mumble my apologies and assure her I was about to visit the supermarket.

'Not to worry,' she says, indicating her basket. 'I'll make some toast.'

bar

It's 1997, and I'm celebrating the twenty-first anniversary of getting into RADA with a glass of champagne with my new friends Tony and Cherie backstage at the National Theatre.

In the intervening couple of decades I've spent nearly all my time shouting in the evenings, as well as the mornings and afternoons: and I've done just about everything: rep, West End, TV, movies, training films, drama role-play, ads, pub theatre, voiceovers, and four separate characters in different episodes of *The Bill*. I've worked with a fair smattering of greats and I've got all the things I feared, as a teenager, that I'd sacrificed for ever: a reasonable income, a car, a couple of modest pension plans and enough left over for the occasional holiday and a meal out. I've even finally bought a house with Julia, mortgage courtesy of a stage-struck building society manager. The *Daily Mail* nearly got it right when they wrote that Julia was bound for Hollywood. It turned out to be Cricklewood.

The final week of Shakespeare's *King Lear* at the NT, in which I'm giving my Duke of Cornwall, is a surreal affair. The production marks the return to the stage for the first time in years of Ian Holm in the title role, and with an all-star cast directed by Richard Eyre it was, until Diana's arrival in a coffin at Northolt airport two Sundays ago, the biggest event in town: but suddenly the play, and everything else during the following fortnight, seems to be viewed only through a Queen of Hearts-shaped prism. Each night since the car crash we've been exploring kingship, deceit and a world spiralling out of control on the stage of the Cottesloe while barely a mile away across the Thames the flowers are piling up waist-deep in Hyde Park.

It's been one hell of a week all in all, but sanity is returning and life is, at last, resuming its old patterns.

The Prime Minister had obviously planned this official visit to *King Lear* months ago: but now, at this rather formal informal drink with the cast in one of the cavernous rehearsal rooms, all the talk is still of Diana's death and how he coped with guiding the nation through the collective emotional meltdown. His replies are modest and disarming, and he's happy to admit that basically he winged it. 'There was no manual to consult,' as he confides to me over a small sherry. Actually it was to Richard Eyre but I was standing next to him at the time.

The conversation straggles on for several minutes: Cherie laughs at something and even briefly touches my shoulder with an elegant hand. But Special Branch officers are soon ushering them away and by eleven o'clock I've shaken hands for the first and possibly only time with a serving British prime minister and am hurrying to catch my train home.

Linda, the legendary and much-loved denizen of the Soviet-style reception desk at the stage door sees me strolling out. 'Message for you, Simmo,' she calls, waving a scrawled note retrieved from my pigeonhole. 'Tim Spall is upstairs in the bar. He was in the audience tonight and said he'd love to see you if you've got a moment ...'

Tim Spall. Apart from a chance meeting in Brighton and a blurted greeting through the crush of a Christmas party in the mid-eighties I haven't seen him for nearly a quarter of a century. History suggests that winners of the Ronson award at RADA tend to sink immediately without trace, but Tim has bucked the trend, developing into one of the country's leading actors – *Auf Wiedersehen, Pet*, a string of high-profile drama projects, and memorable performances in a number of Mike Leigh's films: *Life Is Sweet, Secrets and Lies,* et al. The words 'National Treasure' have even been whispered about him in the tabloids. If the award of the Ronson can't sink him that appellation ought to do the trick.

The backstage bar of the National, situated on the first floor up a forbidding concrete staircase, is a strange hybrid of a place: part drinking den, part green room, part waiting area. During the day it's almost deserted, just a small core of hard drinkers mingling with waiting auditionees distractedly sipping at cups of coffee; but after curtain down it's filled to bursting point with the cast, crew and office staff from three separate auditoria, all desperate for a pint and a catch-up on the latest gossip. Although it stops serving at eleven there's no official chucking-out time, and you can still find people there eking out their pints well after midnight.

The shutters of the bar are already being ratcheted down as I walk in. Tim is talking to a couple of actors he's bumped into from the production of *Guys and Dolls*, which has just finished in the Olivier. He breaks off when he sees me and walks over. It's good to see Tim again – he looks the same as I remember him but healthier, and after a few stilted pleasantries we slip smoothly into conversation, ranging from his impressions of the current production, through news of our RADA colleagues, to the inevitable question which will occur in any meeting between two actors if left alone for long enough: 'What are you doing at the moment?'

Actors develop a sixth sense about this enquiry. Once you've been in the game for a while you can tell just by looking if they're working or not – in other words, you know the answer before you've asked it. So if you think the response is going to be 'Nothing', don't ask in the first place – unless you're not working either, in which case you can provide some symbiotic comfort. The eyes hold the key; a dull sheen, or worse, a smouldering fury, don't go there.

Fortunately tonight it isn't an issue. Tim knows my situation – he's just seen me in it – and it's a safe bet that he'll have some tasty project lined up. In fact it'd be interesting to know what it is. A new Poliakoff play? A sitcom perhaps? A tilt at Hollywood?

'That's what I wanted to talk to you about,' he replies. His normally rollicking responses, delivered in a vibrant south London rasp, are already dropping into something more confidential. He lowers his voice and glances round before continuing.

'I'm doing the new Mike Leigh film,' he mutters.

'Fabulous. When is it starting?'

'It's a bit different this time,' he continues. 'He's doing a historical film. New territory.'

A historical piece? Mike Leigh? It seems unlikely – Leigh has made his reputation on contemporary subjects, each one evolving through months of improvisation by a committed group of actors who may only meet each other towards the end of rehearsals.

'What about?'

Tim clutches my wrist. 'Look, I shouldn't tell you this, but it's about Gilbert and bleedin' Sullivan.'

It's patently a wind-up. And, unusually for Tim, not a good one. The notion of Mike Leigh doing a film about the lives of two Victorian light operetta composers is about as likely as Ray Cooney writing about incest or Harold Pinter composing a poem in praise of Margaret Thatcher. But Tim isn't smiling: he looks deadly serious. 'I'm not kidding, it's about the D'Oyly Carte opera company – all that stuff you used to go on about at RADA. In fact, the moment he told me about it you came into my head. I'm playing some bloke called Richard Temple. Mean anything to you?'

Richard Temple. I haven't heard his name mentioned for a couple of decades, and yet suddenly it all comes flooding back, all that tonnage of useless information from my wasted teenage years. Born 1847, created the roles of the Mikado, Dick Deadeye and Sergeant Meryll. Died 1912. I've got an old gramophone cylinder of him somewhere, singing 'I am a Pirate King'...

'You've got to get seen for it, Mike, you of all people. Tell your agent to put you up for it. But listen ...'

He's hurting my wrist.

'For fuck's sake, don't mention to him that I told you. It's top secret. Only three or four of us have been cast so far and the whole subject matter is supposed to be under wraps. He's terrified if it gets out he'll get begging letters from every am dram in the country. He'll fucking kill me if he discovers I've tipped you off, so if you do get to meet him, keep your—'

A well-known theatre director has spotted Tim and is already moving across to greet him. Within seconds we're surrounded by acquaintances and well-wishers.

When I return from a trip to the loo a few minutes later he's gone.

this morning

A few days before my interview with Mike Leigh, Julia and I are invited on to *This Morning* to talk about 'being together but living apart'. It's the subject of today's special phone-in feature, and Richard and Judy want us to describe our highly personal way of co-existing; namely, living in identical houses roughly a hundred yards from each other. The initial contact has been made through a friend of a friend who's a researcher on the show and who remembered talking to us at a barbecue during the summer. 'You'll get a car to and from the studios, and it won't take very long.' When she offered a couple of hundred quid as expenses it clinched the deal. We've both got tax bills to pay.

Julia and I have got back together. It all began following her trip down the road to check I wasn't putting my head in the gas oven the day after the election. I was never more pleased to see anyone in my life. A couple of weeks later we met for a drink, to be followed in the subsequent weeks by a visit to Hampstead Heath, a Steve Martin film at the local multiplex, a meal at the Turkish restaurant on Shoot-Up Hill, and finally an evening at the finals of the national brass band championships at the Albert Hall.

Slowly, outing by outing, we've brought things round, and although we're still not technically living together, we're now spending every day in each other's company. We've even taken the small but crucial step by jointly purchasing an aluminium waste bin. It's a tiny gesture, but a momentous one. This single gleaming item, now housed in the corner of Julia's kitchen, is our first mutually owned possession, paid for in cash by the both of us over the counter in a simple but profound ritual at John

Lewis in Brent Cross. It's all we have to show for nearly ten years of stop-starting, but it represents real progress. It's our baby.

On the morning of our appearance a smart minicab collects us from Julia's flat soon after 8 a.m., and we're at the south bank studios an hour later. Richard and Judy are on holiday, but we're taken into the studio to meet their stand-ins, John Leslie and Fern Britton. After a few pleasantries we're shepherded away into a nearby reception area. The windowless room is fringed with leather sofas and with a tiny galley kitchen at one end, littered with half-eaten croissants and cups of vending-machine tea. A monitor screwed to the wall shows a live transmission of events in the studio, and for the next twenty minutes we sit with an assortment of various other guests and experts, watching John and Fern being fitted with their microphones and having their collars brushed. We're scheduled to appear in about an hour, sandwiched between a feature on garden conservatories and an interview with a woman who ran into her long-lost identical twin at a Scrabble tournament in Bournemouth.

Soon after 9.30 the programme's resident psychotherapy expert, Dr Raj Persaud, ambles into the waiting room and introduces himself to us. Raj is a studious, intense man in his late thirties with a trademark look of permanent concern. His handshake is soft and persuasive. He asks if he can have a quiet word with us before we go into the studio, and beckons us out into the corridor. As we leave, I glance at the TV monitor; the programme is already on air and Fern is discussing a selection of latest household gadgets with a young bloke wearing too much hair gel.

Once we're out of the room Raj gathers us into a confidential huddle so our darkest secrets won't be overheard by any passing tea ladies. 'I just wanted to get a bit of background information about you both,' he says quietly. 'I know you've spoken to Jane our researcher and she's given me one or two details about your history so that we have something to encourage people to phone in with their own personal experiences, but it would benefit me if I could just run through your story again. You've been together on and off for a number of years, is that true?'

'On and off, yes,' replies Julia crisply.

Raj writes it down. 'And yet you now live a hundred yards apart, and still maintain completely separate houses. And you find that works, do you?' He already sounds unconvinced.

I reply with a long and convoluted response about freedom and independence and respect for one another's space. He smiles knowingly at each new titbit of information.

'And I hear you've recently bought a waste bin.'

We nod.

'I think this is a very important step,' he says gently. 'It's tremendously significant. Would you agree it might be perhaps a sign of things to come?'

Julia flashes a brittle smile and a heated debate ensues. I was supposed to have emptied it two nights ago but forgot, which meant that I overfilled it last night and now the pedal mechanism has stopped working and the bag is wedged in the aluminium cylinder. Julia says I should pay the full cost if we have to get a new one. I maintain that as it's been in her house she has had the benefit of it, so any expense should be shared.

'Well, of course, this typifies the problem,' says Raj. 'You may find it difficult to relinquish your individual ownership priorities. These things can become much more difficult once you reach – um …'

He's saved from expounding further. A floor manager appears from the studio and calls to him. He's needed for his microphone placement.

'That's useful, thanks,' he says. 'I'm sure our viewers will find it all very interesting. What will happen is that we'll have an informal discussion for six to eight minutes, and then I'll be asked to give a personal summation of how I see your situation before we open the phone lines. You don't have to stay for that bit. There's nothing to worry about, really. Just one more thing before I go …'

He turns to me.

'Michael, on the question of sexual fidelity. I understand you're both actors. Have you found that a problem?'

An image of Julia's mother, Winnie, sitting in her bungalow

in Cleethorpes and staring at the TV over her Mellow Bird's and a garibaldi, swims into my head. *This Morning* is one of her favourite programmes. I'm currently engaged in a long and delicate battle of bridge-building with Winnie following my rapprochement with her daughter, and the consequences of her observing the intimate details of her prospective son-in-law's sexual history being dissected for the nation's enjoyment doesn't bear thinking about. Winnie was champion Indian club swinger for the Grimsby area three years running after the war.

'Raj, I think we'd better stop there.'

mike

I really want this job.

Mike Leigh finishes writing a sentence and looks up. 'So,' he says. 'What happened then?'

I've only felt genuine dread a few times in my life.

When I unintentionally hit my schoolmate Robert in the face with a cricket bat. When I had to tell Mr Farmer I was quitting my job as a sales assistant in Gamley's toy shop on the busiest weekend of the year. When I nearly drowned in a boating accident.

And when I told Mike Leigh that at the age of sixteen I became obsessed with the operas of Gilbert and Sullivan at a casting of a film about them. It's his look that does it.

A chilly, syrupy look, like a seeping of battery acid.

'And in fact,' I plunge on desperately, 'I still have possibly one of the largest collections of D'Oyly Carte memorabilia of anyone in the south-east.'

Leigh leans forward.

'No,' he replies with spare, frigid simplicity. 'I have.'

This interview is going terribly wrong. He can sense I've been tipped off and am now trying to wheedle my way into his project by attempting an entirely bogus interest and expertise in the subject matter. I reckon I've got about five seconds to convince him I'm the genuine article. He's already starting to close the pad. Another moment and I'll be back out in Carnaby Street. Then I suddenly remember my afternoon in an upstairs bedroom handling Gilbert's snot-stained handkerchief a quarter of a century ago.

'Actually, I think the biggest collection belongs to an ex-cleric called Peter Joslin who lives near Reading.'

Leigh looks at me for what seems to be an eternity.

Then he sits back and nods. He's turning to a fresh page in his notepad. His pen is once more poised for action.

'You're right,' he says. 'He has.'